Roy Wilkins

Roy Wilkins

The Quiet
Revolutionary
and the NAACP

YVONNE RYAN

UNIVERSITY PRESS OF KENTUCKY

Scholarly publisher for the Commonwealth,
serving Bellarmine University, Berea College, Centre College of Kentucky, Eastern
Kentucky University, The Filson Historical Society, Georgetown College, Kentucky
Historical Society, Kentucky State University, Morehead State University, Murray
State University, Northern Kentucky University, Transylvania University, University
of Kentucky, University of Louisville,
and Western Kentucky University.
All rights reserved.

Editorial and Sales Offices: The University Press of Kentucky
663 South Limestone Street, Lexington, Kentucky 40508-4008
www.kentuckypress.com

Frontispiece: Roy Wilkins (LBJ Library; photo by Yoichi Okamoto)

17 16 15 14 13   5 4 3 2 1

Library of Congress Cataloging-in-Publication Data

Ryan, Yvonne, 1961-
  Roy Wilkins : the quiet revolutionary and the NAACP / Yvonne Ryan.
    pages cm. — (Civil rights and the struggle for black equality in the twentieth
century)
  Includes bibliographical references and index.
  ISBN 978-0-8131-4379-8 (hardcover : alk. paper) — ISBN 978-0-8131-4381-1 (pdf)
  — ISBN 978-0-8131-4380-4 (epub)
  1. Wilkins, Roy, 1901-1981. 2. Civil rights movements—United States—History—
20th century. 3. African Americans—Civil rights—History—20th century.
4. National Association for the Advancement of Colored People—Biography.
5. Civil rights workers—United States—Biography. 6. African American civil rights
workers—Biography. I. Title.
  E185.97.W69R93 2013
  323.092—dc23
  [B]   2013029396

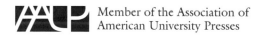

Contents

Introduction

On the morning of September 10, 1981, flags on all government buildings in the United States flew at half-mast to mark the death of Roy Wilkins, former leader of the National Association for the Advancement of Colored People (NAACP), the country's oldest and largest civil rights organization. At Wilkins's funeral the following day, Vice President George Bush and Senator Ted Kennedy joined nine hundred mourners to listen to eulogies from veterans of the civil rights movement, for whom Wilkins's passing represented the end of a momentous chapter in the movement's history. His death had been reported in the nation's newspapers, whose editorials paid tribute to his achievements and his "cool, solid" leadership. But even as soprano Leontyne Price sang "We Shall Overcome" over his coffin, Wilkins was fading from the public consciousness, his achievements and contributions to a crucial period in American history nearly forgotten.

Many of Wilkins's colleagues and peers, including Thurgood Marshall, the NAACP's flamboyant and charismatic general counsel, and Walter White, Wilkins's predecessor, have been the subject of scholarly attention; but Wilkins's contribution to the civil rights movement has so far been ignored in the scholarly examinations of this important period.[1] It was, in a way, his misfortune to lead the NAACP during a period that gave rise to many charismatic figures, including Martin Luther King, Fannie Lou Hamer, Stokely Carmichael, and Malcolm X, who have made compelling subjects for historians and, in King's case, still provide a philosophical and moral standard by which every other leader is judged.[2] Wilkins lacked the oratorical skills that could lift an audience, in part because he appeared to lack the passion to paint a vision of freedom. Instead, he often appeared aloof, patrician, and urbane: more like a sophisticated chief executive of a multinational corporation than of an organization dedicated to righting a set of fundamental injustices.

1

Wilkins spent forty-six years of his life within the NAACP, retiring just four years before his death. Yet despite his position as head of the organization, which he led from 1955 to 1977, he remains an enigma. His position put him at the center of many of the most important events of the civil rights movement, but he features in the movement's historiography only in the context of other players. Most, if not all, significant histories of the movement mention him, but he appears almost as a supporting actor, whose presence mainly serves as a counterpoint to the more interesting players. He is seen, at best, as a paternalistic uncle; more often he is viewed as an aging, difficult, and hierarchical bureaucrat who held his organization back, allowing younger, more exciting groups to take the glory and garlands.

Wilkins was born in 1901, five years after the Supreme Court had enshrined the legal precedent for the separation of the races that, by the time of Wilkins's birth, extended to almost every area of public life.[3] He grew up in St. Paul, Minnesota, among white immigrants from all corners of Europe, and from the age of five attended an integrated school. He felt deeply that black Americans should enjoy the same economic and social opportunities as their white counterparts—his writings and speeches are testament to that—but his approach was almost academic. For Wilkins, desegregation and discrimination were irrational concepts; as a result he often took a detached, intellectual approach to the fight for equality. This detachment should not be confused with disinterest or lack of anger. His career provides many examples of his rage at yet another unjust act, his anger usually expressed through his newspaper columns or his speeches. However, Wilkins invariably looked toward a legislative remedy as the ultimate solution. He abhorred the use of violence as a response to injustice, even while he acknowledged the occasional necessity for armed self-defense. The only rational and effective way to address inequality, as far as Wilkins was concerned, was to ensure that rights were protected through legislation and court rulings. His detachment allowed him to serve as the conduit between civil rights activists demonstrating on the streets of Selma, for example, and the white power structure. He shared with President Lyndon Johnson and the NAACP's Washington lobbyist, Clarence Mitchell, an understanding of the complexity of the legislative process and was particularly adept at negotiating and navigating the corridors of power.

His absence from histories of the civil rights movement is particularly puzzling because Wilkins in fact led two powerful civil rights organizations. In addition to his position as secretary of the NAACP, he led the Leadership Conference on Civil Rights (LCCR), a coalition of religious, fraternal, civil, and labor groups founded in 1950 by Wilkins, A. Philip Randolph, the leader of the Brotherhood of Sleeping Car Porters railway union, and Arnold Aronson, a leader of the National Jewish Community Relations Advisory Council. The LCCR was set up to coordinate various advocacy groups in lobbying Congress and, through their efforts, the organization supported the passage of the landmark civil and voting rights legislation of 1957, 1964, 1965, and 1968. One of the reasons why Wilkins was reluctant to embrace direct action as a primary tactic of the NAACP was that he believed black Americans did not constitute a powerful enough group in the United States to force widespread social and economic change; he argued, for example, that boycotts worked best in communities where African Americans carried significant economic weight but could not be applied effectively in every town or city. Joining forces with the groups affiliated with the LCCR gave the NAACP the ballast it needed to demand congressional action.

Unlike the NAACP, the LCCR was a relatively informal coalition. It also had one simple focus: securing equal rights through congressional action. While each of the member organizations could take whatever action they wanted under its own banner, when representing itself as part of the LCCR direct action was confined to putting pressure on members of Congress to pass civil rights legislation through letters, phone calls, and often visits by LCCR delegations. Despite the importance of the LCCR in securing civil rights legislation, it has thus far has been ignored by historians of the civil rights movement.[4] While this book cannot address this gap, it does examine Wilkins's stewardship of the LCCR and that organization's contribution to the momentous civil rights legislation of the 1950s and 1960s.

Although a "top down" approach to the civil rights movement has been overshadowed in recent years by studies of local activism, studying the workings of organizations like the NAACP, which operated through a network of branches, and the LCCR, which operated at a national level, is important to our understanding of what makes a dynamic, disruptive protest movement successful. The efforts of those courageous and energetic men and women who stood their ground in the face of physical attack could have been wasted without the efforts of those such as Wilkins, who lobbied people in power to bring about change; conversely, those efforts would have been more difficult and far less effective without the moral force of protesters in places such as Alabama and Mississippi. This book shines a light on what happened in the background to change America.

1

The Family Firm

Roy Ottoway Wilkins was born at the turn of the twentieth century, on August 31, 1901.[1] ("Ottoway" was a tribute to the doctor who delivered him, but it was possibly too unusual and was discarded as soon as Wilkins could write.) His grandfather, Asberry Wilkins, had been born a slave but had won his freedom when he was fourteen years old at the end of the Civil War. In Holly Springs, Mississippi, where Asberry had worked as a field hand, there was little opportunity for former slaves to make a living, so he became a sharecropper. With his wife, Emma, he raised five children, of which Wilkins's father, William, was the second eldest. William had ambitions far beyond Holly Springs. He attended Rust College, a local black college, but opportunities were no better for William than they had been for his father, and when he graduated the only work he could find was as a porter. The limitations of life for a young black man in Mississippi angered him, and he constantly challenged the white racism he confronted—often with his fists. One night, after William had been in one too many confrontations, Asberry was warned that his son was in danger. He encouraged William and his wife, Mayfield, a teacher, to leave town immediately. The pair took the first train north in the hope they would find work and a life free of the grinding oppression of the South.

The young couple eventually settled in St. Louis, but opportunities were not much greater in Missouri than Mississippi, and William Wilkins could only find work laboring in a brickyard. Nevertheless, it was enough to allow the couple to move into an apartment. There, Roy Wilkins was born in 1901, followed by his sister, Armeda, two years later and brother, Earl, in 1905. The senior Wilkins was stern and remote, emotionally and

5

physically exhausted by the challenges of the daily realities of life in St. Louis. He began to take more and more comfort in religion.[2] Life became even harder when, within a year of the birth of her youngest child, Mayfield Wilkins died of tuberculosis. As her health declined, she feared that her husband would not be able to look after the children and would, in desperation, send them to his mother in Holly Springs. Having escaped from Mississippi, Mayfield did not want her children to be raised there, so she wrote to her sister Elizabeth who lived in St. Paul, Minnesota, with her husband, Sam Williams, to ask that they raise the three children. The couple agreed, and the children left their father to start a new life in Minnesota. The Williamses adopted the children in 1911; but, although Wilkins saw his father, who became a traveling preacher, only intermittently throughout his childhood, he maintained contact with him and his stepmother until their deaths in the 1950s.

This tragic turn of events shaped Wilkins's life in an unexpected way. The influence of Sam Williams had a profound effect on the young boy. Williams was born in Mississippi but had also gone North to settle in St. Paul, where he found work looking after the private railway car of the president of the Northern Pacific Railroad. As such, he held a position of middle-class respectability in the local community. According to Wilkins, he was "not hard and not soft," but believed in discipline, diligence, and hard work.[3] He advised his nephew that if a black man wanted to advance, he must be educated and neat and have clean fingernails—advice the young Roy Wilkins took to heart.[4] He certainly followed his uncle's thrifty example. As a young boy he had a morning and evening newspaper round, and he financed his college studies with various summer jobs, working in a slaughterhouse and serving as a dining car waiter on the railroad back and forth to Seattle and as a redcap at St. Paul's Union Station. (This latter job led to a lifelong fascination with railways and transportation; Wilkins retained an encyclopedic knowledge of railway timetables, instantly recalling the best route to get from one city to another. In his later years, he often spent Sunday afternoons talking with the redcaps at La Guardia airport, close to his home in Queens, New York.)[5] The fact that Sam Williams owned his own house, had no debts, and put all three of his adoptive children through college was always a source of pride to Wilkins, and throughout his life he was preoccupied with financial security—both his own and the NAACP's. Gilbert Jonas, who worked with Wilkins at the Association in the 1960s and 1970s, describes him as "notoriously tight fisted with the NAACP's money," adding that he was barely more generous with his own.[6] He lived a relatively frugal life—his only extravagances were classic sports cars and occasional vacations in Europe or the Caribbean—and expected a similar parsimonious attitude from his staff.

During Wilkins's childhood, St. Paul's black population was smaller than in many other northern cities, and although hotels and restaurants were segregated, housing, schools, public leisure facilities, and transportation, for the most part, were not. The Williamses were one of the few black families living in their neighborhood, which was populated primarily by Swedish, Norwegian, Polish, German, and Irish first- and second-generation immigrants, many of whom spoke little English. Wilkins's best friend was Swedish, as were the Williamses' immediate neighbors, who treated Wilkins as one of their own family and with whom he kept in contact for many years after leaving Minnesota. An indication of the legacy this neighborhood had on him, as well as a glimpse of his sharp sense of humor, can be seen in a letter Wilkins wrote to Walter White, his future colleague, in 1931 en route to his new life with the NAACP in New York. "We leave here next Friday for ten days in Minnesota," Wilkins wrote, "where I will get in a little golf, fishing, and swimming along with my people, the blond, blue-eyed Scandinavians."[7]

The environment in which Wilkins grew up bore little of the social complexities of rural Mississippi, for example, where class, hierarchy, power, and proximity all played a part in creating the appalling, oppressive conditions in which many black Americans were forced to exist. Although he must have grown up with family stories about his father's flight from likely death in Mississippi and the anger and frustration that followed, on a daily basis Wilkins was shielded to a large extent from this reality during his childhood and school years. While he had attended a black kindergarten in St. Louis, once they were in St. Paul, he and his siblings attended desegregated schools. Wilkins thrived in the classroom. When he enrolled at the University of Minnesota to study sociology and economics, he quickly became involved in the school newspaper and other aspects of college life, despite the fact that there were some restrictions on black students at the university.

Wilkins's entry into college life, that bridge to adulthood, coincided with his first real awareness of the violence of white racism. On June 15, 1920, three young black men who had just arrived in Duluth, Minnesota, as part of a traveling circus became victims of a lynching. The three were part of a group of six men accused of raping a white woman. As news of the alleged attack spread, a mob of thousands gathered outside the jail where the men were held. Some of the mob broke into the building and took away three of the prisoners, who were then tried and found guilty in a mock trial. They were then beaten almost to death and hanged from a lamppost in downtown Duluth. The proximity of the violence was shocking to Wilkins—it took place just 150 miles from his hometown—but he was particularly appalled at the viciousness and hatred of the thousands of white people who had joined in the attacks. The murders challenged Wilkins's view of a group he had previously thought of as neighbors and friends and made him aware of the vulnerability of blacks even in a relatively benign state such as Minnesota. "For the first time in my life," he later said, "I understood what Du Bois had been writing about. I found myself thinking of black people as a very vulnerable *us*—and white people as an unpredictable violent *them*."[8]

Despite Wilkins's plan to study a subject that offered the prospect of secure employment when he graduated, he was far more interested in journalism, which offered a platform from which to challenge attacks like that at Duluth. While in high school, he had edited the school newspaper and regularly contributed poetry and news articles. In his second year at the University of Minnesota, he joined the staff of the *Minnesota Daily,* the college-produced commercial newspaper with a circulation of around 10,000, as the paper's first black reporter. After a year he became night editor of the paper, dividing his time between the classroom and the newsroom for the remainder of his college career.[9] By the time Wilkins left university in 1923, any thoughts of a career in sociology were abandoned, and it was inevitable that he would continue working in and for newspapers.

His professional life began at a small weekly publication called the *Northwestern Bulletin,* which had been founded by a friend of Wilkins. It was a good place to begin but was far too small to contain his ambitions, so when he was offered the chance to edit *The Appeal,* a black newspaper with a proud history of crusading journalism, he seized the opportunity. Unfortunately, *The Appeal*'s glory days were behind it, and the paper had become heavily reliant on advertising and features. Wilkins attempted to revive its campaigning zeal, running more stories about local and national black issues, and he enjoyed the chances the paper gave him to meet important people as they passed through the city; nonetheless it did not offer a big enough platform on which to establish his career as a newsman. When his father heard that the publisher of the *Kansas City Call,* a relatively new black weekly newspaper, was looking for a news editor, he pointed out that his son was more than qualified. Wilkins was hired and given his first assignment—to cover the NAACP convention that was taking place in the city. The *Call* changed Wilkins's life in several ways. Chester Franklin, the publisher, became a mentor to the young journalist and would prove to be a powerful ally during Wilkins's years at the NAACP. In addition, Wilkins's new role would introduce him to a whole new world.

Kansas City was one of the main destinations for thousands of poor, rural blacks migrating from the South; and, as the black population grew, so did the number of restrictive laws and covenants limiting blacks' freedom in the city: all public facilities apart from the trolley cars were rigorously segregated. Conditions were appalling for many of the new migrants: an NAACP study of race relations in the city published in 1925 found inadequate black schools, regular reports of police brutality, and a severe shortage of habitable, let alone decent, accommodation for the rising black population. Wilkins's new position gave him a forum to protest against the racism he saw, heard about, and experienced, and he made full use of it. One of his earliest campaigns was against a school bond issue, which would have allocated almost $1,000,000 to build a new high school for white students, while under $30,000 was earmarked to remodel a factory building for a black elementary school. The *Call* "crusaded and beat the bushes and whipped up community sentiment" in protest. Wilkins calculated that the complacency of those in favor of the issue who would not vote, assuming that the bond issue would pass without any problem, would clear the way for those against the issue to win the vote and defeat the proposal—which is exactly what happened.[10]

Just as his adult life was taking shape, Wilkins suffered three devastating losses. His sister, Armeda, died of tuberculosis in November 1927 at the age of twenty-four. Then, barely two months later, his aunt and uncle died within two days of each other. Wilkins and his brother, Earl, were left on their own. Wilkins's nephew Roger later wrote that a "profound loneliness" marked both Roy and Earl and that no one, possibly not even their wives, was closer to each than the other. Given his very private nature, Wilkins said little about these losses in later years. Although he wrote briefly about it in his autobiography, the sense of loss of home, as much as people, is acute. His main words of tribute to his uncle, however, were that he had died leaving no debts, "a final testament to his belief in self-help"—a model that shaped Wilkins's philosophy for the rest of his life.[11]

Once the family's house was sold, Wilkins brought his brother into the *Call* as an advertising salesman. Earl Wilkins would remain at the paper until his own untimely death from tuberculosis in January 1941. Although the two brothers had been separated by circumstances and distance, this renewed proximity brought them closer, so close that the two brothers even dated sisters for a time. Wilkins was engaged to Marvel Jackson, whom he had met at college, while Earl courted and later married her sister Helen. During their engagement, Marvel Jackson moved to New York to work first for W. E. B. Du Bois at *The Crisis,* then moving to the *Amsterdam News,* where she later became that paper's first female reporter. As she became more involved with the social and cultural life of New York City, Jackson later told an interviewer, she began to have second thoughts about her engagement and came to dread the thought of marrying Wilkins, but was spared any awkward disentanglement by a letter from him shortly before the proposed wedding date. During Jackson's absence, Wilkins had met Aminda Badeau, a social worker who had just moved to Kansas City from St. Louis; in his letter to Jackson, Wilkins confessed that Badeau was apparently three months pregnant. Although he promised to "straighten it out," Jackson quickly took the opportunity to break off the engagement, and Wilkins married Badeau in June 1929. According to Jackson, Earl Wilkins suspected Badeau of tricking his brother; in any case, the couple remained married until Wilkins's death in 1981 but never had children.[12]

Ironically, Wilkins would soon follow his former fiancée to New York. By the late 1920s, he was combining his work at the *Call* with increasing activity within the local branch of the NAACP. Wilkins liked to say his family was entwined with the NAACP almost from its beginnings. As a boy, he sold copies of *The Crisis,* the Association's magazine; and his Uncle Sam was the forty-second member of the St. Paul branch, for which Wilkins served as secretary by the time he was twenty-two. He continued his involvement with the organization when he moved to Kansas City; there he was considered a bright young man who could bring some much-needed new blood into the local branch. He became secretary of the Kansas City branch, leading its contribution to the NAACP's campaign against the nomination of Judge John Parker to the Supreme Court. Parker had been heard to make racist remarks in an early speech, and when his nomination was announced the NAACP mobilized the full weight of its organization against Parker. In Kansas City, Wilkins used newspaper advertisements and his column in the *Call* to wage the battle. When Parker was defeated, Wilkins launched a similar campaign against Kansas senator Henry Allen at the request of the NAACP's national office. Allen, a former governor of the state, was an interim appointment who had voted for Parker's confirmation. Wilkins entered the fight against him "with both feet."[13] He persuaded Chester Franklin to donate advertising space to the campaign against Allen, he wrote articles, he made speeches, and he helped mobilize the state's NAACP branches against the nomination. The campaign attracted widespread black support, and Allen lost his seat to George McGill, the Democratic candidate.

The Parker and Allen campaigns transformed Wilkins's life. They marked a turning point in his move from what he saw as the passivity of journalism to a more active campaign against racism.[14] Wilkins's efforts in the two campaigns impressed Walter White, who at the time was the Association's assistant secretary. He met with Wilkins during several visits to Kansas City, and the two maintained a casual correspondence as Wilkins's reputation as a journalist and activist grew. This contact proved useful when, in 1930, W. E. B. Du Bois invited Wilkins to join the staff of the NAACP as business manager for *The Crisis,* its membership magazine. After much deliberation Wilkins declined the offer; but, despite his self-confessed lack of business knowledge, he had no hesitation in offering Du Bois some suggestions on how to improve the magazine's financial health, most of which focused on the need for better organization. Wilkins's decision to turn down Du Bois's offer was probably wise, because there is no doubt that Wilkins and Du Bois would have been a combustible combination, as subsequent events proved. Nevertheless, the force of Wilkins's opinions made such an impression that the following year, when White was promoted to secretary and began looking for an assistant, James Weldon Johnson, the departing secretary, suggested, "What about that young man who wrote the letter?"[15]

This time Wilkins accepted the position, but only after driving a hard bargain. A number of letters went back and forth between Kansas City and New York as the finer points of the proposed salary were hammered out between the impecunious organization and the ambitious young editor. While the position offered Wilkins a much bigger platform from which to crusade, as well as the chance to build a national reputation, he was not prepared to move from Kansas City for the $3,000 per annum proposed by the Association. After some weeks of negotiation, a salary of $3,300 was eventually agreed upon, and Wilkins took up his new position at 69 Fifth Avenue on August 15, 1931.

Unfortunately, as he later wrote, "the pall of office politics and intrigue was thicker than the smog in Los Angeles" at the national office.[16] Walter White had been secretary for just a few months when Wilkins arrived, and the transition from James Weldon Johnson—the first black secretary of the organization, who had had an extraordinary career as poet, writer, and diplomat and who had overseen the NAACP's growth for a decade—was not an easy one. White had joined the NAACP in 1918, eight years after its founding, as assistant secretary; his pale complexion, blonde hair, and blue eyes belied the fact that he came from a well-to-do black family in Atlanta, but his interest in racial politics was born of bitter experience. White had lived through the Atlanta riot of 1906, which erupted when a mob of 10,000 angry whites, fueled by political race-baiting and false rumors of sexual attacks on white women by black men, killed at least 25 African Americans and attacked black areas of the city (including White's street). In 1918 James Weldon Johnson, impressed by White's energy and his work in the Atlanta chapter of the Association, asked White to join the NAACP's head office as his assistant.

During his time at the NAACP, White had built a reputation as a courageous investigator, making full use of his pale complexion to infiltrate communities where lynchings had taken place in the hope of finding evidence against the perpetrators. But he was a less effective executive. White had acted as temporary secretary in 1929 when Johnson took a year's leave of absence, but uncertainty about White's ability to manage the organization's finances had led the board of directors to establish a Committee on Administration to oversee his activities. Nevertheless, de spite such reservations, White was appointed Johnson's successor at the end of 1930. In addition to funding and revenue problems exacerbated by the Depression, White's tendency to be cavalier in his handling of financial and political matters, while at the same time being a bureau cratic and overbearing manager, created an atmosphere of tension and low morale within the national office. Du Bois was particularly dismissive of White and baited him whenever possible as he competed for funds to keep *The Crisis* afloat.[17]

Wilkins had barely settled into his new life in New York when his ca reer at the NAACP almost ended before it began. Relations finally broke down between Du Bois and White in December 1931. Protesting bud get and job cuts and suspecting duplicity in White's accounting state ments, Du Bois penned a memo challenging the secretary's leadership. Four other senior officials—William Pickens, the NAACP's field secre tary; Herbert Seligmann, director of publicity; Robert Bagnall, director of branches; and the newly arrived Wilkins—signed the document. Citing a list of complaints, the memorandum, which pulled no punches, stated, "These facts illustrate the utter viciousness of the present method of ap pointing the Budget Committee and laying facts before it. . . . We are not acting under the assumption that we have any vested rights in our positions, but, on the other hand, we do not propose to sit down and allow the Secretary and the Chairman of the Board or any other officers of the Association to malign and traduce us without giving us a reason able chance to answer."[18] Wilkins later claimed it made no mention of White "by name," a particularly surprising assertion in light of the final, damning sentence, which read, "We have all had considerable and varied experiences but in our several careers we have never met a man like Walter White who under so outward and charming manner has succeeded within a short time in alienating and antagonizing everyone of his colleagues, including all the clerks in the office."[19]

A coup d'état was only avoided by the efforts of Joel Spingarn, the NAACP's president, who promised to investigate the charges laid against White and Mary White Ovington, the NAACP's chairman and one of its founders. Overcome with remorse, and faced with an ignominious return to Kansas City, Wilkins withdrew his support for the memorandum the following day. The other signatories, except Du Bois, were equally quick to recant. The repentant Wilkins went further by offering his resignation to White the following day, saying, "I am simply sick over the part I took in that awful mess before the Board yesterday. I regret the whole incident, I withdraw all charges and insinuations, and in decency and respect for you, the work of the Association, and my conscience, I hereby tender my resignation to take effect at your pleasure."[20]

After the melee about the Du Bois memorandum, Wilkins steered clear of office politics for the next few months by spending much of his time on the road, meeting members across the country and looking for cases of discrimination that the Association could fight. During these trips, he got to know many of the Association's local leaders, including Daisy Lampkin, an energetic regional field secretary from Philadelphia. Lampkin had arrived at the NAACP in 1930 with a sterling reputation as an activist for civil rights. She had been the national organizer of the National Association of Colored Women, was a vice president of the *Pittsburgh Courier* newspaper, and was a leading member of the women's wing of the Republican Party. She had earned her NAACP stripes by reviving its moribund Pittsburgh branch and organizing the Association's annual conference in 1931, which took place in Philadelphia. Despite a difference in age of almost twenty years, Lampkin and Wilkins became friends and allies almost from the start. The two started working together shortly after Wilkins arrived at the national office, and from that point Wilkins confided in Lampkin for the rest of her long career at the NAACP. She proved to be one of his most formidable supporters as he rose through the organization.

During these early years, Wilkins paid close attention to the activities of branches, prodding the inactive and supporting the vigorous. But his ambitions drove him to look for bigger challenges, particularly in light of the courageous and dramatic investigations that White had undertaken when he was in Wilkins's position. Wilkins's chance came at the end of

1932, when he was asked to carry out an investigation in the heart of the Deep South. For some months, the NAACP had been investigating claims of discrimination against blacks working on federally funded levee programs in Mississippi. Helen Boardman had initially been hired by the board to investigate the allegations. She confirmed that blacks were working for much lower pay than whites, without holidays or overtime, and were sometimes even being charged for water they used. According to Boardman, the overseers at the camps treated the black workers little better than slaves.[21] In one Louisiana camp, thirty black workers were housed in tents the same size as those housing twelve white workers at another camp. No beds were provided for the blacks, so many slept on straw, in the open air, or in nearby barns. At another camp, black workers barely received any pay at all, as the charges for food, shelter, and other expenses often amounted to more than their pay.[22]

When Boardman was unable to investigate further, Wilkins was dispatched to Mississippi with journalist George Schuyler to continue the investigation. Posing as itinerant laborers looking for work, the pair were shocked by the stories they heard and conditions they found. Workers described eighteen-hour days or more for wages of just $1 or $2 per day if they were paid at all, and most worked six days a week—spared only a seventh day of labor by religious restrictions that prevented work on Sundays.[23] Wilkins, in a press release, laid the blame for this situation firmly with the government: "We know now that the army has a group of engineers in every camp on the delta. These engineers live in their tents in the camps. They do business daily and nightly with the contractors. They supervise and pass finally upon all levee constructions. They know exactly, in detail, what the Negro laborers are suffering in these camps."[24]

Shamed into action by the findings, the Senate decided to reopen its investigation, and the NAACP urged its members to support the levee workers in a press release sent to branches: "The Delta folk are helpless. You are not. You can help put millions of dollars in the hands of black workmen on the Mississippi and at the same time wipe out slavery in what is called fondly 'the land of the free.'" The NAACP investigations eventually bore fruit. In October 1933 the War Department announced that contract workers in the levee camps would receive a guaranteed minimum wage and reduced working hours.[25] Wilkins's involvement in the investigation gave him an opportunity to apply his appetite for campaigning in a tangible way. After this, however, he rarely became involved in grassroots activity, although the NAACP made much of this episode in later years in its attempt to refute accusations that Wilkins had done little "in the trenches."

Inquiries into discriminatory hiring practices in government programs such as the levee camps and the Hoover Dam were obvious causes for the NAACP; others, although equally worthy of investigation, were more complex and sometimes either given cursory attention or ignored. The case of the "Scottsboro Boys" began in that fashion, and the consequences of the Association's tardiness in offering support would be felt for many years afterward. The facts were stark but not unfamiliar. In March 1931, nine black youths were charged with the rape of two white women while all were hopping rides on a freight train traveling through Tennessee and Alabama. When the case quickly came to trial in Scottsboro, Alabama, the young men were represented by a white lawyer who had been hired by the nearest NAACP branch, sixty miles away in Chattanooga. Unfortunately, the lawyer was a drunk who met with his clients for a mere thirty minutes before the trial. All but one of the youths were quickly sentenced to death, despite scant evidence that the women had been sexually attacked and the fact that one of the accused boys was physically incapable of rape.[26]

Such a blatant miscarriage of justice should have been an obvious candidate for the Association's attention. But White, possibly out of reluctance to tie the NAACP to a seemingly hopeless case, asked for copies of the trial transcripts to be sent to the head office for examination by the organization's legal committee, which then took one month to review the documents. In the meantime, the International Labor Defense (ILD), the legal arm of the American Communist Party (CPUSA), stepped in and took control of the case. The CPUSA had made a concerted effort to attract black Americans for some years and had developed a program of self-determination for American blacks, which, taken to its logical, albeit unlikely, conclusion would create a separate black state. The CPUSA saw the Scottsboro case as a heaven-sent opportunity to establish the Party in the South and to mobilize a broad working-class base from which to attack capitalism.

The Scottsboro incident erupted shortly before Wilkins arrived at the Association. While he was still in salary negotiations with the NAACP, he publicly took White and the Association to task for their caution in the case. Once he joined the staff, he continued to prod White about why the NAACP was not doing more to counteract the ILD's campaign. Wilkins berated White for having to rewrite ILD press releases and distribute them as NAACP announcements to deflect the increasing criticism from the black press about the organization's silence. In response, after Wilkins arrived at the NAACP, White handed over the Scottsboro case to him; but it was too late. By that time, Wilkins said, the Communist Party had "beaten us [the NAACP] out of the starting gates."[27] Although he remained involved with the case and the Scottsboro Boys, it took many years for the case to be finally resolved. Over the next two decades, the defendants endured several more trials. (One of the group, Haywood Patterson, was sentenced to death in three separate trials and received a seventy-five year sentence in the fourth. Ruby Bates, one of the accusers, dramatically recanted her accusation during Patterson's second trial, but she made a less than credible witness and her revised testimony was laughed at in the courtroom.) It took many more years and trials for justice to be served. In 1937, rape charges against four of the nine (Willie Roberson, Olen Montgomery, Eugene Williams, and Roy Wright) were dropped, and they were released from prison; the remaining five, however, remained incarcerated.[28] Over the next decade, Haywood Patterson escaped from prison twice but was captured and eventually died in prison (sentenced on a different charge) in 1952. Clarence Norris was paroled twice and was eventually released from prison in 1946. Charlie Weems was paroled in 1943, Ozie Powell was released in 1946, and Andy Wright finally left prison in 1950.

Unfortunately, White was more concerned with analyzing the potential challenge to the NAACP's position from a Communist group than with determining how the ILD had succeeded in mobilizing what should have been the NAACP's natural constituency. The ILD's success in mobilizing black Americans highlighted a leftward shift among that group. As historians August Meier and John Bracey argue, the move to the left was strengthened by the migration of blacks from the rural south to the urban north, where the Democratic Party machinery invariably controlled political life.[29] The NAACP could not ignore these changes and was forced to forge new alliances, not least because several organizations on the left, including the Communist Party and the Congress of Industrial Organizations, were also taking up the cause of black Americans. Nevertheless, there were some valuable lessons the NAACP learned from the debacle. Charles Houston, the NAACP's chief counsel, acknowledged that the Scottsboro case illustrated how successful the tactics of mass pressure could be and, Houston said, "It has changed the emphasis of the Negro question from a race issue to a class issue."[30]

By the time of the Scottsboro arrests, the Depression was biting deep into the American economy, and almost everyone, black and white, found life increasingly hard. Finding a solution to this social and economic devastation was the main priority of the new president, Franklin Roosevelt, who took office in March 1933 with a mandate to tackle the appalling economic conditions. However, the president's package of federal programs offered little relief for black Americans. The short-lived National Recovery Administration (NRA), a government agency that existed only for two years between 1933 and 1935, established a series of voluntary sets of "fair practice" codes that were intended to eliminate unfair trade practices, establish minimum wages, limit working hours, and encourage collective bargaining. In principle, this should have gone some way to improving the lot of black Americans, who were among the poorest workers in the United States and who were trapped in poverty by the discriminatory practices of both unions and industry. Sadly, the NRA may have made the situation worse. The minimum wage clause did not apply to agricultural or domestic workers—sectors that employed around three-quarters of black Americans—and the policies would be administered by state and local officials who, particularly in the South, saw no need to change established discriminatory practices.

Blacks were furious—and frustrated—at the way the NRA program was administered, calling it "Negro Rights Assassinated" or "Negro Rights Abused." They felt little better about any of the other "alphabet agencies" set up as part of the New Deal.[31] In an attempt to represent the black worker at congressional hearings on the NRA, John Davis and Robert Weaver, two young black economists, appealed to the NAACP and other groups to join together to finance their lobbying efforts. Supportive of the idea, White, with Wilkins's enthusiastic support, enrolled the NAACP in a coalition of organizations that formed the Joint Committee on National Recovery (JCNR). The loose coalition of about twenty unions and religious and civic organizations came together under the leadership of Davis to fight discrimination in New Deal agencies and programs. Unfortunately, the JCNR lacked funding and resources, and as a result Davis's efforts to lobby and prod had little effect.[32]

In the fall of 1933 Du Bois accepted a temporary professorship at Atlanta University, leaving *The Crisis* without an editor at a critical time. With the Depression tightening the purse strings of even the most generous philanthropists, competition for money intensified, and the magazine had become the battlefield upon which the various political machinations within the NAACP's national office were played out. *The Crisis* was very much Du Bois's creation. Despite being the official organ of the NAACP, the publication reflected Du Bois's own philosophy and interests and had operated on a relatively autonomous basis. Although the magazine had in the past enjoyed periods of high circulation and a healthy bank account, the Depression had reversed its fortunes, and by 1933 *The Crisis* was in a parlous state. Circulation had fallen, bills went unpaid, and demands for funds meant that the Association became more involved in the running of the magazine than Du Bois found palatable. The feud between the imperious editor and the autocratic White did not help matters.

On his departure, Du Bois did what he could to avoid letting *The Crisis* fall into the hands of his nemesis by presenting the Board with a fait accompli. He announced that he had hired George Streator, a former Fisk University graduate, to run the publication as its managing editor; Du Bois would remain editor-in-chief in Atlanta. But because the Association was funding the magazine the board of directors insisted that Wilkins be appointed co–managing editor. It was a terrible combination. The hostility between White and Du Bois simply devolved to their respective deputies. Wilkins resented the extra work and the fact that his duties on *The Crisis* were undefined. Streator meanwhile saw little value in having Wilkins as a colleague and dismissed his contribution to the magazine as nothing but "advice and hot air."[33] Certainly, Wilkins offered Streator little support other than observations and criticisms, which Streator attempted to quash by asking that Wilkins at least take on writing a regular column rather than making ineffectual suggestions. Streator complained that news about branches was being given to the *Pittsburgh Courier*, where Daisy Lampkin was vice president, rather than to him at *The Crisis* and, even more galling, that he was not allowed to attend board meetings (at White's instruction). He even accused White of asking staff to spy on him.[34]

This untenable situation was only resolved when Du Bois resigned from the NAACP in July 1934 following a provocative editorial in which he advocated voluntary segregation as a means of black advancement.[35] To fill the gap, the board initially decided that Wilkins and Streator would continue as co–managing editors. Streator, however, had had enough; he resigned, leaving Wilkins as temporary managing editor until the board could take a more permanent decision at the next meeting in September. Wilkins was reluctant to take on the editorial role. He wrote to the board of directors arguing that he was already doing the work of three people (he was also in charge of publicity following the departure of Herbert Seligmann and another officer) and was unable to take on any further work. But his pleas fell on deaf ears: not only was Wilkins's request ignored, a new editor was not appointed until 1949, when Wilkins was appointed acting secretary.

Unfortunately, the magazine was aptly named. *The Crisis* was in terrible condition, with a number of bad debts, scarce resources, and, Wilkins claimed, no editorial plan.[36] Under Du Bois's direction the magazine explored the political and cultural facets of black life. The activities of NAACP branches were mentioned in a monthly column, and specific campaigns, such as the antilynching battle, were featured when there was something to report; but the magazine was certainly not a mouthpiece for the organization. Wilkins was keen to broaden its appeal by including human-interest stories, more articles about NAACP activities, and "editorial comment written for a much larger public than intellectuals," arguing that if *The Crisis* had broader appeal it could become a self-supporting publication rather than relying on NAACP subsidies.[37] Profiles of black entertainers and artists, such as musician Fats Waller and sculptor Richmond Barthé, running alongside stories such as that of a man who sold 17,000 watermelons a year illustrated Wilkins's new editorial strategy. Readers of *The Crisis* generally approved of the changes. Photographer

Carl Van Vechten was one of the overhauled magazine's more ebullient fans, writing to Walter White, "A very dull periodical has overnight become informative, exhilarating, and entertaining. Is this transformation due to Roy Wilkins? If so he should be blessed by the Pope and given the keys to the city. 678 wreaths of laurel to him and a spray of silver lilies to you, dear Walter!"[38]

Elsewhere there was little to celebrate: the NAACP was fending off criticism from several quarters, not least from Du Bois, who wrote a stinging and very public rebuke of the NAACP's structure; the economic impact of the Depression was taking its toll on finances, and pressure from young black economists to tackle economic issues all prompted the Association to undertake a serious review of its programs. The Committee on Future Plan and Program led by Howard University economist Abram Harris along with a small group of intellectuals, including Rachel Du Bois (no relation to the esteemed W. E. B. Du Bois) and Sterling Brown, was set up and charged with considering "the future program of the Association in the light of changing national and world conditions."[39] In its findings, a summary of which was approved by the annual conference in 1935, the committee proposed a sweeping reorganization of the NAACP's structure that would devolve power to a network of grassroots activists in an attempt to shift the Association's focus from the black middle class and to allow for a greater alignment of black and white workers. This, Harris argued, would help to build an integrated labor movement where decisions to press for legislative reform would be made at a local level rather than by the executive office. Such a move would, in effect, transform the Association's head office into little more than a titular administrative center servicing a national network of workers' groups that advocated a purely economic program.[40]

The potential cost of implementing these recommendations, and their consequences if it restructured along the lines suggested by Harris (including likely unemployment for most of the Association's leadership), meant that the report received little support from either the board of directors or the national office staff. Some of the Association's members, however, were already moving in that direction. The Depression was encouraging an increased political awareness in NAACP branches in northern manufacturing cities, which were beginning to find common ground with some labor organizations. Unions had been given a boost by the passing of the National Labor Relations Act, known as the Wagner Act, in 1935, which protected the rights of workers in the private sector to organize unions, strike, and participate in collective bargaining. However, in spite of this new rapprochement, the relationship between labor organizations and blacks—and indeed between unions and the NAACP—had never been comfortable. The American Federation of Labor (AFL), for example, operated an openly racist policy. Its member unions confined blacks to segregated chapters or excluded them altogether, and employers frequently manipulated blacks into acting as strikebreakers, much to the fury of unions and white workers.

The NAACP had always received numerous complaints from black workers in all industries and regions about discriminatory pay and conditions. For example, in New York City black motion picture operators, working within a union, were restricted to working in cinemas in Harlem, were not paid overtime, and were paid less than their white peers. In the construction industry, black workers reported that union officials colluded with contractors to restrict employment opportunities for blacks. Wilkins cited one instance of a small clothing manufacturer whose workforce was composed primarily of black workers. As soon as the factory was unionized, the union attempted, unsuccessfully, to have all the black workers dismissed in order to employ white women.[41]

Throughout his career, Wilkins frequently used his regular newspaper columns to comment on an event or issue, and this was the forum he used to express his frustration over discriminating labor unions. Citing a recent strike organized by steel workers in Milwaukee with the specific aim of forcing out black workers using the powers granted by the recently passed Wagner Act, he argued that "union labor strategy seems to be to form a union in a given plant, strike to obtain the right to bargain with the employers as the sole representative of labor, and then to close the union to black workers, effectively cutting them off from employment." The solution, he suggested, would arrive when, "sooner than most people think, the rank and file workers are going to scrap the craft union structure, dump the A.F. of L. overboard, and organize industrial unions without a color line. Then we will have a real labor movement in this country."[42] The editorial proved prescient when, in 1935, the Committee for Industrial Organization (later the Congress of Industrial Organizations, or CIO), was formed and from its beginning was open to black workers. The NAACP enthusiastically endorsed the new organization. By the late 1930s, union activists led some NAACP branches and were pushing the organization leftward. By 1940 the composition of many urban NAACP branches had changed beyond recognition: an increasingly youthful and militant presence, driven primarily by labor activists, had replaced the middle-class leaders of previous years.

The influence of this more militant generation was also reflected in the NAACP's head office, where new staff members were eager to push the organization forward with an ambitious legal strategy to secure the constitutional rights of black Americans. From its earliest days, the NAACP had waged a long and patient battle in courtrooms across the United States. By the early 1930s it had secured a series of important court cases, including *Buchanan v. Warley* in 1917, in which the Supreme Court found that zoning ordinances that were racially restrictive were unconstitutional; *Moore v. Dempsey* in 1923, in which the Supreme Court declared that trials dominated by mobs violated the due process clause of the Fourteenth Amendment, and *Nixon v. Herndon* in 1927, which invalidated the "white primary" law that prevented blacks from voting in Democratic primaries in Texas.

The Association had expanded its legal program in 1930 on the promise of $100,000 by the Garland Fund, a philanthropic organization, to fund lawsuits that challenged the segregated education system in the South. Nathan Margold, a young New York lawyer who was hired to manage the Garland program, produced an extensive report, which argued that facilities provided for blacks were never equal, although they were almost always separate, and therefore violated the "separate but equal" precedent established in *Plessy v. Ferguson* in 1896. This, Margold argued, paved the way for a legal challenge, particularly against separate public schools; and he drew up a bold legal strategy. The Depression almost derailed Margold's plan: the Garland Fund lost so much money it was able to give the Association only around a tenth of the promised funds.[43] By the time even this money was available, Margold had left the NAACP. Charles Houston, who by this time was head of Howard University's law school, took on the fight.

Houston had already established himself as a brilliant lawyer. He was the son of a well-regarded attorney who had a successful practice in Washington, DC. After graduating magna cum laude from Amherst College, where he was the only black student in his year, Houston began teaching English at Howard University; but when America entered the war in Europe in 1917, he joined the army as an officer at the age of just twenty-one. On his return from France, Houston entered Harvard Law School, where he became the first black member of *Harvard Law Review*'s editorial board. When his studies in Cambridge ended, instead of resuming his position at Howard, Houston traveled to Spain, to study the country's legal system. While abroad, he took the opportunity to visit Italy and parts of North Africa, where he enjoyed living in a country where he was not defined by his race. Eventually, however, he had to return home, and in 1924 joined his father's law practice in Washington, DC.

While at Harvard, Houston had come to consider the teaching of law as important as the practice of it, particularly in achieving civil rights. He was convinced that developing a cadre of highly trained black lawyers who would be "social engineers" would be crucial to defeating Jim Crow and, with this vision in mind, he joined the faculty of Howard University's law school. Within five years he had become vice-dean of the school and implemented a series of ambitious reforms, thanks to which the school quickly gained a reputation for producing extremely effective civil rights lawyers. By the time he joined the NAACP's legal team he was able to call upon a number of brilliant young black lawyers to put his vision into practice. Over the years they would secure a succession of victories, culminating in the *Brown v. Board of Education* ruling in 1954, which would dismantle the legal framework of segregation.[44]

Houston was more pragmatic than Margold. He knew that a direct challenge on segregation in high schools would be doomed to failure, He instead developed an ambitious legal program that would challenge access to graduate schools. Houston took the long view and with each case aimed to secure a precedent to be used in the next stage of the fight. Thurgood Marshall, one of Houston's students at Howard who had been practicing law in Baltimore, joined the Association in 1936 to help Houston lead the NAACP's litigation program. Marshall's arrival in New York was a boon for Wilkins. The two men were of similar ages, lived in the

same neighborhood, and often traveled to work together, but tempera-
mentally they were very different: Wilkins was cautious, measured, and
bureaucratic, while Marshall was charismatic but disorganized and had an
expression that, Wilkins wrote, made him look like "a skeptical house de-
tective listening to the alibi of a philandering husband caught *in flagrante*
with a lady of the night."[45]

This energetic team fanned out across the country, shoring up support for branches that were flagging under the weight of economic mis-
ery, looking for cases to take to court and plaintiffs willing to fight them,
and drumming up new members. Wilkins kept a diary for a few weeks in
early 1935, and his entries give a flavor of the activities he was preoccupied with during this period. His primary task should have been editing
The Crisis, but more often his days were spent writing press releases, pre-
paring the annual report, dealing with the administration around the antilynching campaign, and, on one occasion, helping to serve a subpoena
on a restaurant manager in Greenwich Village who had refused to serve
Wilkins and two friends on the basis that Wilkins appeared to be drunk.
(When the case came to court the three plaintiffs were awarded $200
each in damages.)[46] He spoke at branch meetings in Ohio, women's clubs
in New Jersey, farmers' groups in Arkansas, and youth groups in New
York; but, as the decade progressed, more and more of his speeches were
to unions, workers' conferences, and employee groups, as the NAACP
tried to fend off challenges from Communist groups, particularly in the
North.

In the mid-1930s a wave of protests swept through more than thirty-
five cities as blacks demonstrated and picketed against stores that were
happy to take their custom but refused to employ black workers. While
some protests were brief, angry, and ineffectual, some "Don't buy where
you can't work" campaigns were successful in winning concessions from
white businesses.[47] A new group, a loose confederation of black and white
organizations known as the National Negro Congress (NNC) instigated
by economist John P. Davis and James Ford, an organizer for the Communist Party, to improve the lot of black Americans, capitalized on this
new militancy. In Chicago in the winter of 1936 the NNC brought together hundreds of participants, including Du Bois, Lester Granger of
the Urban League, A. Philip Randolph, and Ralph Bunche to discuss a

range of subjects connected with the economic uplift of black Americans. Wilkins attended the conference as an observer and, although he was later dismissive of the organization, at the time he praised the NNC's success in involving young people and labor organizations, both groups that the NAACP had yet to attract in significant numbers. He tried to encourage Walter White to align with the NCC on certain issues, but White refused. Thus, an early opportunity to broaden the Association's program and strengthen relations with the labor movement was lost.[48]

Although there was plenty to occupy the NAACP domestically, Wilkins could not help looking at the descent toward war in Europe with fear, interest, and a certain amount of bewilderment. How could America be appalled by the Nazis' treatment of Jews in Europe but not be equally appalled by the treatment of black Americans at home, he wondered. "If it is a disgrace to make one race scrub a sidewalk in Vienna, is it not equally a disgrace to issue passes without which Negro Americans cannot even walk certain streets of a large southern city?" Wilkins summed up the dilemma thus: "Until a Negro can study medicine at the University of Michigan we cannot make a convincing argument why Jews should be permitted to study at Heidelberg."[49]

The obscenity of segregation became personal for Wilkins in January 1941, when his brother Earl died at the age of thirty-five of tuberculosis. Before his death, Earl had spent three years in a sanitarium and was left a semi-invalid by his illness. Wilkins flew immediately to Kansas City to join his sister-in-law, Helen, his nephew, Roger, and his father. Roger Wilkins later described his grandfather weeping at the loss of one son and being comforted by his only remaining child. Roger also recalled that his father resented William Wilkins's abandonment of his young children. If Roy Wilkins shared that view, he made no mention of it. His anger instead was reserved for the fact that his brother was laid to rest in a segregated graveyard. Forty years later, he described his feelings in his autobiography. "From across the Atlantic and Pacific," he wrote, "World War II was blowing closer and closer, but white America was not yet ready to accept a Wilkins or any other Negro as an equal—not even in death."[50]

By the time the Japanese attacked Pearl Harbor on December 7, 1941, Wilkins had been a part of the country's preparations for war for some time. At forty years of age, he was too old to qualify for conscription, but when war looked inevitable Fiorello La Guardia, New York City's mayor, had asked him to serve on a local draft board. With the outbreak of war, the old dilemma between patriotism and protest resurfaced. The blatant discrimination in the US military, where even blood supplies were segregated, as well as inequities in war industries and city housing projects, to cite just a few examples, made a mockery of the call to protect democracy abroad. Nevertheless, as they had in every other conflict in American history, many black Americans felt a patriotic duty to fight for their country.

New organizations emerged, acting as pressure groups to challenge discrimination in the war industries. Although these groups lacked the organizational structure of the NAACP, they proved to be the first real challengers to the Association. In May 1941 A. Philip Randolph, leader of the Brotherhood of Sleeping Car Porters, one of the first predominantly black unions, called for one hundred thousand African Americans to participate in a March on Washington to protest against discrimination in factories producing military hardware. Randolph made efficient use of the NAACP's branch network to mobilize the public, and the threat of tens of thousands of angry blacks on the streets of Washington helped prod President Roosevelt into issuing Executive Order 8802, which created the Fair Employment Practices Committee (FEPC) to combat discrimination in the defense industry and government.[51] The order stated explicitly that, "there shall be no discrimination in the employment of workers in defense industries or government because of race, creed, color or national origin."[52]

Strong words these may have been, but despite suggestions from some quarters that this was the most important federal mandate since the Emancipation Proclamation, it was mostly a symbolic victory. Still, the FEPC is notable for several reasons. For the first time since the Civil Rights Act of 1875, the federal government issued a mandate against discrimination, which in itself provided an impetus for both black leaders and the black community to renew their efforts to obtain equal rights. The cooperation between blacks and a government office was also unique. In addition, the provisions that instructed employers and government agencies to ensure "equitable participation" were forerunners of affirmative action programs. Nevertheless, the entire existence of the FEPC was precarious. Roosevelt refused to give the commission the power to prosecute violations. This impotence was exacerbated by the absence of congressional approval and funding, thanks to continued southern political objections.

Although the organization that arose out of Randolph's initial call, the March on Washington Movement (MOWM), was short-lived, its proposals on the use of nonviolent, direct action anticipated the modern civil rights movement.[53] As Harvard Sitkoff argues, despite the underlying philosophy of nonviolence, Randolph's strident rhetoric was a departure from the more conciliatory approach of more traditional organizations such as the NAACP. "His readiness to threaten rather than implore, to demonstrate rather than confer, became the model for others to follow," noted Sitkoff; and in doing so, Randolph forced the NAACP along with him.[54] Randolph's movement inspired the NAACP to mobilize those groups that had a vested interest in the FEPC, the continued existence of which had become a priority for the Association. Therefore, the NAACP joined forces with Randolph in spite of fears that the activities of his organization would overlap, or even overtake, those of local NAACP branches.[55]

Whether he was dissatisfied at the prospect of spending many more years as White's deputy or was concerned about his financial future, given the precarious nature of the NAACP's income, when Wilkins was offered the editorship of the *Amsterdam News,* a New York–based black weekly newspaper, in 1941, he took the offer very seriously. As editor of a newspaper such as the *Amsterdam News* Wilkins would have had a powerful platform within the black community, but the reach of the black press was narrow. In a letter to White he confessed that he was concerned about the lack of financial stability and security at the NAACP and looked to his boss for assurances that more concerted attempts would be made to solve the problem.[56] To keep Wilkins in place, White appealed to his deputy's ego: "As editor of *The Crisis,* and a top ranking official of the NAACP," White told Wilkins, "you occupy a place in American life of prestige greater than you possibly could do as editor of one of a number of papers. Prestige and honor butter no carrots nor pay any rent, I know, but they are intangible which are not valueless."[57] White's approach worked: Wilkins remained at the NAACP—though perhaps with some regret when he was faced with finding a solution to some of the organization's systemic problems.

A study commissioned by the NAACP's Committee on Administration in 1941 confirmed Wilkins's concerns about the organization. The final report described an autocratic approach by the national office that did little to help the NAACP work as an effective organization. The committee argued that the structure of the national office was not conducive either to closer involvement with branches or even as a simple conduit of information. Worse still, it argued that the national office's tendency to view branches simply as moneymaking operations led to the branches' only intermittent involvement rather than sustained and effective support of the Association's program.[58] Little was done to address these problems, although in May 1942 the Association's national officers attended a weekend conference to discuss some of the difficulties facing the organization. In preparation for the conference, members of the senior staff were asked to consider their priorities and come up with suggestions about what the program should cover.

Wilkins's proposals suggest several common themes. He was concerned about an apathy within the organization that hindered the creation of a more dynamic activity program; a lack of coherent planning; and, most important, a confusion not only on the part of the branches and departments but also within the national office about the NAACP's methods and aims.[59] His biggest fear was that other groups, particularly the Communists, would steal a march on the Association. He cited, as an example, the Veterans Committee Against Discrimination, which the NAACP had allowed to "take the play away" from the organization when it picketed the Senate in protest at the possible closure of the FEPC. Branch members needed work to do, Wilkins argued, and "If the NAACP does not give them work, they turn to other organizations that do offer activity in the cause."[60] Wilkins took a keen interest in the Association's branch network, and in 1942 it was even proposed that he fill the vacant role of Director of Branches, a position eventually given to Ella Baker. Although he rejected the suggestion, he offered several ideas on how the organization of NAACP branches could be improved, including breaking up larger branches into smaller neighborhood units to encourage a more diverse base and local leadership. The suggestion provoked much discussion but, as was often the case with the NAACP's more introspective exercises, nothing was implemented.

Ella Baker, who would become a pivotal leader of the civil rights movement in the 1950s, had joined the NAACP in 1940 as field secretary and became Director of Branches in 1943. She echoed some of Wilkins's frustrations. During her brief tenure at the Association, she implemented a series of important programs, including leadership training and workshops, and had traveled constantly during her time at the organization, sometimes at great personal risk, to build up the branch network. As Patricia Sullivan notes, the efforts of Baker and her colleague Madison Jones were crucial to the development of the NAACP at a turning point in its history, and their reports from the field brought the membership to life for those working in the national office.[61] Unfortunately, her vision of a membership that was organized at the grassroots and that drove the NAACP's program was at odds with that of Walter White, who saw the Association's branch network as a reflection of the national office's power.[62]

Even when Wilkins finally got his chance to lead the NAACP, temporarily, in December 1944, he had little opportunity to put any significant changes into effect. While White was on a tour of the South Pacific to examine the conditions of black troops, Wilkins did what he could to impose his authority on the organization. He was particularly tough on those he saw as dangerously autonomous, such as Leslie Perry, the administrative assistant in the NAACP's Washington office, who was castigated for sending out correspondence without consultation with the head office. For the most part, however, Wilkins acted as caretaker, carrying out his usual administrative duties while also overseeing some of the Association's legislative priorities, especially the prospective federal and state FEPC bills.

The scale of the Association's task in achieving equal rights had always been enormous; but as the end of the war approached it became clear that the conflict had changed the outlook of many black Americans and that they would no longer be satisfied with a gradual approach to equality. Any difficulties between Wilkins and White that might influence the effectiveness of the organization would therefore take on far more importance than a simple personality clash would normally imply. The NAACP had little idea of the profound effect World War II would have on American society as a whole and the Association's constituency in particular. The process of boosting black participation in the war effort, and in particular in the military, provided a salutary lesson in what could be achieved in the fight for equality.

When war broke out in Europe in 1939, there were just over 7,600 blacks serving in the Army and Navy and only five black officers. In the Army, black soldiers were restricted to four African American units, and in the Navy they were only allowed to be mess men.[63] A concerted effort by the NAACP and other groups had quickly borne fruit. Black combat units were created, and all military units were opened to black soldiers, though still on a segregated basis. This was far from ideal, but it was progress of a sort. By the end of the war, approximately 1,000,000 African Americans had served in the armed forces, including more than half a million in Europe, where their presence was, for the most part, met with equanimity by many of the communities in which they were based. This was in stark contrast to the segregation in place in the military camps. Having fought courageously for democracy abroad, black veterans had no intention of settling for second-class citizenship when they returned home.

2

Treading Water

The war years transformed the NAACP almost in spite of itself. By 1946 the Association had 1,073 branches and over 450,000 members, a remarkable increase of over 200,000 during the preceding three years.[1] Southern branches, in particular, showed a surprising vigor. In South Carolina, for example, membership grew from 800 in 1939 to 14,000 in 1948. Through its alliance with labor groups, it had broadened its base, begun to move away from its traditionally middle-class roots, and established itself as the principal, but by no means only, voice for a broad range black interests.[2] There were hints, however, that the NAACP's focus on litigation and legislation was no longer enough to satisfy its members' impatient desire for change.

Wilkins recognized that the NAACP was unprepared for such dramatic growth. "We had a big membership—five hundred thousand members and twelve hundred branches—and a large income," he later recalled, "but we didn't know how to use them."[3] Wilkins suggested to White that three areas in particular were badly in need of urgent repair if the Association was to make the best use of its sudden growth: the branch department, which Wilkins called inefficient; the youth department, which "continues to be a mystery"; and the membership department, which he said was struggling to cope with the influx of new members.[4]

Underlying the picture of chaos painted by Wilkins was the sense that the Association was unsure of its direction in the postwar world. Wilkins had already warned White in September 1945 that the NAACP urgently needed to strengthen its existing program and structure. He reiterated his concerns in March 1946 and issued several stark warnings. The NAACP's lack of direction was a serious problem, he said, and if it was not rectified, the NAACP was at the mercy of other groups. Wilkins warned White that "the Communists, as I have mentioned, are active. The Urban League has been quietly hiring better prepared staff members than we. They are doing a good job and the League is opening new offices and expanding in other ways. Some Interracial Committees are attracting the support of people who ordinarily would be with us—your friend from Media, PA, told me the other day when she was in the office that the Media Interracial Committee has completely taken the play away from the Media branch."

Ultimately, Wilkins told White, "We have to be about the business of perfecting a militant action membership or we may wake up some fine morning to discover that we are but a shell with a few score thousand faithful dues-paying members."[5]

Ella Baker, the NAACP's tireless director of branches, bore the brunt of this confusion. Unfortunately, the working relationship between White and Baker had worsened just at this pivotal time, leading Baker to resign in May 1946. In a three-page letter of resignation, an angry Baker directed a number of stinging criticisms at White, describing a culture where "an almost complete lack of appreciation for the collective thinking of the staff seems to prevail." She complained about the absence of staff meetings, the bureaucracy that hindered the smooth running of the office, the lack of consultation with staff members, and an atmosphere of suspicion and duplicity that caused "a disproportionate amount of staff energy [to be] consumed in fighting a sense of futility and frustration." As a final, damning indictment of the Association's national office, Baker closed by saying, "I came to the Association because I felt that I could make a contribution to the struggle for human justice and equality. I am leaving because I feel that there must be some way to do this without further jeopardizing one's integrity and sense of fair play."[6] Wilkins was hospitalized at the time of her departure. He sent Baker a short but regretful note about her resignation but said nothing about her charges of a confused, demoralized, and discouraged staff, although he had warned White shortly before Baker's resignation that the Association's lack of direction meant Baker had had "little to build upon except the general position of the NAACP."[7]

Baker's depressing portrait of an organizational culture steeped in paranoia, political intrigue, and obfuscation was in part a result of the deteriorating relationship between Wilkins and White. They went to great lengths to appear cordial and loyal in public but by the early 1940s suspicion and jealously governed their working relationship. The ambitious Wilkins had spent a decade as second in command and was frustrated. He resented White's extensive travels, lobbying, and self-publicizing and was increasingly bitter. When John Hammond, a board member who was no fan of the assistant secretary, accused Wilkins of making disparaging remarks about White while at a cocktail party, Wilkins responded with a vehement denial. Unfortunately, White's obvious lack of support for his deputy throughout the affair led Wilkins to complain to Daisy Lampkin of White's nefarious motives in trying to oust him through accusations of disloyalty. "There have been several incidents in the past year," he wrote, "which have seemed to indicate that Walter is very reluctant to have anyone assume the power of what we have chosen to call an executive director, a person who could keep his hands on the whole Association's program and push it along on all fronts with appropriate authority granted by the Board."[8] Wilkins's complaints, though self-serving, exposed a genuine problem: the difficulties at the top of the NAACP were having a negative effect on the development and running of the Association's program.[9]

Adding to Wilkins's dissatisfaction was White's apparent lack of interest in what he considered routine administrative tasks and his assistant's frustration at playing second fiddle. In principle, the combination of White's ability to forge connections with the great and the good and Wilkins's attention to the detail of the organization should have been an ideal combination. In reality, however, White's egocentric leadership style meant that few responsibilities of any importance were delegated to his deputy. Wilkins's equally large ego was constantly thwarted by having to defer to White, and he had little power to effect some of the more pressing changes that needed to be made.

The carnage of World War II had prompted a desire among world leaders to find a common forum within which international disputes could be resolved peacefully through negotiation and cooperation rather than conflict. In April 1945, representatives from fifty governments and numerous nongovernmental organizations, including the NAACP, had gathered in San Francisco to draw up the United Nations Charter. The postwar map was constantly being redrawn as colonial imperialism gave way to independence and a wave of freedom spread through Africa and Asia. Black Americans watched as country after country was liberated from colonial masters, feeling both hope and despair that equality and freedom in their own country were still elusive.

White initially led the Association's delegation, which had been invited as an unofficial observer; but when he was called back to New York, White handed this responsibility over to Wilkins. While in San Francisco, the NAACP delegation met with various government representatives from Asia, Africa, and the Soviet Union who were sympathetic to the NAACP's cause. Doubtful, however, that the American government would fully represent the interest of its black citizens, the NAACP delegates helped draft a proposal that called for an end to inequality and imperialism, but a concerted effort by the United States, with the help of Britain and France, thwarted attempts to add specific provisions on racial equality.[10]

Although the sight of so many countries shedding the colonial yoke offered some cause for optimism and inspiration, the growing mood of militancy among black Americans demanded that the Association focus on its domestic agenda.

Wilkins and White both had thoughts on what should be done, but came to different conclusions. When, in September 1945, White proposed adding several new positions, including a church secretary, a labor secretary, and opening a Hollywood bureau, possibly to be led by Langston Hughes, Wilkins rebelled—by memorandum—arguing not only that no program had been developed for the proposed departments but also that these additions risked adding to the already top-heavy bureaucracy of the organization. Not only that, he argued, the required funds would be better spent in strengthening the Association's floundering department of branches, particularly in regions where membership numbers had increased dramatically. "For the first time in many years we have a large membership in the state of Texas alone, to say nothing of the other South Western states . . . We have the largest state conference of branches in the

Association in the state of Virginia and, for the first time in history, a large and tremendously alert membership in South Carolina, with a greatly increased number of branches in Florida, yet we are doing nothing to establish a regional office to tie these people into the national program."[11]

Unfortunately, Wilkins had little time to deal with the NAACP's organizational problems. In June 1946, he was diagnosed with colon cancer and immediately admitted for surgery. Several months of recuperation followed. As a result of the surgery, Wilkins had to have a colostomy. In his autobiography many years later, he vividly recalled his fear at the diagnosis, and possibly even more at the long-term treatment: "I was forty-five at the time, I had been married seventeen years, and I wondered what Minnie would think about having a freak for a husband."[12] While there is no record in the NAACP, Wilkins, or Spingarn archives about any illness of Wilkins's other than the cancer, Carolyn Wedin, in her biography of Mary White Ovington, refers briefly to a mental breakdown suffered by Wilkins around 1946.[13] It is highly possible that the intense atmosphere at 20 West Fortieth Street, the NAACP's national headquarters, combined with Wilkins's first brush with his own mortality may have prompted a nervous collapse. Certainly, it would hardly be surprising if such an episode provoked a psychological crisis; but, in keeping with his very private personality, Wilkins said nothing about his illness publicly, either at the time or in later years.

He returned to duty on October 1, 1946, only to be faced with a crisis over White's declining health. While on vacation in February 1947, White suffered a serious heart attack and was forced to recuperate for three months. He returned to the office in April but agreed to a reduced workload, with Wilkins taking on some of White's responsibilities. Now secretary in all but name, it was Wilkins's good fortune that 1947 turned out to be an "exhilarating" year, with encouraging signs of progress in both the judicial and executive branches. In the courtroom, Thurgood Marshall and his legal team were moving through the next stage in the NAACP's desegregation battle by demanding equal admittance and participation for black applicants to graduate schools.[14] Marshall was also in the process of organizing a campaign against restrictive covenants and brought together a coalition of nineteen organizations, including the American Jewish Congress, the AFL, and the CIO, to join with the

NAACP in filing amicus curiae briefs supporting black plaintiffs in four cases challenging housing discrimination.[15]

There was also a sign of support from the White House when Harry S. Truman became the first president to address the NAACP's annual convention, which took place in Washington, DC, in June 1947. Standing on the steps of the Lincoln Memorial, the president told the 10,000-strong crowd, "Recent events in the United States and abroad have made us realize that it is more important today than ever before to insure that all Americans enjoy these rights. And when I say all Americans—I mean all Americans." Truman challenged the South to change its ways, and promised that the federal government would act if the states did not. "We can no longer afford the luxury of a leisurely attack upon prejudice and discrimination," he asserted. "There is much that State and local governments can do in providing positive safeguards for civil rights. But we cannot, any longer, await the growth of a will to action in the slowest State or the most backward community. Our national government must show the way." He spoke of the need to remove the barriers to opportunity and of the right to a decent home as well as to education, adequate medical care, a fair trial, equality at the voting booth, and freedom from violence and intimidation. Building a strong case for democracy meant, the president said, putting America's own house in order, and this was a matter of urgency. Wilkins took Truman's words—and his presence at the occasion—as a symbol that the fight against segregation finally had the support of the federal government.[16]

Truman's speech was aimed as much at an international audience as the NAACP members standing at the monument. By the time he spoke at the Lincoln Memorial, the "iron curtain" between East and West had been drawn. Four months before his address to the NAACP convention, Truman had stated what he saw as America's role in the new global order during a joint session of Congress. The Truman Doctrine, as the speech became known, promoted the United States as a champion of those countries threatened by a spread of Communism, and was delivered in response to increased tension in Greece and Turkey, both of whom were facing a Communist threat. In a sentence unintentionally laden with meaning for America's racial situation, the president said, "I believe that it must be the policy of the United States to support free peoples who are resisting attempted subjugation by armed minorities or by outside pressures."[17]

The NAACP tried to link the principles of the Truman Doctrine to civil rights at home in a petition to the United Nations Commission on Human Rights in October 1947. The petition, entitled "An Appeal to the World: A Statement on the Denial of Human Rights to Minorities in the Case of Citizens of Negro Descent in the United States of America," had been drafted primarily by W. E. B. Du Bois, who had at that point returned to the NAACP. Du Bois accused America of "failing to practice what it preached and argued that the racism at work in the United States had become an international issue, in part because of the failure of the American government to deal with the problem. Ultimately, the petition argued, the United Nations was the only body capable of demanding justice for black Americans.[18] Fearing that diplomats would simply ignore the petition, Du Bois leaked it to the press. This unleashed a storm of controversy, which was exacerbated when Du Bois told reporters that the violent repression of blacks in Mississippi posed more of a threat to the United States than did Soviet Russia.

Although the petition fell foul of Cold War politics, the political imperative to improve the racial situation in the United States was gaining ground, particularly within the State Department, which proved to be a surprising ally to the NAACP. The Soviet Union was making much of America's racial problems, and the thorny question facing the government was what to do about those problems.[19] When Truman's advisory committee published its findings in its report, entitled *To Secure These Rights*, in December 1947, it exposed the appalling extent of America's racial inequality in detail. It explicitly condemned segregation and made a series of recommendations, including the establishment of a permanent FEPC, antilynching legislation, federal protection of voting rights, and ultimately the eradication of Jim Crow.

The report appeared just before the presidential campaign began, and the race was already proving to be tight. In an attempt to capitalize on the national debate about civil rights sparked by the controversial report— and to attract the important black vote, which could prove crucial in key northern states—in January 1948, in his State of the Union address, Truman referred to the report and signaled his intention to act on civil rights. True to his word, in July the president issued two executive orders that desegregated the military and instituted fair employment practices in the federal government, despite the political risks in an election year. Truman's gamble in courting the black vote—and White's gamble in supporting the president—paid off when he won a stunning and surprising victory against the Republican candidate and frontrunner Thomas Dewey, thanks in part to large numbers of black votes in the crucial North and Midwestern states.

Once safely back in office, Truman sent an ambitious civil rights package up to Capitol Hill that included antilynching provisions, better protection of voting rights, and a permanent FEPC. Unfortunately, although the 1948 election gave control of Congress back to the Democrats, the president was still unable to get his legislation passed. Prospects for any further civil rights legislation dimmed further when some Republicans joined forces with Dixiecrats to tighten the rules required to end a filibuster. As the bill spluttered to a halt, the Truman administration decided to postpone the fight to the next session. The NAACP's members were disgusted and passed a resolution at the 1949 annual convention in Los Angeles charging Congress with betraying the civil rights mandate given to it at the previous election. The resolution also called on the Association to mobilize a mass conference with other groups to ensure the safe passage of the legislation.[20] Wilkins was suspicious of the motives of those proposing the resolution, believing that it was a direct criticism of the Association's leaders, and particularly of him, and that it was being put forward either in the hope that such a move would be a failure and therefore prompt demands for a new leader or that any such conference or mobilization would be overtaken by the left wing of the organization.[21] Nevertheless, a response from the Association's leadership was required soon.

Just when the NAACP needed cohesive leadership, however, it was plunged into a new period of squabbling and dissent. In June 1949, White offered his resignation; but, hesitant to leave a vacuum at the head of the organization, the board of directors instead persuaded him to take a leave of absence for one year. Yet White had little support outside of the national office. Members were still angry at his maneuvers to push Du Bois out of the NAACP the previous year. Problems had simmered between the two men since Du Bois's return to the Association in 1943 as director of special research. Age certainly had not tempered the now elderly Du Bois's intellect or energy, or his dislike of White. The two men bickered and argued constantly about matters as mundane as office furniture and as important as the NAACP's future direction.

The situation was finally resolved, albeit only by an irreparable breach. In the fall of 1948, during the presidential campaign, Du Bois had accused the Truman administration of deliberately thwarting any discussion of civil rights during a United Nations conference in Paris earlier that year, and he was appalled at Walter White's acceptance to serve as a consultant to the US delegation. He told White, by memorandum, that NAACP participation in the conference was tantamount to collusion, that it tied the Association far too closely to the "reactionary, warmongering colonial imperialism of the present administration," and that it would be a tragic mistake for the NAACP to attach itself to the "Truman bandwagon."[22] In his response to Du Bois, White called the accusations "ridiculous" and said that "no commitments as to policy have either been asked or given" by the administration. On the contrary, he argued, the Association would likely be among those who disagreed with aspects of US foreign policy, as it had in San Francisco in 1945.[23] Although Du Bois had some supporters on the board, his fate was sealed when his memo was leaked to the *New York Times*. George Streator, Wilkins's old nemesis from *The Crisis* who was now working on the newspaper, quoted liberally from the memo, including Du Bois's assertion that Eleanor Roosevelt had said she would resign from the delegation if the issue of civil rights was brought up at the conference.[24] At the next board meeting on September 13, the board decided that Du Bois's contract would not be extended when it expired at the end of the year. Thus, ignominiously, Du Bois's forty-year connection to the NAACP was ended, and the Association lost its elder statesman.

This unhappy episode was still a contentious issue for many NAACP members as the next scandal erupted in April 1949, when White announced that he had divorced his black wife, Gladys, in order to marry Poppy Cannon, a white journalist. A slew of letters to the national office from branches and individual members protested White's actions, although some, such as the Minnesota State Conference, suggested that the secretary should be judged on his professional, not private, actions.[25] That controversy was compounded by an article White wrote for *Look* magazine in which he argued that a new chemical that could lighten skin color could be the way for black Americans to "get the fair treatment" they had always wanted.[26] After these controversial moves by White, Wilkins looked like a safer pair of hands to steer the ship; so, after twenty years in the wings, with White's yearlong leave of absence Wilkins finally got an opportunity to lead the NAACP, if only temporarily.

Although it appeared Wilkins had the support of the NAACP's board, with White's departure the political machinations at the head office became even more intense. Speculation about White's future began almost as soon as the door closed behind him: just a month after his leave of absence began, George Streator in the *New York Times* reported that White was probably too ill to return to the Association and described a growing battle between the pro- and the anti-Wilkins camps, both of which were mustering forces should White not return. More than that, Streator claimed that White had been asked not to attend the Association's annual conference so that Wilkins could establish himself as leader in White's absence. He also implied that if White did not return, moves were under way to elect Wilkins in his place and avoid any kind of leadership coup by more left-leaning members.[27]

Driving much of the dissent in the anti-Wilkins faction was the frustration felt in some of the NAACP's more activist branches, particularly around the New York City area. Members in these branches adhered to the more militant attitude that had taken hold in the period immediately following World War II; they were angry at the slow pace of change and the hesitancy of the Association's leaders to take more direct action to force the issue of equal rights. Trouble had been brewing for some time, but when White left, it came out in the open in a disagreement between Lindsay White, the newly elected head of the New York City branch, and Wilkins over the direction of the NAACP. After an exchange of letters between Lindsay White and Walter White, and then Wilkins, leveling accusations of high-handedness on the part of the national office on the one hand and equally damning claims of branch inefficiency on the other, the dispute became far more serious when it escalated into a bitter row between Wilkins and two prominent judges, Hubert Delaney and Jane

Bolin, who were both members of the national board and leading members of the troublesome New York branch.

After hearing that Judge Delaney had met with leaders of the branch to listen to some of their concerns, Wilkins accused the judge of a conflict of interest and of abnegating his responsibility as a national officer. Delaney responded with equal vigor, arguing that Wilkins's attitude illustrated the problem—that an autocratic national office was failing to recognize the importance of the branches to the Association. This attitude, Delaney claimed, had contributed to a precipitous decline in membership. Membership, which was claimed to be around 500,000 at the beginning of 1948, had apparently fallen to as low as 383,000 by the end of the year, and Delaney argued that the fall was even more dramatic: that membership levels were closer to 150,000.[28]

Wilkins replied with an air of outraged hurt and, of course, rejected Delaney's charges. He attributed the membership decline to several factors, but mostly to the doubling of the membership fee (to $2). Attempting to counter Delaney's accusations of the Association's autocracy toward the branches, Wilkins argued that the most dramatic fall could be seen in those branches that had the greatest autonomy. A further area of contention was the fact that Jane Bolin had not been nominated again as a director but had, instead, been offered a vice president position, which did not carry any voting rights. Delaney and the New York branch accused Wilkins and his staff of a variety of nefarious plots to prevent Bolin's reelection; this prompted heated denials from Wilkins. It didn't help that Bolin and Wilkins had already crossed swords at an earlier board meeting, when the judge questioned Wilkins's administration of the annual conference.

When reports of the disagreement appeared in the *Afro-American* newspaper, Wilkins suspected an internal leak and called a meeting with Thurgood Marshall, Madison Jones, and church secretary Walter Offutt to discuss how the newspaper could have gotten the details. Notes from the meeting show how rife with paranoia the national office had become. Wilkins suggested that a staff member must have encouraged Bolin to raise questions publicly and promised to fire anyone found leaking information either to the press or to board members. Offutt complained that there was little privacy within the national office, while Jones claimed that the report in the *Afro-American* was undermining the NAACP's reputation. Even the usually pragmatic Thurgood Marshall was not immune from the atmosphere of mistrust: he claimed that papers had been stolen from files kept in his desk. Wilkins had little time for any broader discussion. He warned the attendees that he expected their loyalty, then promptly closed the meeting.[29]

The dispute did little to position Wilkins as a responsible leader but, ironically, matters were brought to a head by an event that represented a significant step forward for the NAACP and also offered Wilkins an opportunity to distinguish himself as a leader in his own right. After the Truman administration's civil rights agenda fell victim to southern obstruction, the Association's members demanded more coordinated action. A resolution passed at the 1949 annual convention called for the NAACP to join forces with other sympathetic groups to lobby for the passage of legislation. At the close of World War II union leader A. Philip Randolph had established an organization called the National Council for a Permanent FEPC. The council brought together labor, fraternal, civic, and civil rights groups, but had proved to be ineffective and by 1949 was falling apart. Although their views on what should be the main priority differed slightly, both Randolph and Wilkins believed that the prospect of civil rights reform was too important to lessen the pressure on Congress. Together, using the skeleton of Randolph's organization as a starting point, they called for a National Emergency Civil Rights Mobilization Conference to take place in Washington in January 1950.

Wilkins was chairman of the steering committee and as such was responsible for accreditation to the event. Shortly before the conference began, he announced that members of communist or communist-affiliated groups would not be welcome. This decision was made by all the sponsoring groups, some of whom had already conducted anticommunist purges within their own organizations; nevertheless, the decision was controversial and, as a result of the ruling, applications from some delegates, including several from New York area branches, were rejected. The stated explanation for these rejections was that the applications were not in order, although the implication was that Communists were alleged to have infiltrated the branches that had submitted the applications.[30]

If one simply looked at the numbers, the conference was a great success: over four thousand delegates from thirty-three states and representing around fifty organizations congregated in Washington to lobby their congressmen. Those who could not attend were encouraged to write or call their representatives in Washington and meet with local politicians where possible. The gathering attracted the attention of the press and was widely reported. Given this success, Wilkins expected to be greeted with applause by the board when he returned to New York. Instead, far from receiving congratulations, he instead had to face difficult questions concerning his administration of the event. At the first board meeting following the conference, Wilkins was challenged by Delaney and John Hammond, a well-known jazz record producer and both a prominent member of the NAACP's board of directors and a member of the executive committee of the New York branch, about the problems in accrediting members from some of the Association's branches. Delaney accused Wilkins of violating the provisions of the 1949 conference resolution and of exceeding his authority. When a motion to commend Wilkins on the success of the mobilization was taken, both directors refused to ratify the resolution.

Over the next few weeks, relations worsened. Lindsay White made strenuous complaints to Louis Wright, the chairman of the NAACP's board of directors, about the poor treatment given to delegates from New York. In addition, and far more damning, he accused the credentials committee of racism, claiming that white members of the committee refused to accredit black delegates and argued that it was "ludicrous" for black members to be denied the right to participate in a civil rights conference by their own organization. Even worse, White implied that the CIO had demanded such a policy in return for its donating $5,000 to the event. Wilkins, naturally, denied the accusation and insisted that the board carry out an inquiry as soon as possible.[31]

Before the next board meeting, Wilkins drafted a fifteen-page statement citing a number of episodes that he claimed undermined, either deliberately or inadvertently, the reputation of both the NAACP and himself. Before submitting the statement, Wilkins sought the opinion of Henry Lee Moon, the NAACP's public relations director, about the document. Moon was blunt, telling Wilkins, "If the dissemination of information is its sole objective, it is altogether adequate. If the creation of an unbridgeable cleavage is desired, it is masterful. If, however, the development of a climate in which the association can be preserved as a strong and unified whole is the purpose, it is as dangerous as the H-bomb, and potentially as capable of destroying the initiator as the intended victim."[32] Wilkins paid little attention to Moon's recommendations, however, and sent the statement almost unchanged.

Wilkins may have had vociferous critics on the board and in the press, but he also had powerful allies. Arthur Spingarn, president of the NAACP, spoke in his favor at the meeting, and another great supporter, Daisy Lampkin, proposed a motion rejecting a request by the New York branch for an investigation or reprimand of Wilkins following the mobilization in Washington. Lampkin's motion passed by 13 votes to 3 (the dissenters included Delaney and Hammond), and the vote almost brought this particular episode to a welcome close.[33] It was not quite over, however. In March 1950, Jane Bolin had the last word when she resigned from the NAACP. In her resignation letter to Spingarn, Bolin called the Association's program "sterile and barren" and accused its national officers of having a "contemptuous and scornful" attitude to the branches. She also was exasperated by the preoccupation with Communists, which, she believed, had become such a distraction that the Association was devoting more time and attention to Communism than to black Americans.[34]

Judge Bolin was correct in her assertion that the preoccupation with rooting out Communists was a distraction. However, anticommunist hysteria turned a spotlight on liberals of all persuasions; and, given the antipathy in many quarters to the notion of equality, those who were active in, or even sympathetic toward, civil rights became easy targets for investigation and victimization. It was all too easy to become caught up in the hunt for "reds under the beds," and both Wilkins, who had possibly learned some lessons from the mobilization fracas, and Marshall warned against waging a "witch hunt." Delegates at the NAACP's annual convention in June 1950 took matters into their own hands by calling upon the Association not only to investigate branches where infiltration by Communists was suspected, but also to confiscate the charter of branches under suspicion and expel members who were found to be "under Communist or other political control and domination." This simply exacerbated the dilemma of practicing the very kind of discrimination the Association was committed to fighting.[35]

However important the perceived threat of communism infiltration was felt to be, it was not the most pressing issue facing the organization at the time. Walter White was due to return in June, and the question about whether to accept his resignation was still unanswered. Claiming he was now strong enough to return to work, White wrote to the board of directors in March 1950 to lay the groundwork for his return. Making a none-too-subtle dig at Wilkins—and making full use of the fear of the Communist threat—he said, "I have encountered reports of dissension and disruption in the NAACP which convinces me that in this most critical period the NAACP's enemies are attempting to 'divide and conquer' us." Upon discovering he was "heartbound" to the organization, he added, he had decided to withdraw his resignation and dedicate himself to leading the organization—as only he could—through this turbulent period.[36]

A decision about White's return was to be taken at the May board meeting. As the deadline approached, Wilkins became increasingly reluctant to hand back power. In public, he rejected the idea of rivalry between himself and White, saying that any such competition was simply an invention by the press.[37] But he struck a different note in his personal correspondence. In a letter to Edward Dudley, the American ambassador to Liberia, in April 1950, the strain on Wilkins was evident. "A lot of stuff has been flying back and forth," he wrote, "initiated by some people who persist in regarding this as a contest between Walter and myself. This is, of course, a lot of nonsense but I have become so tired of attempting to explain it only to see what few remarks I make distorted and misinterpreted that I am simply letting things ride. Some things that are going on are pretty nasty and sneaky and the situation is not too comfortable for me but some kind of decision will be reached one way or the other by June 1."[38]

White's supporters were cheering from the sidelines. While he was traveling, Walter White's wife, Poppy, kept him fully updated on events at the national office, and she spared little detail about the bickering and factions at work there. The press also relished the speculation. Shortly before the meeting, the *Afro-American*'s front page asked, "NAACP Crisis Set?" and described, with some accuracy, the behind-the-scenes machinations that had taken place over the past several months. Neither Wilkins nor White received a ringing endorsement from the newspaper; instead, it argued that the Association should begin paying more attention to its members—and to the man in the street—than who should occupy the secretary's office. Other newspapers, undoubtedly fed information by one faction or another, also enjoyed the intrigue and had no hesitation in laying bare the battle between Wilkins's and White's factions in their pages.

Wilkins's position had been weakened in March by an assertion by longtime board member and former first lady Eleanor Roosevelt that he had written to her to criticize White's marriage to Poppy Cannon. The alleged letter from Wilkins angered her to such an extent that she resigned from the board, although she had previously tried to offer her resignation some months before, citing pressure of work. After heated denials from Wilkins (and it does seem highly unlikely that he would have written such a letter to such a prominent and respected ally of White's, whatever his views), Mrs. Roosevelt admitted that she was unable to find the letter and that "it may have been from someone else." However, she still refused to say unequivocally that Wilkins had sent no such note, blaming instead her disorganized filing system for the difficulty in finding it rather than the fact that it might not have been sent at all.[39] Such a dismissive response demonstrated the low regard in which she held Wilkins and did not offer him much cause for optimism as the May board meeting approached. But he had no intention of giving in quietly. Shortly before the meeting, he wrote to Maceo Smith, head of the Texas state conference of NAACP branches, that if questions continued to be raised about his trustworthiness and integrity, he would "take off the gloves and stage a fight that will make all these skirmishes look like pillow taps."[40]

White's leave of absence had prompted the board of directors to commission Judge William Hastie, a board member of some years' standing and a friend of Walter White, to review the leadership structure of the national office. When the board gathered in May, it first discussed Hastie's report. In addition to giving the board and the chairman more authority, Hastie proposed that the secretary's duties be separated into internal and external functions. Internal operations, such as the day-to-day management of the Association and its budget along with the appointment of all staff below the rank of junior executive, would be directed by an administrator, while an executive secretary would be responsible for public relations and the appointment of junior executives and any senior executive not appointed directly by the board. Both positions would report directly to the board, but the executive secretary was marginally considered the senior officer.[41] Sensing a way to keep both senior officials quiet, Hastie's recommendations were passed by unanimous vote.

Attention then moved to the question of White's return and whether he should resume his duties as executive secretary, albeit under Hastie's new structure. The argument went back and forth between those board members who did not want White to return and those who did. The heated debate lasted for more than four hours. Both sides had powerful supporters: Eleanor Roosevelt argued strongly for White, while Arthur Spingarn and Alfred Baker Lewis argued equally strongly against him and for Wilkins.[42] Eventually, a close vote—16 to 10—brought White back into the organization as executive secretary but put Wilkins in a more powerful, if difficult, position than when White left the previous June.

In the midst of this unrest the one area of the Association that was functioning successfully was its legal department. The NAACP's plan to desegregate public schools was quietly gathering strength, driven by the Association's sister organization, the Legal Defense and Educational Fund, better known as the Inc. Fund, or LDF. Led by Thurgood Marshall, the Inc. Fund was originally the NAACP's legal arm, but had separated from the Association for tax reasons in 1940.[43] The Association's legal team had developed its long-term strategy under the leadership of the NAACP's first counsel, Charles Houston. Since the early 1930s, the team had conducted a patient, methodical campaign and had won a succession of increasingly important victories. The graduate school challenge culminated in 1950 when, in *Sweatt v. Painter* and *McLaurin v. Oklahoma State Regents*, the Supreme Court upheld the NAACP's contention that separate graduate school facilities were inherently unequal. On the same day, the Court also ruled in *Henderson v. United States* that segregated dining facilities on railroad dining cars violated the interstate commerce act and, while avoiding the thornier question of "separate but equal," abolished the practice of curtains, markers, or any other signs that discriminated on the basis of race.[44] *Henderson* was particularly significant because the Truman administration filed an amicus curiae brief in support of the plaintiff, an indication that the government was at least ready to challenge segregation in the courts, if not in Congress. Thurgood Mar-

shall considered all three decisions to be "replete with road markings telling us where to go next."[45] Those markings would lead to what Wilkins
would call "one of life's sweetest days."

On May 17, 1954, the Supreme Court dismantled the legal framework
supporting segregation in its unanimous decision in *Brown v. Board of
Education,* declaring that racially segregated public schools were unequal,
which ultimately made segregation per se illegal. Marshall called the national office with the news of the unanimous decision, then made his way
back to New York to celebrate with the staff.

There was much to celebrate. The verdict had been far from a foregone conclusion. In fact, shortly before the announcement, Wilkins had
drafted two versions of a press release, one announcing regret at a decision that would have left segregation intact, and the other expressing
delight at an opinion that invalidated segregation. Everyone hoped that
the latter would be the one ultimately used; nevertheless, the unanimity
of the decision was an unexpected surprise. The ruling, however, was
not entirely good news. Although the Supreme Court justices had taken
a brave decision, the court failed to set a timetable for implementation,
thus leaving room for the southern states to devise various ways to circumvent the instruction. The situation was made no clearer when the
Court issued a subsequent decision a year later, in *Brown II,* in which it
instructed school districts that had not already begun to implement desegregation plans to do so "with all deliberate speed."[46]

Understandably, Wilkins and Marshall thought that *Brown* would
prove to be the beginning of the end of the battle for equal rights. Unfortunately, it proved to be simply one victory—albeit a significant one—in
a longer war. Wilkins had had very little to do with the progression of the
legal case, although in many of the tributes paid to him on his retirement
and later, in obituaries, he was closely identified with the case and, in
some reports, mistakenly credited with overseeing its victory. He would,
however, become heavily involved in the campaign to ensure compliance
with the ruling. Within a month of the decision, still euphoric from the
victory, the NAACP held a "jubilation" conference in Atlanta to devise
an implementation strategy.[47] With the framework for segregation now
legally removed, the Association now had to shift its focus toward chang-

ing public attitudes, emotions, and traditions in order to win support for equal rights legislation and litigation. This would have to take place block by block in local communities rather than on a national level if the *Brown* ruling was to be successfully implemented.[48]

This task would occupy much of the NAACP's attention and resources over the next few years, leaving it unprepared when the fight for freedom unexpectedly moved from the courtroom to the streets; and it would be Wilkins's battle to fight. On March 21, 1955, Walter White died of a heart attack. He had spent the day working on a manuscript and visiting the NAACP office, where he chatted with staff about upcoming issues. He had been ill for several months but had recently taken a monthlong vacation in the Caribbean to recuperate and returned looking relaxed, healthy, and keen to get back to work. His sudden death not only came as a shock, it also reopened the position of executive secretary. Wilkins, along with Clarence Mitchell, who led the NAACP's Washington office, and Thurgood Marshall were suggested as possible successors to White. All three candidates had their strengths: Marshall was still basking in the success of the *Brown* decision. He was charismatic, highly respected, and a passionate defender of civil rights. Clarence Mitchell, on the other hand, had an extraordinary grasp of the minutiae of the legislative process and knew how to wield friends and influence people to help further the cause of civil rights. Wilkins brought almost a quarter of a century's knowledge of the NAACP. He had traveled to branches across the country and, as administrator, been responsible for the relatively smooth operation of the Association for the past five years—clashes with the board notwithstanding.

One of Thurgood Marshall's biographers has claimed that competition between Marshall and Wilkins for the position of executive secretary led to an escalation of tension between the two men, but there is little evidence to support this assertion.[49] On the contrary, in his initial reorganization plan presented to the NAACP's board in September 1955, Wilkins requested that Marshall, "with whom the Secretary frequently confers," be named associate executive secretary.[50] When Marshall married Cecile Suyat in December 1955, Wilkins gave the bride away, and was named godfather to Marshall's first son the following year.[51] In reality, for all the strengths of Marshall and Mitchell, and despite Wilkins's faults, it would have been almost impossible to appoint anyone other than Wilkins to the position without risking more internal turmoil; so it was almost a formality when, on April 11, 1955, the board unanimously voted that Wilkins be appointed executive secretary, effective immediately. No doubt as a result of the difficulties surrounding White's leave of absence in 1949–1950, the board went to great lengths to present a united front. Wilkins's nemesis, Hubert Delaney, who acted as secretary for the board meeting, even went so far as to say, "There has seldom been an instance where the Board acted with greater dignity and with more unanimity based upon their desire to see the Association close ranks and move forward under the leadership of an Executive Secretary who would not be handicapped by factional strife within the Board."[52] Finally, after twenty-four years, Wilkins was the undisputed head of the NAACP with the full backing of the board of directors.

During the heady but brief honeymoon period that followed, Wilkins was described as astute, scholarly, courageous, diplomatic, and, all in all, more than qualified to lead the Association into what was sure to be a time of challenges.[53] Even the usually critical black press sang the praises of the new leader. The *St. Petersburg Times* called Wilkins "a quiet fighter" while the *Pittsburgh Courier* claimed he was "the most qualified man who has ever been chosen to this exalted position." The Chester, Pennsylvania, *Times,* on the other hand, was more circumspect in its approval: "Wilkins will bring to his new position the resilient tact of a polished diplomat." Wilkins's old employer, the *Kansas City Call,* congratulated the board, which "would not have found a more seasoned NAACP man to run its national organization than Wilkins."[54] An extravagant photographic spread in *Ebony* magazine showed an energetic and dynamic Wilkins striding purposefully to high-level meetings, consulting with NAACP staff at the office, and relaxing at home with his wife, Minnie.[55] As executive secretary of the NAACP Wilkins was one of the leading voices of black America, the first point of contact for presidents, politicians, and civic leaders. And with the *Brown* ruling still fresh, it must have seemed to Wilkins that the long battle to secure equal rights was almost won. The Association's membership, while far fewer than its postwar peak of half a million, was still significant at over 305,500; its finances were relatively healthy; and the NAACP was still the most important black organization in the United States. In short, it appeared to be unstoppable.

3

A Strategy for Freedom

Shortly after becoming executive secretary of the NAACP in April 1955, Wilkins laid out some ambitious goals for the next few years: "By 1963 [the hundredth anniversary of the Emancipation Proclamation] we definitely expect that segregation in education will be completely out in most areas, and on its way out in the die-hard areas." He also said he expected all public housing to be desegregated and segregation in private housing to be largely dismantled. Using the desegregation of the armed forces and the *Brown* ruling as examples that progress was being made, Wilkins anticipated "very much less discrimination" in the labor market and in leisure and transport facilities.[1] As for the Association itself, Wilkins was hesitant to make any organizational changes. He complained that the branch, public relations, and accounting departments were "functioning below their potential" and needed to be improved, but offered few specific recommendations. He did, however, propose that the pre-1950 organizational structure, where responsibility for administration and staff lay with the executive secretary be restored, thus combining the responsibilities that Wilkins had as administrator with his new position, thus consolidating power back in the hands of the executive secretary.

Reviving the original structure meant more power but also more work; yet Wilkins was reluctant to delegate work to his staff. His opinion of those working at the head office was not high; he suggested that some were competent, or just "competent enough" but lacking initiative; others he simply accused of idleness.[2] After looking outside the Association, Wilkins eventually found a loyal and dedicated deputy in John Morsell. The cerebral Morsell arrived at the Association with a distinguished academic record: a master's degree in social legislation from Columbia University in New York; a doctorate in sociology, which he obtained while working for the New York City welfare department; and valuable expertise in social science research. Wilkins knew of Morsell through his work with Minnie Wilkins at the welfare department. Nevertheless, Morsell was surprised when Wilkins approached him in November 1955, initially, Morsell thought, to discuss possible candidates for the position. Instead, Morsell suggested himself for the position because, as he told Wilkins: "I had never been very active but I had always revered it [the NAACP]. I was brought up with the *Crisis* magazine in my house as a kid," he added, and "I would consider the chance to work for the NAACP as an unparalleled opportunity if there were any way in which I could help."[3]

There was plenty to do. In May 1955, the Supreme Court handed down what should have been a ruling that established a timetable for implementation of the decision. Instead, in *Brown II,* the Court decreed that school desegregation should be implemented "with all deliberate speed," thus giving the more recalcitrant states no reason to rush to comply. The right to vote was still being denied to many blacks in the South, and their attempts to register were frequently met with violence and intimidation, which went unchallenged by the authorities. It took the brutal death of a teenage boy to illustrate to the world the appalling oppression under which many black Americans lived and how difficult Wilkins's goals would be to achieve.

Emmett Till, a fourteen-year-old from Chicago, was brutally beaten to death in the summer of 1955 for allegedly whistling at a white woman while staying with relatives in Mississippi. At Till's funeral, his mother insisted on an open casket so the world could see the boy's injuries; and photographs of his face, beaten to such an extent it was unrecognizable, were published in *Jet* magazine. Wilkins represented the anger of many when he said, "It would appear from this lynching that the State of Mississippi has decided to maintain white supremacy by murdering children." The woman's husband and his half-brother were accused of Till's murder. They were quickly brought to trial, but acquitted after barely more than an hour's deliberation by the all-white jury. The verdict provoked outrage almost everywhere outside of the South, prompting calls for boycotts, demonstrations, and other forms of action as black anger grew.

Eventually, the NAACP had to issue a response to what it called the "Mississippi terror." While it was unable to pursue the legal case once Till's killers had been acquitted, Wilkins said there was plenty that the Association's members could do to prevent more atrocities. Wilkins saw Till's murder as part of the endemic problem of American racism and believed that responding to a single event would ultimately have little effect. He therefore called for civil rights legislation, improved law enforcement, voting rights, an end to economic reprisals against those who sought equality, and the elimination of "racial discrimination from all phases of American life." To continue with the lobbying, research, and political and educational action, Wilkins argued, money was needed. It was, he said, the responsibility of anyone who believed in democracy to strengthen the organization that challenged the South's racist practices.[4]

It is impossible to identify one particular event as the catalyst for the civil rights movement, but Emmett Till's murder has been cited as a pivotal moment. *Brown* had encouraged and motivated the NAACP's constituency, but the manner of Till's death—and the absence of any justice—angered blacks to the point where something more than lawsuits and legislation was demanded. Proof that black Americans were ready to challenge the white power structure on their own terms came within months of Till's murder. On December 1, 1955, Mrs. Rosa Parks, a seamstress in Montgomery, Alabama, refused to give up her seat to a white man on a local bus. Montgomery's practice of segregation in public transportation, whereby blacks who boarded a bus took seats at the rear and whites who boarded sat at the front and, as the bus filled, took seats toward the back, which blacks would then be expected to vacate, had long been a source of anger among the city's black community, and Mrs. Parks's arrest as the result of her refusal to give up her seat galvanized the local black community. E. D. Nixon, a former president of the Montgomery branch of the NAACP who had worked with Mrs. Parks in the organization, acted quickly to bring together the city's black leaders. Nixon and Jo Ann Robinson, who led a local group called the Women's Political Council, proposed a one-day boycott of the city's buses in protest. On December 5, 90 percent of Montgomery's black community stayed off the buses. The Montgomery Improvement Association (MIA) was quickly formed to mobilize local sentiment and extend the boycott, with a young preacher, Martin Luther King Jr., appointed as its leader. Several previous attempts had been made to challenge the status quo in the city, but the boycott took the NAACP completely by surprise. Rosa Parks's arrest paved the way for a legal challenge to the segregated public transport system in the city, an outcome that would ordinarily have been a perfect opportunity for the Association. However, the speed with which the local black community banded together to arrange the boycott and elect a leader, without any direction from the Association, gave the NAACP little time to respond.

In February 1956, after negotiations between city and company officials failed, the MIA sought the assistance of the NAACP in attacking Alabama's bus segregation laws. Robert Carter, Thurgood Marshall's deputy, was dispatched to assist the black lawyers in filing suit in federal court. Wilkins had strong misgivings about the use of boycotts as a weapon, but he could not fail to see that the Montgomery activists had quickly captured national attention and that the NAACP, already committed to helping the boycott leaders, had to play a more prominent role in events. He sent a telegram to branch leaders across the South, urging them to cooperate with local ministers and groups to raise funds that should be sent either to King or to the NAACP's national office. The latter would use such funds to support the "legal action now pending in court challenging segregation statutes."[5] Wilkins also reassured King that the Association would continue to support the protest by taking on all the legal costs for those arrested, including Mrs. Parks, and put the NAACP's legal staff at their disposal. In addition, Wilkins promised that the Association would assume the majority of costs associated with the legal challenge against Montgomery's segregated buses and, if necessary, provide emergency financial aid for weekly expenses.[6]

Inspired by Montgomery, some other NAACP branches proposed holding bus boycotts in their cities to support the Alabama protesters. Wilkins quickly put a stop to the idea of any NAACP-sanctioned boycotts. His discomfort with direct action generally, and boycotts in particular, was based on his belief that, as a minority group, black Americans lacked the economic and political power to secure change through these kinds of methods, and therefore they were at best pointless and at worst dangerous. He frequently argued that Gandhi's use of similar tactics against the British was successful in India because Indians were the majority group and therefore could wield enormous economic power. Boycotts such as that in Montgomery, Wilkins felt, could work only on a local scale, in cases where the black population was numerous enough to have an economic impact. This was the case in Montgomery and in other cities such as Baltimore, where the NAACP had waged a long campaign against a local theater, but Wilkins's concern was that the success of the Montgomery protest would encourage similar, but much less successful, demonstrations elsewhere, and that these demonstrations would deflect the Association from its strategy of litigation and lobbying, as well as risk punitive white reprisals that would place the NAACP in a vulnerable position.[7]

The MIA was already posing a potential threat to the NAACP's finances and position. Some were confused about who was financing the Montgomery boycott, and donations for the boycott sometimes were sent to the NAACP, which was providing legal support to the protestors. In a telegram to Franklin Williams, the Association's West Coast representative, Wilkins warned that if branches in the region raised funds for the national office, "there must be no quarrel over funds for legal defense in Lucy case and other activity which must be taken to win University of Alabama case and to combat entire Southern situation but we will not quarrel with Montgomery Improvement Association over who gets funds. It must not conflict with Montgomery effort or confuse public or antagonize church leaders. Repeat not antagonize church leaders."[8]

Wilkins's reference to the "Lucy case" illustrates the Association's problem in trying to balance support of a very public boycott with the many other calls on its resources at the time. The Autherine Lucy case was one such example. Lucy had applied to the University of Alabama's graduate school in 1952 to study library science. When her application was rejected on the basis of her race, she approached the NAACP, whose lawyers took the case to the Federal District Court in northern Alabama. There the judge found against the university, a decision later upheld by the Supreme Court. When Lucy finally enrolled in February 1956 she was prevented from entering the university's dormitories and dining areas and was forced to face a baying mob for four days as she tried to attend classes. By the time the Montgomery boycott was in full swing, Autherine

Lucy had been suspended by the school, which claimed it could not guarantee a safe environment, and the NAACP was fighting the suspension in court. Unfortunately, Lucy lost the case and was expelled from the university within weeks of her enrollment amid claims from the school that she had slandered the university.[9]

The NAACP's lawyers were more successful in challenging the city of Montgomery: the boycott was eventually resolved in November 1956, when the Supreme Court, in answer to a petition filed by the NAACP, upheld an earlier ruling that city and state bus segregation was unconstitutional.[10] For Wilkins, this was a vindication of the NAACP's belief in the process of law, and he reminded King frequently in later years that it was litigation, and not direct action, that secured the victory in Montgomery. He never acknowledged that, as the *Brown* ruling was proving, court decisions on their own rarely prompted societal reforms, certainly as far as race relations were concerned. It took the quiet and dignified processions of the black citizens of Montgomery, walking miles to and from work in relentless summer heat and cold winter rain, to shame the city council into negotiations and give the NAACP's lawyers the moral authority as the legal team challenged the city's discriminatory transportation policy through the courts.

After the victory in Montgomery several NAACP branches wanted to wage similar protests elsewhere, but it would take more than one successful protest to change Wilkins's mind. He debated the efficacy of direct action over litigation with James Peck, a civil rights activist, in an exchange of letters that began in early 1958 and would continue intermittently over the next ten years. Peck argued that the court case "certainly was not the major [factor] in the Montgomery situation. Without the peoples' protest action, the buses would still be segregated, despite the court case—just as interstate buses in the South remain segregated despite the Supreme Court."[11] Wilkins rejected Peck's argument: "Montgomery had a happy combination of elements that would make a boycott successful, and such a combination does not exist everywhere."[12] Furthermore, Wilkins defended the Association's reliance on legal action as one of its primary means of agitation. "Legal victories rooted in the law," he wrote, "form the basis on which other methods can proceed toward accomplishment."[13]

Nevertheless, Montgomery represented a new development in civil rights protest, where a legal challenge emerged out of a direct action protest rather than vice versa, where NAACP lawyers found suitable plaintiffs and cases to challenge discriminatory statutes as part of a carefully plotted legal strategy. Montgomery forced the Association to become reactive, attempting to secure a legal precedent following a protest or providing legal support for protesters.[14] These new circumstances did nothing to dent Wilkins's belief that political action rather than direct action was the most effective route to securing equal rights; but securing their rights directly was a seductive idea to many of the NAACP's members. Wilkins made the case for the Association's traditional methods at its annual convention in 1956, saying, "We must intensify the use of political action in the final surge to full equality. The use of purely political action against us by certain southern states is ample evidence that we, too, should resort to this activity on our behalf. . . . If politics can be used for increasing corporation profits, there is nothing wrong with using politics to secure human rights. Everyone tries to use politics for his benefit; you can use it for yours. Don't stammer and don't apologize. Use your vote in behalf of civil rights."[15]

As part of this attempt to build political strength, Wilkins hosted a three-day National Delegate Assembly for Civil Rights in Washington, DC, in March 1956. The conference brought together fifty national organizations and two thousand delegates under the umbrella of the Leadership Conference on Civil Rights (LCCR) to lobby for civil rights during the presidential election year.[16] After the flurry of activity around the Civil Rights Mobilization in 1950, when it did not even have an official name, the LCCR had then languished as an idea for two years, when it was said to exist only in Arnold Aronson's desk drawer. It was revived in 1952 to lobby for a revision to the filibuster rule, and the group had been meeting intermittently since then, but without any formal constitution, organizational structure, or even budget (participating organizations voluntarily contributed dues but no specific amount was stipulated). It also had had no successes. Nevertheless, the coalition presented an impressive front to Congress and the main political parties.

The idea of the LCCR underpinned Wilkins's belief that black Americans could only become stronger if they were part of a much bigger group; but, more than that, as historians August Meier and John Bracey argue, the fact that the LCCR was led by the NAACP "marked a radical transformation" of the Association's strategy and priorities. Historically it had relied upon the relationships forged by its national officers with co-operative individuals in positions of power; this new approach made use of the resources of dozens of religious, civic, and fraternal organizations and their constituencies.[17] Kevin Schultz argues that joining forces with other groups also changed the NAACP's legislative focus, from antilynching and poll-tax legislation to issues such as securing a permanent FEPC and jobs for black Americans.[18] Although the LCCR failed in its attempts to kill Rule 22, the congressional procedure that allowed a filibuster to be ended only with a two-thirds majority, or win a permanent FEPC, as the 1950s progressed the coalition grew in strength and importance and would prove pivotal in the passage of the landmark civil rights legislation of 1957, 1964, and 1965.

The LCCR became a significant part of Wilkins's life. As its head, he became the public face of at least fifty organizations, which would stand him in good stead in the corridors of power. For example, when President John F. Kennedy wanted a civil rights leader to be the liaison for lobbying for civil rights legislation, he chose Wilkins, possibly because he represented so many groups that none could claim to be ignored.[19] With such a broad coalition, the new organization could exert much greater pressure on legislators than the NAACP on its own.[20] And, as important, its wide range of members meant that the LCCR's lobbying efforts were not restricted simply to racial issues, making it more difficult for those opposed to equal rights for black Americans to obstruct legislation aimed at addressing discriminatory laws.

The Association began to wage its legislative battles with Clarence Mitchell, the director of the NAACP's relatively new Washington bureau, executing the Association's legislation strategy through the Leadership Conference as its legislative director.[21] But by 1956, the political landscape had changed to some extent. The Montgomery boycott, the murder of Emmett Till, and southern resistance to school integration had finally begun to provoke a change in public opinion among white Americans. At the same time, black voters were becoming an attractive and increasingly powerful constituency, particularly in an election year; but their loyalty to the Democrats had been hard to dent. Recognizing the electoral potential in winning the black vote, attorney general Herbert Brownell proposed a package of legislation that included the creation of a civil rights division in the department of justice and federal authority to investigate instances of voting discrimination.

Encouraged by President Eisenhower's announcement that he would support civil rights legislation, the LCCR mobilized forces for a three-day conference in the nation's capital. Much of the agenda was given over to the testimonies of black southerners. The words of people like Gus Courts, a grocer and president of the Belzoni, Mississippi, branch of the NAACP, who had been shot and injured because of his attempts to register local blacks to vote; and L. C. Blackman, a black contractor whose business had been boycotted and his life threatened by the Ku Klux Klan after he had campaigned for school desegregation in Elloree, South Carolina, gave weight to the importance of passing effective civil rights legislation. At the end of the conference, delegates announced a list of eight measures on which they wanted federal action, including the establishment of a permanent FEPC and a civil rights division within the Department of Justice; and the battle commenced.

Although the LCCR had impressed some on Capitol Hill, the executive branch was still slow to respond to its pleas. President Eisenhower was not completely indifferent to civil rights. He had established the President's Committee on Government Contracts (PCGC) in 1953, under the chairmanship of Vice President Richard Nixon, in an attempt to tackle discrimination in companies working on government contracts. Another Eisenhower structure, the President's Committee on Government Employment Policy (PCGEP), was established two years later to eradicate employment discrimination within the federal government. The PCGEP operated along similar lines as the FEPC in that it had no powers of enforcement but could investigate complaints and pursue solutions.[22] Both were encouraging signs from the White House, but Eisenhower's belief in gradual change was an impediment to any serious progress.

The presidential election of 1956 offered meager hope of any change in the White House. During the campaign, the president said little about civil rights, although Eisenhower spoke of his success in eliminating segregation in federal offices and of progress in reducing discrimination among companies under government contract. But he repeated his belief that desegregation had to be implemented gradually, driven by a change in attitude rather than through the imposition of law. Wilkins had no intention of absolving Eisenhower of his responsibility. He argued that black Americans needed the protection that could come only through comprehensive civil rights legislation and stressed the importance of some form of meaningful congressional action. Somewhat melodramatically, in his keynote address to the National Delegate Assembly for Civil Rights in March 1956, he said, "A considerable part of the free world's hope for survival and peace depends upon first, what we do and say and how we do and say it, and secondly and more decisively, what our Congress does and does not do in the next four months before adjournment for the 1956 campaign."[23]

That summer Wilkins appeared before both the Democrat and Republican resolutions committee in an attempt to secure commitments to civil rights legislation from both parties. He repeated the call for the eight measures proposed by the LCCR earlier in the year; but most important, Wilkins argued, was protecting—and upholding—the right to vote. At one point during his testimony, Wilkins took a bar of soap and asked members how many bubbles were in that bar, as one southern registrar had asked black registrants; but it was a wasted gesture. The parties made scant concessions to civil rights in their platforms. Wilkins was more than disappointed: "Both parties gave the Negro the royal runaround on civil rights. The Democratic plank smelled to high heaven; the Republican plank just smelled. If the final judgment were to have been made on those two planks alone, black voters would all have done much better going fishing that November," he later wrote.[24]

Wilkins's concern about voting rights was justified when voters cast their ballots in November 1956. Only 37 percent of blacks eligible to vote did so nationally, and even fewer, 21 percent, did so in the eleven southern states (excluding Texas)—an appallingly low number, due in large part to the difficulties in simply registering to vote.[25] Still, although the total number of black voters was relatively small, the political importance of those votes was not lost on either party. But it was not clear which party had the upper hand. Black voting patterns showed a sharp shift toward the Republicans in the South, while northern blacks remained loyal to the Democratic Party, reflecting the political realities of each constituency. Wilkins told E. Frederic Morrow, who in July 1955 had become the only black member of Eisenhower's administration when he was appointed Administrative Officer for Special Projects, that the Republican Party likely could have won at least 65 percent of the Negro vote and potentially three-quarters for at least the next three presidential elections if the party had unequivocally supported the *Brown* decision.[26]

Not for the first time, a breach of sorts began to appear between the preoccupations of the NAACP's leaders and those of its members, who were more concerned with direct action than federal inaction. The Montgomery boycott had demonstrated that ordinary people could take direct action in their own communities, and that this promised more immediate results than the seemingly endless battle to circumvent Rule 22 in Congress, for example, which was the main topic of conversation during the Association's annual convention in San Francisco when the issue of mass action was brought to the floor. A resolution was passed to "broaden the NAACP's program by all lawful means and recommend that the board of directors give careful consideration to the Montgomery model." Wilkins, however, was not to be dissuaded from his view that the Association should remain focused on pressing the three pillars of government on desegregation, and leave direct-action protest to King, albeit with financial and rhetorical support from the NAACP.[27]

King's emergence as a national leader posed a more personal problem for Wilkins. The two men could not have been more different. Where Wilkins was cautious and reserved, King was bold and dynamic; and King's oratory, rooted in the emotional cadences of the preacher, was in stark contrast to Wilkins's far more restrained delivery. King was the passionate and visionary leader, while Wilkins was the rational pragmatist. When the latter spoke of legislation, law, and the political process, as he often did, his words were important, but rarely inspiring. By contrast, King addressed the NAACP's delegates and electrified his audience with a call to protest even if it meant jail—or death. The contrast was not lost on commentators. The *Amsterdam News*, a frequent critic of Wilkins, damned him with faint praise, calling him "the methodic kind of workman who handles the administrative details," and allowing that he had done a good job at those details. This hardly described the kind of leader capable of inspiring a sea change in national opinion.[28]

Wilkins could ill afford the distractions of King, boycotts, and the transitory attentions of the press. The *Brown* decision had unleashed a vicious backlash against the NAACP throughout the South. As L. C. Blackman's testimony at the LCCR conference had highlighted, any activity that promoted school desegregation could be physically and economically devastating for individuals. But the governments of Alabama, South Carolina, and Louisiana were particularly ingenious in finding legal mechanisms that attacked the NAACP. They unearthed a variety of archaic statutes to prohibit or curtail the Association from operating in their states. There was an almost admirable deviousness in this strategy: If the states had used violence to curtail the Association's activities the federal government may have been forced to step in, but by demanding members' names and by making it difficult for NAACP lawyers to operate in the states, plaintiffs were prevented from coming forward, the Association was embroiled in costly litigation, and local people were dissuaded from becoming members.

Robert Carter, the NAACP's legal counsel, thought that the Association had overestimated the ability of the *Brown* ruling to "box in" segregation and underestimated the racism that existed "outside that box"; the southern states tried their best to prove Carter right.[29] By the end of 1956 the NAACP was fighting for survival in Florida, Louisiana, Alabama, North Carolina, Texas, Georgia, and Virginia. A raft of lawsuits was needed not only to force compliance with the school integration order but also to fight several of the state actions against the Association. The lawsuits also put additional pressure on the often inadequate and untrained leadership in many of the Association's southern branches. As Wilkins wrote later: "The only way to begin was to begin. The real question was 'Where first.'"[30]

Louisiana, with perhaps unintentional irony, adapted a statute originally designed to curtail the Ku Klux Klan to demand that the NAACP file its statewide membership lists with the Louisiana secretary of state. Although several branches did file the requested lists with the appropriate authorities, the Association was enjoined eventually from conducting business in the state for several months while the NAACP challenged the statute in the federal courts. When the Association in Louisiana finally resumed its operations at the end of 1956, it was in a significantly weakened condition, with only 1,698 members across the state—a fraction of its 13,190 members in the previous year.[31]

Alabama followed Louisiana's lead almost immediately, and to even more devastating effect. The state's government was particularly exercised over the NAACP's financial support of the Montgomery boycott and by its legal support of Autherine Lucy's attempt to enter the University of Alabama. It retaliated on May 31, 1956, with a demand that the organization register with the Alabama secretary of state; the following day, "without notice or hearing," Judge Walter B. Jones of the 15th Judicial Circuit Court in Montgomery issued a temporary restraining order and an injunction forbidding the NAACP to operate in Alabama, saying he intended "to deal the NAACP . . . a mortal blow from which they shall never recover."[32] The Alabama government also ordered the NAACP to submit its membership list for the state; this was a more complex requirement, and the debate about whether to comply with the order caused a number of arguments at the Association's head office. Wilkins and Carter were adamant that filing the lists with the state authorities could endanger members' lives and livelihoods. Marshall was equally adamant that the NAACP should comply with the legal instruction.[33] Wilkins and Carter's argument prevailed, and when the NAACP refused to acquiesce it was fined $100,000 for contempt of court. Eventually, the Association was banned from the state completely for nine years.

Other states used similar methods. Virginia, for example, passed a series of statutes prohibiting fund-raising for litigation and also issued restrictions that, in effect, barred a lawyer in the state from taking on an NAACP case. State officials also requested access to the Association's membership lists. That request was denied by Wilkins, who told John Boatwright, the secretary of the Association's lavishly named Committee on Offenses Against Administration of Justice: "The slightest danger of revelation of the identity of our members would cause a substantial and injurious curtailment in the size of our membership"—exactly the effect intended by the request.[34]

In Florida, the NAACP was forced into a lengthy and costly battle with the Florida Legislative Investigation Committee, better known as the Johns committee after its chairman, state senator Charley Johns. The Johns committee was set up by the state legislature in 1956 with a broad mandate to investigate individuals and organizations that might be "inimical to the well being and orderly pursuit of their personal and business activities by the majority of the citizens of this state." Although this primarily meant Communists, the first organization in its sights was the NAACP. The committee interrogated many of the Association's leaders in the state, citing dubious evidence from witnesses who alleged communist involvement in NAACP operations and demanding access to its membership lists for the state. When the Association refused to comply, it quickly became embroiled in a legal battle, which eventually reached the US Supreme Court and was finally resolved in 1963, when the court found for the NAACP.[35]

Georgia began an inquiry into the Association's finances to assess whether it owed the state any taxes, and when the NAACP refused to comply with an order to release its account books, it was fined $10,000. The effect, as Roy Wilkins pointed out to Daisy Bates, was "to keep us so busy defending the Association and spending our money that we will have no time or resources left to push the program."[36] By May 1957 eight states had implemented some kind of impediment to the NAACP's operations.[37] By 1958, the NAACP's budget was the largest in its history, but the cost of the continuing legal battles for its survival, and for school desegregation, combined with the costs of the voting and registration campaign across the South put the Association in a precarious financial situation and made the competition for members even more fierce.[38]

Although the Association survived these challenges, the constant fight had a devastating effect on its resources and on the morale of its members. Even in states where the NAACP was not fighting for its life, branches stagnated; and the effects of the lawsuits began to take their toll on morale, both at the head office and among the Association's members. Wilkins described the strains on all concerned to William Walker, a newspaper editor based in Texas: "Although the NAACP is far from knocked out in the South (we are barred from only one state, Alabama), our people are jittery and we are groggy. The opposition cannot do us any permanent damage in the long run, but they can carry on a war of irritation which will make our members and prospective members uneasy."[39] Describing these events as a "war of irritation" was an understatement. It would take almost eight years and several trips to the Supreme

Court before the NAACP was allowed to resume operations in Alabama. While the Association was tied up in legal challenges, the officials in that state, Marshall admitted, "have us exactly where they want us," which was in limbo.[40]

The fight in Texas had repercussions that went beyond the effect on membership figures and finances. In September 1956 the state's attorney general, John Ben Shepperd, took out an injunction to prevent the NAACP from operating in the state.[41] Using an arcane charge of barratry (the initiation of groundless litigation for the purposes of harassment or financial gain), state troopers seized membership lists from the homes and offices of branch officials, who were then questioned about their roles in the Association's lawsuits in Texas. On appeal in October 1956, state judge Otis Dunagan allowed the NAACP to continue operations but prohibited the Inc. Fund from soliciting plaintiffs or offering them financial support, in effect noting the two as separate entities. The state also accused the NAACP of being a foreign corporation and claimed the organization had failed to pay the proper franchise taxes.[42] At a subsequent hearing the following May the injunction was made permanent. This unleashed a barrage of arguments between the Inc. Fund and its sister organization on how to retaliate.

Marshall, Wilkins, and the board disagreed over the question of whether to appeal the ruling. Marshall endorsed the view of W. J. Durham, the local lawyer hired by Wilkins to represent the NAACP, that the Association should accept the injunction, mainly because hearings had uncovered the fact that the Association had agreed to pay $3,500 per year to plaintiff Heman Sweatt during his lawsuit against the University of Texas Law School in 1950, an act that probably violated the state's barratry law.[43] The board of directors, however, agreed with one of the local branch leaders, who argued that the Association should appeal on the basis that not doing so would imply that the NAACP had violated the law.[44] Wilkins too thought that an appeal should be lodged, telling Marshall that doing so would be "for the sake of the troops," who might be upset at the suggestion that the NAACP had sailed close to the edge of propriety.[45]

Following a direct appeal by Durham, the board did eventually heed its legal counsel's advice and the Association resumed normal activities;

but the arguments left a bitter taste, particularly between Marshall and some members of the board.[46] The disagreement over the Texas case highlighted the tension that sometimes arose between the NAACP's focus on public relations and the Inc. Fund's focus on the rule of law.[47] A process to finally separate the two organizations began in March 1956 when the Internal Revenue Service (IRS) raised questions about the Inc. Fund's tax-exempt status. Marshall was summoned to Washington for what turned out to be a "most discouraging meeting," where he was asked numerous questions about the relationship between the NAACP and the Inc. Fund. The depressing conclusion was that the IRS was likely to deny any extension to the Inc. Fund's tax-exempt status, with the additional threat of a congressional investigation.[48]

The IRS investigations provided a convenient excuse to separate the two branches and allowed Marshall at the same time to stage a "one-man coup" to rid the Inc. Fund of what he saw as troublesome ties with the NAACP; accordingly, in 1957 the two groups separated.[49] The Inc. Fund moved to new offices outside of NAACP headquarters, Marshall became director-counsel of the Inc. Fund, and Wilkins became unpaid secretary for the Inc. Fund and was the only officer serving on the boards of both organizations. Unfortunately, while the break may have been a good move for the Inc. Fund, for the NAACP the division was a recipe for confusion and conflict. For several years following the split, the Association was to a large extent a cause without a legal program: it had a small legal team with which to conduct its cases at a time when litigation was a fundamental part of its function. It competed with the Inc. Fund for donations, but fund-raising was made more difficult by the understandable lack of clarity in the minds of both staff and the public about which organization was responsible for what litigation. An internal report on the NAACP's legal program and its relationship to the Inc. Fund in 1961 suggested that there were, in effect, two legal entities of the NAACP, each with different aims, that difference being exacerbated by the limitations imposed by the IRS and also by the rulings in some states that the Inc. Fund restrict itself to requests for legal assistance from lawyers or potential plaintiffs. It could not, or would not, accept direct requests from branches.[50]

Momentum for some kind of action on civil rights by the Eisenhower administration and Congress gained speed with the comfortable reelection of the president in November 1956. Eisenhower used the first State of the Union address of his second term to announce that his administration intended to pursue the civil rights legislation that had initially been drawn up by Brownell the previous year. Wilkins was unimpressed. He had little confidence in Eisenhower and complained loudly that the president had failed to mention, let alone condemn, the wave of racially motivated violence currently sweeping through the South. In a pointed statement to the *New York Post*, Wilkins berated Eisenhower for refusing to make a speech in the South on behalf of civil rights, and expressed hope that eventually "the President will express as much concern for innocent victims of bombings and other terror in the South as he has for the Hungarian victims of Soviet terrorism."[51]

In truth, any legislation was likely to fall foul of the filibuster, so Wilkins, as chairman of the LCCR, renewed the fight for a means to weaken Rule 22 and limit its potential to damage any potential legislation. Consultations began with sympathetic congressmen in the hope that enough support could be gathered to strike when a new session of Congress convened at the beginning of January.[52] There was a tiny loophole in Senate procedure, by which only on the first day of a new congressional session—in this instance, January 3, 1957—a motion to change Senate rules could be passed by a simple majority. Unfortunately, although a vote was taken that day, Rule 22 survived intact; but thirty-eight senators supported the move to abolish the rule, giving Wilkins hope of more support in the future.[53]

Whatever Wilkins's reservations, as the administration's civil rights program began to take shape, it became clear that this was the best opportunity the NAACP had ever had to obtain effective civil rights legislation. The process of getting a civil rights bill through both houses of Congress was both complicated and delicate, often resembling a game of Snakes and Ladders, with every gain blocked by another obstacle. Its path was made only slightly easier by a tilt in the balance of those leaning toward reform.[54]

Wilkins devoted all his energies to the challenge of ensuring the legislation's successful passage. He began a campaign to garner support for the legislation even before the bill was sent up to Capitol Hill, appearing in front of House and Senate committees to highlight many of the areas that demanded reform. He took a conciliatory tone with the House Judiciary Committee, assuring its members that black Americans were willing to compromise but that any legislation must protect the voting rights and personal safety of those campaigning for civil rights. But he was far more defiant when he testified at a Senate Judiciary Subcommittee hearing. There he bluntly warned senators that the patience of black Americans would not last if the civil rights bill was not approved.[55] In June 1957 the House of Representatives passed the bill, with a vote of 286–126. H.R. 6127 had emerged from the House with just two minor amendments.[56]

Although the bill's successful passage through the House was an encouraging sign, it was clear that its way through the Senate would be much tougher. To rally support, Wilkins wrote to NAACP staff to emphasize the importance of the next stage. "It may well be that the next few weeks will be the most important in the legislative career of the NAACP," he asserted. "While it is going on, the civil rights fight in the Senate is the number one item of business before all of us: everything else takes a temporary second place."[57] He cajoled branch members to intensify the pressure on their congressmen to support the legislation by sending letters and telegrams. Most importantly, he encouraged the NAACP's members to cultivate and extend relationships with sympathetic politicians so as to create a bipartisan coalition that would support the bill. Wilkins urged delegates at the 1957 annual NAACP conference in Detroit to lobby their senators whether they were friendly, lukewarm, or hostile.[58]

Meanwhile, Wilkins spent much of his time during July and early August working in Washington with Clarence Mitchell to build congressional backing for the legislation or traveling across the country to speak at rallies, branches, and civic lunches. Radio commercials featuring a bipartisan group of senators were broadcast on almost one hundred radio stations in support of the bill. Wilkins and Mitchell also guided the lobbying strategy, while Wilkins, in his capacity as chairman of the LCCR, coordinated the response of the participating organizations.[59] However, regardless of the pressure exerted by the NAACP and the LCCR, the success or failure of the bill depended primarily on the Senate's majority leader, Lyndon Johnson.

Up to this point, Johnson had displayed scant commitment to civil rights, and his Texas background gave little reason for optimism.

Wilkins, who later became one of Johnson's most trusted advisers on civil rights, described him as the "Br'er Fox of the Senate," saying, "you never quite knew if he was out to lift your heart or your wallet."[60] The Senate leader was particularly adept at maneuvering legislation through the complex congressional process. He told Wilkins that he was only interested in voting rights, and that the most contentious element of Part III of the bill, which allowed the attorney general to pursue violations of civil rights, would have to be deleted if it were to pass. To soften the southern bloc, Johnson proffered a jury trial amendment, which would allow a trial by jury for anyone indicted under the new law. Given the blatant disregard for justice displayed by southern juries when assigned to any case involving an element of race, such an amendment would virtually nullify Part III.

Wilkins, Mitchell, and the coalition of supporters from other organizations were disgusted. In allowing the Justice Department to prosecute civil rights violations, Part III remedied a long-standing problem. As such, Wilkins considered it to be one of the most vital elements of the legislation. Now, it appeared, its sacrifice was the price demanded by the southern bloc if a filibuster was to be avoided. The leadership of the LCCR convened to consider its response and discuss whether it should continue to support the amended bill. At the meeting, Wilkins argued that the decision to support the bill involved three issues: Was the present bill better than nothing at all in helping more blacks register to vote? Should the Association fight to restore Part III at the risk of killing the bill completely? And, if the Association accepted the jury trial amendment, how should it explain its decision to its membership, and what would the likely reaction be if the bill proved to be unworkable?

Wilkins also considered the perspective of black voters. He argued that if no bill were passed, Democrats would get most of the blame while Republicans could at least fall back on their stronger voting record on civil rights. If a weak bill were passed, Republicans would still receive much of the credit and could even claim that Eisenhower would have supported a stronger bill, safe in the knowledge that he would be required to do no such thing. Wilkins argued that although Democrats in states that had a significant black electorate would escape heavy punishment, black voters would likely punish Johnson if he were a candidate in the 1960 election.

Vice President Nixon, on the other hand, had thus far suffered no loss of reputation in the battle; on the contrary, black voters persisted in believing that he was a strong advocate of civil rights—unlike Senator Kennedy, who, Wilkins concluded, had identified himself further with the southern bloc.[61]

The Civil Rights Act passed in spite of the longest filibuster speech in the Senate's history, as well as numerous other tricky obstructions. Even in its watered-down state, it was the most significant piece of civil rights legislation to emerge from Congress since 1875 and at least promised some protection of voting rights. Moreover, its passage demonstrated that even the most tenacious attempts to derail the legislation could be beaten. As he anticipated, however, Wilkins's decision to back the bill provoked a barrage of criticism from almost every corner. As the bill approached its final hurdle, Wilkins braced himself for the inevitable backlash. In a memorandum to NAACP staff he said that although everyone who had lobbied for the bill wanted something much stronger, the weakness of the current legislation might prove to be a bargaining tool by the 1960 election: "The point is, that with a bill we are in a better position to campaign than we would be without a bill."[62]

Supporting the legislation was a big gamble for Wilkins. While the NAACP was unlikely to lose a significant number of members in protest, not least because there were few other places for them to go, the tortuous wheeling and dealing that only resulted in a weak bill gave weight to the argument that direct-action protests were a more effective way of securing equal rights. If the NAACP maintained its stance that legislation and favorable court rulings, rather than boycotts and mass action, were the best means of winning full equality, it needed credible action from Congress.[63] Unfortunately, the Civil Rights Act wound up being as ineffectual as its critics feared. Numerous cases of voting discrimination failed to be prosecuted under the new law, despite their being submitted to the Department of Justice.

As the Civil Rights Act was being signed into law, the governor of Arkansas, Orval Faubus, inadvertently provided a stark illustration of the necessity for federal action. Faubus had been relatively liberal in his attitudes to integration until he found himself in a tight gubernatorial race in the 1956 elections. School integration seemed the perfect issue with which to advertise his newfound segregationist credentials. Arkansas had been one of the few southern states voluntarily to draw up school integration plans in several cities, although the Little Rock school board had drawn up demanding admissions criteria for black pupils wishing to transfer to the city's Central High School. The result was that, from an initial pool of around two hundred black pupils, only nine were eventually allowed to begin the new school year in the high school.

Before school opened in Little Rock, however, Faubus announced that he had ordered the National Guard to surround the campus, claiming that violence would erupt if the black children tried to enter the school.[64] When the teenagers arrived at the gates on the first day of term they had to fight their way through a hostile crowd that jeered and pushed them, only to find that the armed guardsmen at the entrance of the school refused to let them in. By using state troops to oppose a federal statute, Faubus had instigated one of the most serious constitutional crises to face the United States since the Civil War, creating Eisenhower's worst domestic nightmare. Even worse was the image of one of the black students, fifteen-year-old Elizabeth Eckford, who, carrying her schoolbooks and holding her head up high, faced a violent, hostile mob of braying, screaming protestors alone—an image that was broadcast on the evening news programs.

When the White House failed to respond to the developments in Arkansas, Wilkins warned the president that such inaction would undermine federal authority; still, Eisenhower did almost nothing for three weeks. The president met with Faubus, but failed to meet with black leaders. In a letter to Adam Clayton Powell, Wilkins was scathing in his criticism of the president: "I have great difficulty in speaking calmly about the role of President Eisenhower in this whole mess. He has been absolutely and thoroughly disappointing and disillusioning from beginning to end."[65] Eisenhower was finally forced into action when federal district judge Ronald Davies enjoined Faubus and the National Guard from obstructing the desegregation process at the school. As a result, the governor withdrew the troops, leaving the nine black children unprotected in a highly volatile situation. At that point the president federalized the National Guard and sent the 101st Airborne Division into the city to restore order and protect the black students for the remainder of the school year. Faubus promptly responded by closing Little Rock's schools. The NAACP protested, and Inc. Fund lawyers took the case to the Supreme Court, which invalidated Faubus's decision, reaffirmed *Brown*, and dismissed attempts by Faubus and his legislature to circumvent the desegregation order.[66] The governor made one last attempt to avoid desegregation by holding a referendum in the city on whether schools should be desegregated or remain closed. The city overwhelmingly voted for the latter, and Little Rock schools did not reopen until 1959.

President Eisenhower finally met with a group of the main civil rights leaders in June 1958. In spite of Wilkins's poor opinion of Eisenhower, he was keen to keep the president's tenuous goodwill. Wilkins acknowledged Eisenhower's role in integrating the military and in proposing the 1957 Civil Rights legislation, but then argued for the restoration of Part III as part of a new civil rights bill, saying that this was the "most effective and bloodless way" to dispel the problems that were plaguing the South. Martin Luther King Jr. asked Eisenhower for a presidential pronouncement in favor of desegregation, arguing that it would set a moral tone for the country, and suggested a conference, to be led by the president, at which peaceful methods of achieving desegregation could be discussed. Then, in contrast to the soothing words of the rest of the group, Lester Granger of the Urban League warned the president that the bitter mood of black Americans showed "more signs of congealing" than at any other time he could remember. Not only did the president decline to discuss the proposals put forward, he responded petulantly to Granger, saying he was "extremely dismayed" to find that blacks were bitter despite the efforts of his administration and went on to suggest that more executive action on civil rights might only result in more bitterness.[67]

Surprisingly, White House aide Rocco Siciliano described the meeting as an "unqualified success—even if success in this area is built on sand."[68] The civil rights leaders, by contrast, found it disappointing. The group left the Oval Office with only a promise that the president would consider the recommendations the group had proposed and a vague agreement to the suggestion for a conference on civil rights.[69] At a press conference following the meeting, Wilkins and his colleagues attempted to sound more positive about the outcome of the meeting—only for Wilkins to be baited by Louis Lautier, a black reporter, who wondered whether he had been brainwashed by the president.[70]

The fact that King was now considered one of the most important civil rights leaders demonstrated just how quickly he had risen to prominence. He attended the White House meeting as head of the Southern Christian Leadership Conference (SCLC), a new organization formed in early 1957 by King and other religious leaders.[71] Although it differed in both structure and tactics from the NAACP, the SCLC posed the first significant threat to the older organization, particularly in regions where the Association's operations were prohibited or curtailed. This was especially true in Alabama, where the state's legal reprisals had wiped out the NAACP and left a vacuum, which the SCLC began to fill with a network of local affiliates, making it difficult for the NAACP to reestablish itself if and when the federal courts sustained its appeals against the state court injunctions.

John Brooks, the NAACP's director of voter registration, was dispatched to observe an early SCLC meeting and report back to the national office. He said that participants were careful not to be publicly critical of the NAACP, but much was made of the fact that, unlike the NAACP, SCLC leaders were based in the South rather than New York or Chicago. Brooks concluded, "The Southern Christian Leadership Conference has a small hard core of leaders that would like to take over the NAACP's leadership in the South. They are willing to use our staff, our branch officers and our members to build their organizations for this purpose."[72] The gauntlet had been thrown down, and Wilkins and his colleagues were only too quick to accept the challenge.

Despite King's protestations that the SCLC had no wish to step on the NAACP's toes, the fact that the two groups were operating in the same communities meant it was inevitable that they would rely on the same pool of organizers and appeal to the same, small pool of members. Some NAACP officials also supported SCLC, or attempted to. For example, when Medgar Evers, the NAACP's field secretary in Mississippi, became involved with an SCLC group in his community, Wilkins hastily told him to make his excuses and withdraw quietly; but he did encourage Evers to continue to collaborate with the SCLC on projects that the NAACP thought useful.[73]

Although the SCLC could not compete with the organizational structure and breadth of the NAACP, it captured the imagination of many blacks who might, under other circumstances, have become involved with the Association; and competition for publicity, members, and revenues exacerbated tensions in the relationship between the two groups. In public Wilkins, Marshall, and other NAACP leaders spoke warmly of the new organization and its leader. In private, however, they resented both, not least because the emergence of the SCLC revived old criticisms of the NAACP: that it was too cautious and reliant on litigation at the expense of other potentially more successful methods of achieving equal rights.

It is ironic that while Wilkins was fending off accusations from some quarters that the Association was too moderate in its approach, the NAACP was accused by others of being a militant group and pushing change too quickly. As television became a ubiquitous presence in American homes, these debates were increasingly broadcast on a national scale. While Wilkins lacked the charisma of King, his analytical approach was well suited to the new medium, and he became a frequent spokesman for the civil rights movement on television. The importance of TV as a platform for the NAACP became apparent when Chet Huntley, a television commentator, argued in an NBC broadcast in February 1959 that desegregation would be best served if the "militant" NAACP withdrew from the fight and left the field clear for "moderate" black organizations. The Association, backed by over two hundred calls from outraged viewers to NBC, immediately demanded equal air time to respond to Huntley's assertions. The network proposed a thirty-minute live debate the following week between Roy Wilkins and Thomas Waring, editor of the Charleston, South Carolina, *News and Courier* and an infamous segregationist. Each would be given ten minutes to make his case. The NAACP argued that ten minutes was not long enough, but reluctantly agreed; and, in the few days before the broadcast, the organization prepared a detailed and eloquent rebuttal to Huntley's comments.

In his ten minutes, Wilkins said that the NAACP's response to school desegregation had been a calm and reasoned call to its members to petition their local school boards. The "loud" noise of desegregation, he said, came from southern politicians and newspapers determined to maintain the racial status quo. The NAACP, he argued, rejected violence; in fact, its members had been the victims, rather than the perpetrators, of violent attacks. Asking black Americans to renounce their constitutional rights would mean that "we and our children sit by the side of the road while others zoom past us into the space age."[74] Wilkins's brief appearance was met with widespread acclaim and provided invaluable publicity. And it was a battle worth fighting. Huntley's show could well have been many viewers' introduction to the NAACP, and Wilkins's calm, articulate appearance belied accusations of his organization's being a militant one. In addition, as Aniko Bodroghkozy points out, his appearance also allowed the NAACP to reach a bigger black audience.[75]

Wilkins found himself increasingly called upon to defend his attitude to boycotts and other forms of direct action. Stanley Levison, a longtime member of the NAACP and a close confidant of King, was particularly critical of the Association's reluctance to embrace mass action. He called upon Wilkins to appeal to the "ordinary person who does not attend dinners, who hasn't $15, $50 or $100 for a ticket or a tuxedo, but who has zeal, energy and native talent which cannot be bought but can be given without cost if we ask for it."[76] James Peck of the Congress of Racial Equality (CORE) also took Wilkins to task, arguing that he should take the initiative in pursuing boycotts and, more importantly, move to expand the sphere of NAACP activities outside of litigation and lobbying and embrace nonviolent protest. If the NAACP did not make these changes, Peck warned, "Some other organization (or organizations) may well have to develop to fulfill this need."[77] In response, Wilkins simply reiterated his belief that the success blacks had experienced in Montgomery was ultimately the result of the lawsuit, not the mass action, and argued that the threat of white reprisals, particularly where against a group that was as outnumbered as black Americans, made the advocacy of actions such as boycotts wantonly dangerous.[78]

This argument, however, centered on armed self-defense, while it was nonviolent protest that provided one of the most serious—and unexpected—challenges to Wilkins's relatively new position as head of the NAACP. It was a paradox of the nonviolent movement that many activists, including King himself, believed that carrying weapons or having guns in their homes were sensible precautions in states as dangerous as Mississippi and Alabama. Wilkins himself took a pragmatic view of armed self-defense as an understandable response when faced with white violence. But that pragmatism was tempered by a fear that meeting violence with violence could draw unwelcome attention to the Association. That was exactly what happened in the case of Robert Williams.

When Williams became president of a moribund NAACP branch in Monroe, North Carolina, in 1956, he was almost the only member. To drum up support he canvassed pool halls, bars, beauty parlors, and street corners. Soon the branch had over two hundred members.[79] Among the branch's activities, Williams and other members organized self-defense networks to protect themselves against the Ku Klux Klan and other hostile groups. Williams's troubles with the national NAACP began in October 1958 when one of two young black boys, aged eight and ten years old, kissed a white girl with whom they were playing—an infraction for which they were arrested and detained for six days while their families' homes were attacked by Klansmen. Williams and his colleagues launched a national publicity campaign that attracted the attention of the Socialist Workers Party (SWP), a Trotskyite group, which eagerly took up the case and helped Williams to publicize the incident both at home and abroad, much to the embarrassment of the United States government and the NAACP.

Williams made matters worse by attacking the NAACP publicly, telling a meeting in Cleveland, for example, that he had formed an organization called the Committee to Combat Racial Injustice because the Association had failed to act effectively in the "Kissing Case."[80] Matters came to a head in May 1959 when, following the rapid acquittal of a white man accused of raping a pregnant black woman, Williams stated that as there was no court protection for blacks in the South, they must defend themselves from white attacks. He told news reporters at the courthouse that it was time to "meet violence with violence." Unfortunately, Williams's fighting talk provided ammunition for the NAACP's detractors, who cried that the organization was a revolutionary front advocating violent rebellion. The branch leader, however, was far from contrite: he told Wilkins that not only had he made the remarks, he was about to repeat them on television. Wilkins did not want Williams's comments associated with the NAACP and suspended him pending ratification (or otherwise) of his suspension at the NAACP's annual convention in New York City in July 1959. To separate itself from Williams, and very probably to discredit him prior to the convention, the NAACP published a booklet entitled "The Single Issue in the Robert Williams Case," which claimed that the main issue was about Williams's call for "mob action," not his call for self-defense.[81] By the time the convention opened, the debate had widened into a critique of the national leadership's attitude toward any kind of mass action, whether nonviolent or retaliatory.

The stage was set for a showdown. In the weeks leading up to the convention Wilkins, Marshall, and other NAACP leaders waged a campaign to isolate and discredit Williams. Williams, for his part, had attracted the support of a number of disenchanted NAACP members who wanted to prod the leadership into more direct action. Still, he was outmaneuvered. At the convention, forty speakers took to the podium to denounce Williams and call for his continued suspension. Using every political trick at his disposal, including exerting pressure on Daisy Bates to denounce Williams publicly, Wilkins eventually succeeded in winning the suspension vote. But the episode exposed a potential division in the relationship between the NAACP's branches and its national office, as demands for more action in the face of the white backlash against *Brown* increased.[82]

Wilkins was also facing questions from the black press about his ability to lead the NAACP. In the spring of 1958, James Hicks of the *Amsterdam News* published a series of essays on the theme of black leadership, with Wilkins as the focus.[83] Hicks was damning in his criticism. He argued that Wilkins was just the latest in a long line of black leaders motivated by a need to "belong" to the white power structure. Hicks called for "forceful, aggressive leadership," but charged that Wilkins was so keen to belong to the white establishment that he had become hesitant in challenging discrimination. Hicks also argued that the leftward inclination of the NAACP's board caused Wilkins problems in getting access to the Republican White House and so hindered his ability to persuade either the executive branch or Congress on civil rights matters. Then again, even if Wilkins had such access, Hicks reasoned, his need to belong hampered his ability to take tough decisions.[84] The main evidence Hicks gave for his assertions was the 1957 Civil Rights Bill. "Eight months after Roy agreed that a half loaf of Civil Rights was better than no bread at all, the watered down civil rights law, and the Commission which it established, is virtually dead. Actually, because of the compromise, it hasn't really ever been born."[85] Rather than leading his people, Hicks challenged, Wilkins was simply running to keep up with the unstoppable force that was black America's drive for freedom. "Roy can't stop running any more than any other so-called Negro leader can stop running today—for he knows that the minute he stops he will get run over by the steamroller. But this is not leadership. For Roy himself hasn't the slightest idea where the steamroller is going."[86]

Within the NAACP some branches were already taking charge of the steamroller. In the summer of 1958 a group of NAACP's youth branch in Wichita, Kansas, angry at the discriminatory policies in place at Dockum's, one of the biggest drugstore chains in the area, had planned a sit-in protest at its local store. The president of the local NAACP branch, Chester Lewis, notified the head office of the protest the day before the sit-in began, but, rather than support, received a reply from Herb Wright, the national youth secretary, stating that the NAACP would not endorse sit-ins or any other form of mass action. Sit-in protests were not NAACP tactics, Lewis was told.[87] The protests took place anyway and within four weeks had succeeded in forcing Dockum's to change its policy across Kansas. The victory in Wichita launched a wave of equally successful sit-in protests across the state. But despite this success, the Wichita protests received little immediate recognition from NAACP leaders. Certainly they made no move to harness this energy and expand the Association's program to include more direct action.

The Kansas protests presented Wilkins with an uncomfortable dilemma. By ignoring instructions from the head office, the Wichita branch set a risky precedent that Wilkins would not wish to see emulated anywhere else; but the fact that the young people had secured a dramatic victory far more quickly than a court case ever could was obvious. The protests also brought publicity, which in return could win popular support and more members. But this was not enough to persuade Wilkins and his colleagues. Thus, in not acknowledging the shift to active dissent, the NAACP missed a golden opportunity to capitalize on the activism of their youth branches and lead this burgeoning wave of protest.[88] The Kansas protests were localized and relatively small; once they had achieved their aim, they died out, giving Wilkins and his colleagues little reason to expect that sit-in demonstrations would become more widespread. How wrong they were.

4

Politics and Protest

As 1960 began, Wilkins's primary concern was ensuring passage of a new civil rights bill that would extend voting rights. The presidential election due to take place in November of that year promised change only inasmuch as both parties admitted the need for action on civil rights. Unfortunately, neither had the appetite for the fight that would be required to pass any meaningful legislation. When a new civil rights bill was initially proposed in 1959, Wilkins called for the support of NAACP branch officers, but warned them that Lyndon Johnson's first priority was to maintain a united Democratic Party prior to the election and that he would sacrifice stronger legislation to ensure electoral success.

But even before the legislation reached the Senate floor, four young black students brought the fight for equality back to the streets. On February 1, 1960, in Greensboro, North Carolina, Ezell Blair Jr., David Richmond, Joseph McNeil, and Franklin McCain deliberately took their seats at the local Woolworth's lunch counter. As expected, they were refused service, but the four remained at the counter until the store closed, promising to return the following day, when they would resume their protest. Within five days, more than 500 students had joined the protests at Woolworth's and Kress stores in the city. The students were organized as effectively as any Dixiecrat filibuster. They took turns occupying stools and made sure that protestors constantly took up most of the seats at the lunch counter. Within a week, similar protests were taking place across the state; within two weeks, sit-in protests were taking place in four states; and by the end of March, sit-ins had occurred in sixty-nine cities across the southern and border states—taking everyone, not least the NAACP, by surprise.[1]

The history of the civil rights movement is littered with false beginnings, but the scale and speed with which the sit-in protests spread across the South was breathtaking and transformative. As August Meier and Elliott Rudwick argue, the protests "speeded up incalculably the rate of social change in the sphere of race relations; broke decisively the hegemony of the NAACP in the civil rights arena and inaugurated a period of unprecedented rivalry among the racial advancement groups; and made non-violent direction action the dominant strategy . . . for the next half-decade." The sit-in protests also shifted the balance from one generation to another. Students, both white and black, now became the face of protest, changing its form and pace. The NAACP had to run fast to keep up.[2]

Within three weeks of the Greensboro protest Wilkins wrote to NAACP members to assure them of the Association's support for the protestors. Initially, this involved paying bail money and other legal fees for protestors arrested during the sit-ins, but he also encouraged local branches to offer whatever other assistance they could. Falling short of outright encouragement to join the demonstrations, branches were urged to send letters and telegrams of protest to the presidents of Kress and Woolworth's, to hold protest meetings, and to form small groups to visit their local Kress and Woolworth's stores and warn them that they may be subject to economic boycotts if blacks were not served at lunch counters in the stores.[3] Reflecting the different circumstances facing protestors in the South and members elsewhere in the country, Wilkins's message was a little more vigorous to youth councils and college chapters in the North. Those groups were directed to picket Woolworth's, Kress, and other stores that operated discriminatory policies.[4]

The implications of such a dramatic turn of events did not go unnoticed by commentators. A front-page article in the *New York Times* suggested that the protests indicated "a shift of leadership to younger more militant Negroes," which would likely "bring an increasing use of passive resistance" as a protest technique. Shaken by these prospects, on the day the article appeared Wilkins called an emergency meeting with Gloster Current and Herbert Wright to discuss the new situation.[5] Shortly after that, a three-day staff conference was hastily convened at the Motel on the Mountain in upstate New York to discuss the policies, programs, and strategy of the Association. Just before the meeting, John Morsell asked participants to think about the NAACP's program and strategy; he posed questions such as whether the Association should be membership based, whom it appeals to, the role of mass action, and collaboration with other groups.[6]

Legal counsel Robert Carter argued that the NAACP faced a systemic problem—and a dilemma. The Association should, he said, build a community-action organization to help branches become better equipped to tackle discrimination in their communities. But the question for Carter was, first, how to devise such a program on a national level, and then how to communicate and implement such a program at branch level. Mildred Bond, who had revitalized the NAACP's life membership department, proposed that the Association focus less on litigation, publicity, and petitions because these tools were too "tame for the times"; instead, she argued, the organization should concentrate on lobbying and possibly on militant protest. But, she added, careful consideration must be given to the Association's generally conservative branch leaders and supporting organizations before adopting such a dramatic new program.[7] Calvin Banks, the NAACP's program director, and labor secretary Herbert Hill shared the view that the Association must become a mass organization with better connections to local black communities. Both complained that the current branch structure was inadequate, with many branches not even holding regular meetings.[8] Gloster Current, the director of branches, was the most positive. He offered mainly tactical suggestions because, in his view, the Association was on its way to reaching its various goals, with a few problems remaining in housing, public accommodation, voter registration, education, and equality in the South.[9]

Shortly before the conference, Wilkins devised an action plan in response to a statement from some of the drug stores targeted by sit-in protesters, which continued to refuse service to black customers. His "racial defense policy" instructed members to boycott any store that operated segregated lunch counters across the United States. Not all branches responded enthusiastically to this idea.[10] Some were already galvanized by the protests, but others were paralyzed by caution and fear; thus, any call to action, however mild, was met with mixed results. In those communities plagued by malaise, the Association often looked as if it were following in the footsteps of a more active organization rather than instigating direct action protests of its own. For example, five months before the Greensboro protests, the local NAACP youth council in Nashville asked branch leaders for their cooperation in launching a sit-in demonstration, but were turned down because "the NAACP has more important things to do than to try and eat a hot dog downtown."

This rebuff led the group to work with the Nashville Christian Leadership Council (NCLC), an affiliate of the SCLC, which was ultimately credited with the protest, despite the NAACP's involvement.[11] Episodes like this did not just extract a price in terms of publicity and recognition. After the Nashville protest, for instance, membership of the local branch dwindled within a year. Current attributed the decline to dissatisfaction in the black community that the NAACP had not been militant enough because the local leaders were old, conservative, and "tended to have a grandfather's viewpoint about aggressive activity."[12]

As the protests spread, it became clear that a coordinated effort was needed to consolidate the action. Ella Baker, who by 1960 was the executive director of SCLC, organized a conference in Raleigh, North Carolina, under the auspices of, but not led by, the SCLC. Baker proposed that the students form a new group rather than affiliate with an existing organization. Out of that suggestion came the Student Nonviolent Coordinating Committee (SNCC), which would challenge Wilkins and the NAACP many times in years to come. Surprisingly, discussions about the shortcomings of the Association took up much of the discussion at the conference. One of the most outspoken of those attending was James Lawson, who gave the keynote address. Lawson, a young theological student who had long been committed to nonviolence, had spent over a year in prison for his refusal to fight in the Korean War and three years in working as a Methodist missionary in India; he had been involved with the NCLC since 1958. A persuasive speaker, Lawson was clearly frustrated at the slow progress on civil rights. He called the sit-in protests "a judgment upon middle-class conventional half-way efforts to deal with radical social evil" and explicitly criticized the Association's lobbying and litigation strategy.[13]

It was rare for another activist to criticize the Association so publicly. Lawson's explicit repudiation of the NAACP's techniques and goals captured the attention of the national press and incensed Wilkins. He was particularly angry that Lawson had not been rebuked by Martin Luther King, and he wrote a furious letter to King, complaining that his silence suggested that Lawson's views were shared by others in the SCLC and going on to explain the extent of the NAACP's involvement with, and support of, the sit-in protests.[14] Lawson, rather than King, replied to Wilkins's allegations and, however critical his comments at the Raleigh conference, addressed Wilkins in a tone that was respectful, if not deferential. He went to some lengths to assure Wilkins that the newspaper reports were greatly exaggerated and reaffirmed his support of the Association through his own membership and through his collaboration with local branches. Wilkins offered Lawson no reprieve. He pointed out that an SCLC organizer repeated some of Lawson's arguments against the NAACP at another conference two weeks later, thereby exacerbating the criticism Lawson had made about the Association's activities.

Wilkins told Benjamin Mays, the president of Morehouse College and a former teacher of King's, that he believed King had encouraged Lawson to apologize because he was anxious not to exacerbate any tensions between the two organizations.[15] Indeed, King had considered adding Lawson to the SCLC payroll but changed his mind for fear of alienating Wilkins.[16] Nevertheless, as Wilkins told Mays, he was frustrated at the attacks from those he thought should have been allies: "We just don't believe that other people have to get ahead by kicking the NAACP in the teeth and our people are getting pretty tired of acting like a good-natured St. Bernard dog while other people snap at us and disseminate sentiment that washes away our public support as we remain dignified, cooperative and calm."[17]

The NAACP had always been quick to respond when its position was threatened, but it had never faced the kind of challenge that the new groups and their tactics now posed to its fundamental philosophy. As the students clearly had momentum on their side, the NAACP rapidly expanded its youth organization. Henry Lee Moon, Gloster Current, and Herbert Wright all urged Wilkins to call an emergency conference on youth and civil rights, which they believed would give the Association the lead in organizing and coordinating tactics nationally. With some foresight, Wright warned Wilkins, "If the Association does not act immediately to sponsor it, I am afraid that we may be out-maneuvered by some other organizations."[18] But conferences were neither wanted nor needed by the young protestors—they demanded action.

Louis Lomax explained the new power structure that was emerging in an article published in *Harper's* magazine in June 1960, saying, "the demonstrators have shifted the desegregation battle from the courtroom to the market place, and have shifted the main issue to one of individual dignity, rather than civil rights." The thesis of Lomax's article, "The Negro Revolt against 'The Negro Leaders,'" was that the sit-in protests had sounded the death knell for the kind of middle-class leadership exemplified by the NAACP.[19] The traditional organizations such as the NAACP had become "servants rather than catalysts," Lomax argued, because the protests, with the violence and retaliation that accompanied them, had induced a feeling of "old-fashioned revival" that allowed black Americans to take up the fight themselves rather than having to wait for the NAACP to wage the battle.[20]

Direct-action protests highlighted one of the systemic difficulties for the Association. In theory, NAACP strategy was developed by the board of directors and ratified by the members at the annual convention. However, in practice, as executive secretary, Wilkins played a large part in directing the organization's program, while implementation depended to a large extent on the activism of local branches. In Savannah, for example, members of the local youth branch instigated sit-in protests with the support of NAACP leaders in the city. These expanded into "wade-ins"—an attempt to desegregate public beaches—while adult members of the branch waged a very successful economic boycott, which cost city merchants over $1 million during the first month and continued for nineteen months until an agreement was reached with city leaders in October 1961.[21]

In other areas of the South, however, the picture was much bleaker. Rifts developed between branch officials, who were often more conservative and cautious than their national counterparts, and members who were keen to play their part in the civil rights struggle. In New Orleans, for example, local NAACP leaders undertook boycotts and picketing—albeit with some hesitation—but refused to initiate sit-ins. Frustrated by this tenuous approach, the youth branch began to work with local members of the Congress of Racial Equality, better known as CORE, a small, inter-racial organization formed in 1942, and other groups, to the fury of Wilkins. But Wilkins was even more furious with the local leadership, and subjected Arthur Chapital, the branch president, to an extraordinary reprimand for being too cautious and not encouraging the activist demands of younger members, thereby forcing them into alliances with other groups. "The organizations that you are going out of your way to help has members who are busy creating the impression that your Association is no good and they are spreading this so well that some people who usually give money to us are not doing so." Chapital earned a further rebuke from Wilkins when he tried to explain that the New Orleans branch had decided not to stage sit-ins following legal advice. To this Wilkins responded, "If NAACP branches, composed of cautious adults, and if NAACP local legal advisers, conservative and anxious to maintain a local reputation, are going to hold our branches back in the face of the demands of the times, then we will see other groups stepping in and taking over while the NAACP dies a slow death . . . While you are 'holding back' CORE and other groups are coming forward and picking up the energy, imagination and daring among our young people that we are carelessly throwing to one side."[22]

The Association's funds were dwindling fast as the demonstrations, and the cost of bailing out protestors, increased. Wilkins sent out an urgent call to branch officers in April 1960 asking branches to increase their memberships: "If your branch had 500 members in 1959, get at least 600 in 1960." Citing the sit-in protests as a spur to activity he added, "Don't let our young people down. They are supplying the courage; let us supply everything needed to keep that courage working."[23] But the financial pressures worsened as the sit-in protests continued. In Memphis, Durham, and all of South Carolina, for example, the Association paid bail and other legal fees, which in Memphis alone amounted to $4,400, most of which came from the branch's own funds.[24] The rise in protest activity also demanded more resources: telephone and telegraph bills, for example, stood at $16,000 for the first half of the year rather than the $10,000 that had been budgeted, leaving the Association in a dangerous financial situation.[25]

The impending presidential campaign gave Wilkins an opportunity to operate in more comfortable and familiar territory. He challenged both the Republican and Democratic parties to adopt effective civil rights planks in their election platforms, proffering the growing importance of the black vote as a carrot, which, he warned, would be lost by any politician or party that wavered on civil rights.[26] It was no idle threat: the NAACP estimated that around five million blacks were registered to vote, with the potential to tip the balance in crucial congressional districts in twelve states, so each of the candidates needed to court the black community.[27] Of the main candidates, John F. Kennedy and Lyndon Johnson were old acquaintances of Wilkins from the battle for the 1957 Civil Rights Act. Richard Nixon was a familiar figure, too, thanks to his role as vice president in the Eisenhower administration; but Wilkins had had little, if any, contact with Henry Cabot Lodge, Nixon's running mate. Wilkins was ambivalent about each of them; in fact, the best endorsement Wilkins was prepared to give any of the candidates was to say that Kennedy was "helpful" to the Association.

Although the NAACP's congressional report card on the candidates showed that Kennedy had voted in favor of civil rights motions more often than not, he had "strayed off the reservation" on a part of the 1960 civil rights bill.[28] Worse, Kennedy had voted with Johnson for the jury trial amendment of the 1957 Civil Rights Act, and Wilkins found this difficult to forgive or forget. Relations between the two had soured further in 1958 when Wilkins had been highly critical of Kennedy during a speech he gave in Pittsfield, Massachusetts—almost on the senator's home ground. He attacked Kennedy's support of the jury trial amendment, as well as his "fraternization" with southern congressmen, citing a photograph of Kennedy with his arm around Marvin Griffin, the governor of Georgia and a vehement segregationist, as evidence of the candidate's duplicity on civil rights. Kennedy was furious. He immediately wrote to Wilkins, pointing out his consistent support for civil rights and accusing Wilkins of using a fictitious photograph to embellish his attack. Wilkins, in an unforgiving mood, replied that no senator outside of the South should have voted against Parts III and IV of the Act and warned that, although black voters were pragmatic enough to realize the political imperative in keeping southern support, the fact that Kennedy had been "hailed by the Dixiecrat leaders of South Carolina, Georgia and Mississippi, which, with Alabama, are the 'worst' states on the Negro question," disturbed the black constituency, whose support could not be taken for granted.[29]

Kennedy's efforts to make peace is a measure of the perceived importance of the NAACP and its ability to influence its members, and it was in Kennedy's best interests to restore good relations, not least because his advisers were alarmed at polls showing a sharp decline in black support for Kennedy since Wilkins's attacks had begun.[30] The senator made overtures to local black politicians in Massachusetts, to members of the black press, and to Kivie Kaplan, a member of the NAACP's board and a constituent of Kennedy's in Boston. The peace campaign worked up to a point: Wilkins was persuaded to issue a letter praising Kennedy's record. But he was not placated so easily. He refused Kennedy's invitation to meet and discuss the issue, claiming pressure of work. Even worse, at a press conference prior to the opening of the Association's annual convention in 1960, Wilkins went out of his way to praise Nixon's stance on civil rights, going so far as to suggest that the vice president was responsible for "prodding" the Eisenhower administration into action on the matter of discrimination in government contracts and speculating that Nixon had "done something behind the scenes" to ensure passage of the 1960 Civil Rights Act.[31] Not content with praising Kennedy's rival, Wilkins attacked Kennedy yet again in his address to the convention; but the senator's careful campaign to woo the black press was beginning to have some effect, and Wilkins's comments became less and less damaging.[32]

Johnson found it equally difficult to win Wilkins's favor. As the Senate leader lobbied for the presidential nomination, Wilkins said, "I think fewer colored people would vote for Johnson than for any other candidate."[33] But when Johnson was named the vice presidential candidate, Wilkins had to temper his views. Although Johnson's nomination was disappointing, Wilkins decided to give him the benefit of the doubt. "He doesn't have any personal prejudices," said Wilkins, and "may not do as much as I would wish, but he'll get something done, just as he got through a civil rights bill."[34] The two had collaborated to some degree on the passage of the 1957 Civil Rights Act, and Wilkins thought the Senate leader self-interested and pragmatic, and more altruistic than Wilkins's public comments initially suggested. He knew Johnson as a shrewd politician who could provide Kennedy with the legislative experience the Massachusetts senator lacked. He was therefore worth a gamble.

Appearing as head of the LCCR and the NAACP, Wilkins testified before the platform committees for both parties to make the case for action on civil rights legislation. Supporting the statements of Wilkins and other LCCR delegates was voluminous research conducted by J. Francis Pohlhaus, Washington counsel for the NAACP, who produced a set of working papers for the LCCR and platform committee members. For the paper on discrimination in agriculture, for example, Pohlhaus gathered Department of Agriculture statistics to compare education, longevity of work experience, pay, and other factors in counties with majority black or white populations and counties where the races were equal in number, and demonstrate where systemic discrimination occurred. Similar papers on discrimination in veteran affairs, education, employment, health services, travel, housing, and the military provided compelling evidence, in a form that was hard to challenge, for civil rights reform.[35]

Civil rights advocates were rewarded with propositions that exceeded the most optimistic hopes, and the fact that the platforms were very similar to the LCCR's own proposals pleased Arnold Aronson, who took it as conclusive evidence of the organization's effectiveness.[36] Wilkins also took heart from the "interest, attention and controversy" surrounding the testimonies, which suggested that the issue of civil rights was no longer sidelined as a minority issue but was now seen one of the most important—and pressing—domestic matters facing the nation.[37] Although both platforms were encouraging, the Democratic program went further than the Republican counterpart in calling on all branches of government to take responsibility for ensuring equal rights. The Democrats listed a specific set of goals, including the elimination of discriminatory barriers to voter registration, the establishment of a permanent FEPC and a permanent Civil Rights Commission, an end to discrimination in federal housing programs, and powers for the attorney general that were first outlined in the contentious Part III of the 1957 civil rights bill. The most dramatic proposal was a call for a detailed plan, to be submitted by every school district, for "first step compliance" with the school desegregation ruling by 1963.[38] During his testimony, Wilkins had used a proposal by the school board of Dallas, Texas, to comply with the *Brown* ruling by

1973 as evidence that the gradual approach to integration was not working.[39] The fact that this provision remained in the plank, despite protests from the southern wing of the party, was a sign that change was in the air.

The Republican plank promised to prohibit housing discrimination, establish a commission on equal job opportunities, stipulate that six high school grades should constitute qualification enough to vote, authorize the attorney general to file civil injunction suits in school desegregation cases, and remove discrimination in federal facilities or procedures. However, the plan rejected a target date for school desegregation plans, arguing that recalcitrant school districts would simply view a target as an excuse for further delay until 1963. The most important difference in the Republican plank was a promise to attempt to change the filibuster rule, Rule 22.[40]

Long and bitter experience had shown that promises meant little, however, and Wilkins spelled out why neither party could be trusted on civil rights in a letter to one correspondent: "The Democrats are handicapped by their southern wing. Their conservative wing, largely from the Middle West, handicaps the Republicans. Kansas, Nebraska, Iowa and South Dakota each have two Republican Senators and these eight men vote against civil rights nine times out of ten. Add to these one Republican Senator from Indiana, one from Maryland and two from New Hampshire who also vote against civil rights most of the time and you can see that our problem is not limited to one party."[41] Nixon's political alliances also gave Wilkins cause for concern. He told Texas newspaper proprietor Carter Wesley that he was afraid that Nixon might get to the White House supported by a coalition of northern and southern conservatives, the latter of which included "negro-haters and catholic-haters," in which case any hope of civil rights legislation would be lost.[42]

As Election Day approached, both Nixon and Kennedy continued to make overtures to black voters; but when, shortly before the election, the Kennedys intervened to secure the release of Martin Luther King, who had been sentenced to four months hard labor by a Georgia judge for a minor traffic violation, black candidates were won over "in droves."[43] Kennedy became president with a winning margin of less than one percent of the popular vote. The NAACP was quick to attribute part of his victory to the strength of the black vote. The Association's own analysis, based on spot checks conducted nationally, found that black voters gave four- and five-to-one majorities to Kennedy, evidence that black support "was the essential difference between defeat and victory."[44] Black voters were particularly important in states such as Michigan, New Jersey, and Pennsylvania, which had all voted for Eisenhower in the 1956 election and where the final outcome in 1960 was especially close. In the South the margin of victory was overwhelmingly on Kennedy's side in Louisiana and Georgia. The race was closer in Texas, North Carolina, and South Carolina, but black votes still helped to carry these states for Kennedy.[45]

Wilkins left Kennedy in no doubt that black support came with a price, but the prospects for executive action were not good. Even before he took office Kennedy made it clear that he was not going to risk splitting the party and squander the rest of his political agenda for the sake of civil rights legislation; he would use executive orders rather than legislation to tackle discrimination.[46] Shortly before his inauguration, Kennedy called a meeting with Wilkins and LCCR secretary Arnold Aronson and, after listening to their complaints and doubts about the executive order strategy, suggested they send some proposals to Theodore Sorensen, Kennedy's special counsel and adviser. The report they submitted to the White House contained a number of strong recommendations, including calls for ending federal involvement in any program that practiced discrimination and creating a general Federal Civil Rights code to encompass the entire executive branch and look at the eradication of discrimination in all federal departments and agencies. But their suggestions met with little success, leading Wilkins to complain bitterly to Sorensen that the administration was merely Eisenhower with "a toupee added for a less naked effect."[47]

While still a candidate, Kennedy had asked Senator Joseph Clark (D-PA) and Congressman Emanuel Celler (D-NY) to draft an ambitious civil rights bill that he could introduce soon after taking office. However, once in the White House, Kennedy withdrew his support, in part because the administration claimed there was "very little pressure" for new civil rights legislation.[48] The president's fear of the southern bloc clearly outweighed any political capital to be gained from the good opinion of black voters, but such a swift abandonment of civil rights after the promises of the campaign was hard to swallow. Wilkins immediately wrote to the organizations involved with the LCCR to lobby the president and disprove his claim. However, if the strong case made by the LCCR during the campaign had not given Kennedy the courage to support legislation, lobbying the White House at this stage was surely futile.

Wilkins was deeply disappointed at the swift reversal. During a speech in early February he could not resist chiding the Kennedy administration for not supporting a change to the filibuster rule, which could have passed with executive backing, and for the new composition of various congressional committees, which were heavily populated with nonbelievers in, and in some cases outright opponents to, the civil rights cause. Abandoning civil rights so quickly and so visibly, Wilkins argued, meant that the chance of passing meaningful legislation was now remote, and whatever tentative, piecemeal attempts might be made by the administration would be inadequate at best.[49] Some of Kennedy's advisers also thought that the president had wasted an opportunity and, worse, had been tactically inept in conceding the fight to the southern democrats even before the battle had started, with the president now having to try to repair the damage.[50]

Wilkins's other course of action was equally ineffectual. He wrote a furious but resigned letter to Harris Wofford to protest and reject Kennedy's argument that he did not want to jeopardize the rest of his legislative program by forcing a battle on civil rights: "It is plain why the civil rights legislative line was abandoned but nothing was accomplished by this maneuver. It did not save the minimum wage bill from gutting and it will not save other legislation."[51] More to the point, Wilkins pointed out, abandoning civil rights ambitions at this stage did nothing to save other parts of Kennedy's agenda. He argued that, if Kennedy had stood up to the southern bloc at the start of the congressional term, supported the vote on the filibuster, which would have passed, and tried "whacking" rather than "wooing" the senators blocking any legislation, the way would have been clear if or when Kennedy decided the time was right to support a civil rights bill.[52]

Making the prospect of civil rights legislation even more remote was the fact that the new Congress was likely to be even more of an obstacle than in previous years. The reform of the House Rules Committee added five members, including a congressman from Alabama whose record, Wilkins said, "was just what an Alabaman's record is supposed to be: 100 percent negative" and two "veteran obfuscators on civil rights" from Ohio and Tennessee.[53] The new composition of the committees that would review potential civil rights legislation was as bad, made up of many southern or border-state politicians unsympathetic to civil rights issues. Wilkins used Cold War rhetoric in an attempt to shame—or scare—the White House into action. "Western democratic society is under heavy attack," he asserted. "The United States is supposed to lead the West in preserving freedom in the world, but we find ourselves hobbled by the inequities in our own house, by our political cynicism and by our moral lapses."[54]

For the most part, relations between the NAACP and the White House appeared to be as poor with the Kennedy administration as they had been with the previous incumbent's, but there was some cause for hope with the appointment of Robert Weaver, the NAACP's national board chairman, who was named administrator of the Housing and Home Finance Agency and the first African American to hold a cabinet post. The administration also sometimes used Wilkins himself as a sounding board on civil rights issues. Sorensen, Wofford, and Louis Martin, a black newspaper publisher who had recently been appointed deputy chairman of the Democratic National Committee, were well aware of the tensions and rivalries within and between the various civil rights groups, and they encouraged the president to meet with some civil rights leaders more than others. During the early months of the Kennedy administration, Wilkins met with the president at least twice and also attended a state dinner at the White House. Moreover, when he proposed that the president meet with an NAACP delegation prior to the Association's annual convention, Wofford suggested that such a meeting would support Wilkins's leadership and, at the same time, dispel accusations that the president was avoiding formal meetings with black leaders. Louis Martin argued that a meeting between Wilkins and the president would strengthen Wilkins's leadership "at this critical time," although it is unclear whether Martin was concerned about a challenge from inside or outside the Association.[55]

As the sit-in protests dwindled, the administration's claim that there was little pressure to push for civil rights legislation appeared to have some validity. Even the University of Georgia was integrated when two students, Charlayne Hunter and Hamilton Holmes, became the first black students to enroll at the institution in January 1961. Although their enrollment was not without incident, the two managed to register for and attend classes (they graduated two years later). But any illusion that all was quiet on the civil rights front was shattered on May 4, 1961, when two buses, each containing an interracial group of thirteen protestors, set out from Washington, DC, with the intention of arriving in New Orleans on May 17, the anniversary of the *Brown* ruling. The "Freedom Rides" had been planned and executed by CORE. It had conducted a similar trip, a "Journey of Reconciliation," in 1947, following the Supreme Court's decision in *Morgan v. Virginia*; but a new court decision in 1960, *Boynton v. Virginia,* which extended the prohibition of segregation in interstate travel to include terminal facilities, inspired CORE to resurrect the model to test the *Boynton* ruling.[56]

The earlier protestors had traveled as far as North Carolina; but the Freedom Riders of 1961, led by James Farmer, who had left the NAACP and was now CORE's national director, were more ambitious. They intended to drive straight into the lion's den: the Deep South states of Georgia, Mississippi, Alabama, and Louisiana. Wilkins was initially doubtful about the Freedom Rides, calling them a "joy ride."[57] Farmer, however, knew that he would almost certainly need the NAACP's legal and financial support if the CORE protestors were jailed; and, after the success of the sit-ins, Wilkins was well aware that nonviolent protests had captured the attention of the nation and demanded the Association's approval. He was content to support the sit-in protestors publicly almost from the beginning, in large part because of the protesters' connection with the Association. But the Freedom Rides had been organized and executed, without NAACP involvement, by another organization that, although significantly smaller than the NAACP, had the potential to attract publicity and funds away from the Association. Most disturbing to Wilkins was the Freedom Riders' seemingly deliberate provocation of white violence, which he feared would antagonize a White House that was already showing scant support for civil rights issues.

CORE approached NAACP branches and other organizations along the route to ask for help when protestors arrived in their towns and cities; the requests met with varying degrees of enthusiasm. The NAACP's branch leader in Greensboro, North Carolina, was a keen advocate of the Freedom Rides and welcomed the group with open arms, as did leaders in South Carolina, Tennessee, and Georgia. In Richmond, Virginia, however, branch officers were less hospitable, calling the rides a publicity stunt that was overshadowing desegregation work already under way through the NAACP, and they refused to cooperate.[58] Mississippi, as ever, was a special case. Like his Virginian counterparts, Medgar Evers was also concerned that the protests would conflict with the desegregation protests that the NAACP was already working on, including activities the Association was planning around the anniversary of *Brown*. However, he was always willing to cooperate with other groups, even if he had to be careful to protect the hard-won NAACP network in the state. He tried to dissuade the group from entering Jackson because local branches had just launched "Operation Mississippi," a coordinated protest program, which aimed to desegregate various public facilities and increase voter registration. Evers argued that any additional demonstrations by another group would damage local efforts and suggested—politely—that the Freedom Rides not stop in the state and continue their journey to Alabama, where the Association could not operate. Nevertheless, Evers and his colleague Aaron Henry, the state president of the NAACP, organized a Freedom Rider committee to support the riders as they passed through the state.[59]

As anticipated, violence erupted as the buses entered Alabama. At Anniston, about sixty miles north of Birmingham, one of the buses was set on fire, forcing the riders to disembark into a waiting crowd of angry Klansmen, who were only prevented from attacking the riders by local police. The second bus got as far as Birmingham, but was met by an armed mob that had a full fifteen minutes to attack the Freedom Riders before police intervened. In both cities, the brutality of the attacks on the protestors shocked the nation. Equally shocking to many outside the South was the tacit approval given to the mob by law enforcement officials in the city. When the local police chief, Eugene "Bull" Connor, was asked why no policemen had been on hand when the riders arrived in the city, he said that most of them had been visiting their mothers, as it was Mother's Day.[60] Wilkins repeatedly assured the Freedom Riders of the NAACP's financial and moral support, but he was also quick to emphasize that "solid, basic legal moves are necessary if there is to be a foundation for other action." He continued, "Affirmative action by judicial, legislative and executive means is indispensable. This is still a nation of law. If we colored people hold the white people of the South to law and the Constitution, we cannot sneer among ourselves at the law and the legal processes."[61]

The Freedom Riders displayed extraordinary courage and, while Wilkins may have disliked the use of the Freedom Rides as a tactic, he admired Farmer's "desperately brave and reckless strategy" to provoke the Kennedy administration.[62] Farmer was one of the few people that Wilkins appears to have respected and liked; when the CORE leader was sent to the notorious Parchman state penitentiary in Mississippi during the summer of 1961, Wilkins paid a surprise visit, presenting Farmer with a gift of two books, including *To Kill a Mockingbird,* and a promise of help from the NAACP. According to Farmer, his visit was not simply of practical help; it boosted the morale of the imprisoned group. Wilkins may have hoped that Farmer might have been persuaded to accept bail and leave the prison, but Farmer and his group were not to be persuaded. During the 1960 protests, CORE activists had adopted the tactic of refusing bail when arrested on the grounds that accepting bail would involve collusion or cooperation with a racist system. The group revived the tactic when Freedom Riders were arrested in Jackson. Following Wilkins's visit, Farmer said, conditions in the jail improved encouraging him to "stay awhile" longer.[63]

Conscious of criticism that the Association had been slow to respond to the wave of direct-action protests, Wilkins issued a statement on the NAACP's position on the Freedom Rides shortly after they began. He said that people had a right—if not a duty—to test enforcement of the Constitution as well as the right to challenge unconstitutional state laws or customs, while the government was obliged to protect citizens who attempted to enjoy their constitutional rights. He proposed that all NAACP student members test the principle on their journeys home from college that summer.[64] The South Carolina State Youth Conference took up the instruction with enthusiasm and instructed all its youth and college units to board buses at various points throughout the state, as did student leaders in Atlanta, who planned to ride as far as Jackson.[65]

But he was more skeptical about the efficacy of staying in jail rather than paying bail. Wilkins told NAACP members in Jackson, "We do not believe that you can test a law and get it thrown out by staying in jail. After one spends thirty or sixty or ninety days in jail, the law is still on the statute books and still constitutes support for segregation."[66] The Associated Press and other media organizations interpreted Wilkins's comments as a rebuke of direct-action protests, prompting a hasty clarification of the NAACP's position in the press. Nevertheless, the debate about which tactic or group was most effective continued in the editorial pages of black newspapers. William Walker of the *Pittsburgh Courier* warned the Association that the dramatic revival of CORE signaled a "realignment of groups and supporters" and that, "Unless the NAACP watches out, it is liable to be relegated to the second spot of importance." The *Cleveland Call and Post,* which was generally more sympathetic toward both Wilkins and the NAACP, took a more supportive view, arguing that for all the reckless, courageous drama of the CORE protests, the NAACP was still expected to do the "legal mopping up."[67]

Wilkins's comments were in part an attempt to navigate the tricky legal position presented by the demonstrations. Sit-ins and other protests were not always directed at public accommodations and so did, in some cases, violate trespass laws. The NAACP held to the principle that the law should be both observed and complied with even in the midst of protest. However, Wilkins's comments in Jackson implied that the Freedom Riders were challenging unconstitutional laws, when in fact the challenge was to the federal government to assess the extent of executive support for laws that had already established constitutional rights. The Freedom Riders thus tested the principles of the NAACP's philosophy as much as the federal government's willingness to uphold constitutional rights.

For President Kennedy the protests, and more particularly the violence of the white reaction that they provoked, were an international embarrassment.[68] Wilkins had warned Theodore Sorensen in February that blacks were impatient with the administration's inaction on civil rights, but little was done until the Freedom Rides forced Kennedy to pay attention.[69] Attorney General Robert Kennedy demanded that the Freedom Riders call off the protests. But as one of the objectives of the rides was to push the administration into action, the group refused to comply. Wilkins met with Robert Kennedy, but the attorney general was equally determined not to commit federal troops to protect the protestors.[70] Even after the violence in Anniston and Birmingham, he hesitated to provide federal protection.

The administration finally took action when John Seigenthaler, a Justice Department official and personal friend of Robert Kennedy, was brutally beaten by a white mob. Finally, the president sent in US marshals—although not federal troops—to protect the riders. Wilkins hoped that at last the protests had begun to "bend the Administration or at least . . . convince the Administration that perhaps the policy agreed upon was not as adequate as the president had thought at the outset."[71] By summer's end 360 riders had been jailed, but the tactic of choosing to refuse bail almost backfired. The state of Mississippi imposed high bail fees, and CORE was soon buckling under the weight of over $300,000 of legal costs. The organization was only saved by Thurgood Marshall's generous donation of $300,000 of Inc. Fund cash.

The Freedom Rides propelled CORE, and James Farmer, onto the national stage, turning the small organization into yet another competitor to the NAACP.[72] Ultimately, however, CORE posed less of a long-term threat to the NAACP than did SCLC, so Wilkins was more forgiving of Farmer and his organization. Wilkins's respect for Farmer was not shared by some of his colleagues, however, who distrusted CORE. Even before the Freedom Rides revived the organization Gloster Current dismissed its tactics and questioned its motives. He told Wilkins of increasing friction in one Kentucky town where the NAACP and CORE appeared to be competing for attentions of the black community. Current suggested that the NAACP consider very carefully whether it could or should cooperate with CORE.[73] Although Current was not alone in his suspicion of the new group, he was considered likely to be the anonymous source that described CORE as "a bunch of loonybirds and crackpots" in a *Time* magazine article in early 1962.[74]

The problem of competition grew worse once the Freedom Rides brought an influx of activists into the South. In Richmond, for example, the president of the local branch of the NAACP complained to Current that CORE and the NAACP often had the same members, who competed to raise funds for the organizations separately. She also maintained that some of CORE's tactics were damaging projects that the NAACP was trying to implement.[75] Even worse, there was some confusion in the mind of the public about CORE's relationship to the NAACP. The national office received numerous requests for CORE literature, help in setting up a CORE chapter, and offers for donations to CORE. To some extent, recognition was a problem for all of the groups. Protests such as the sit-ins were rarely conducted under obvious signs that they were a CORE or an SCLC or an NAACP demonstration. This made it difficult for the general public or the media to distinguish one group from another, with the result that the competition for public recognition, and therefore funds, became increasingly important.

Wilkins took every opportunity to criticize other organizations whenever he could do so while at the same time avoiding any hint of a rift between the groups. In an interview with a French news agency in 1962, for example, Wilkins swiftly reduced SCLC to a loose organization composed mainly of church members in the South, and CORE to a "small, trained striking force dealing with one problem in one particular manner at one time in one locality." Black Muslims were described as a rather amorphous organization whose members were dedicated to a separatist philosophy that offered no value to the broader civil rights battle, although Wilkins acknowledged that they were a disciplined group. SNCC did not merit a mention. After he had put the other groups in their place, Wilkins suggested that the NAACP incorporated "all techniques, not just one technique of a march or a demonstration or a picket—we use all those also—but we use legislation, we use political action, we use the courts, we use the boycotts, we use all the things that one uses to protest and make progress in this field."[76]

By the early summer of 1961 the Freedom Rides had begun to dissipate, although some protests did continue into the fall. By then the Kennedy administration had finally stepped in and asked the Interstate Commerce Commission (ICC) to ban segregation in interstate transport. The ICC concurred, and the order went into effect on November 1, thus signaling a major victory for CORE. But despite his intervention with the ICC, Kennedy remained reluctant to take any strong executive action on any other civil rights issues. His hesitation presented the administration with a difficult political dilemma. It was clear that the tide of public opinion, and of events, was moving swiftly toward desegregation. The problem for Kennedy was how to support those forces and defuse the growing anger among blacks while at the same time not alienating southern Democrats, whom he deemed essential to achieve his legislative goals.

Voting rights helped solve a large part of that dilemma, because it was an issue that almost everyone could support. The Kennedy administration persuaded SNCC, CORE, and the other civil rights groups to participate in voting registration programs rather than direct action, temporarily rescuing the administration from an increasingly embarrassing situation. Gradually, the Voter Education Project (VEP) took shape and was finally launched in the spring of 1962 with unofficial but significant support from the White House. The program brought together each of the civil rights groups, including the Urban League, and was coordinated by the Southern Regional Council (SRC), a biracial organization. Funding was provided by several liberal nonprofit foundations, among them the Taconic Foundation, which donated the lion's share of the more than $870,000 budget.[77] The funds were to be distributed among five national organizations and local projects in the South.[78] Robert Kennedy negotiated with the Internal Revenue Service to secure tax-exempt status for the VEP; but even when funding issues had been successfully resolved, persuading the organizations to cooperate in such a joint venture required persistent diplomacy.

The NAACP viewed the VEP with caution. While the extra funds would be welcome it was, as usual, reluctant to enter into a project that was controlled by another organization. The Association had expanded its existing voter registration program in 1957, and by 1962 had two full-time staff members, John Brooks and W. C. Patton, who worked alongside field secretaries and volunteers in communities in Tennessee, Florida, South Carolina, Georgia, Louisiana, Arkansas, and Texas as well as in northern cities such as Baltimore.[79] Some of the NAACP's leaders were doubtful about the VEP's potential for success; and it was hardly surprising that some of the most voluble criticism came from John Brooks, who was particularly disdainful of other groups, which, he claimed, were planning to use the additional funding to build their own organizations at the expense of the NAACP. Brooks even suggested that Wiley Branton, a black attorney from Arkansas who had been designated to run the program, was mainly interested in using the program to further his own career.[80] John Morsell echoed some of Brooks's concerns: "Not the least of the irritations," he wrote in a memo to Wilkins, "is that the only voter campaign in existence (ours) is in effect equated with the unrealized aspirations of five other groups, any one of which can exploit the vagaries of the press to its advantage and our detriment."[81] Clarence Mitchell was even more dismissive, arguing that the involvement of other groups was unnecessary and that the NAACP should simply have been offered the money directly.[82]

There is some ambiguity about Wilkins's own view of the VEP. Two meetings were scheduled to discuss proposals, but he did not attend the second gathering, citing a prior commitment, and sent Henry Lee Moon in his place. Stephen Currier, head of the Taconic Foundation, suspected that this indicated a lack of interest and said as much to Wilkins, who quickly sent an apology assuring Currier of his support for the project. Nevertheless, he also took the opportunity to spell out some of the NAACP's expectations of the VEP. He made three assumptions: that the program would not be used to support direct-action protests or recruitment drives for other organizations; that the SRC would not exercise "arbitrary" authority over the programs conducted by participants; and that the program would demand financial statements and accountability.[83] Thus, Wilkins agreed to the NAACP's participation, but only under strict terms expressly designed to protect his organization. He was particularly concerned that the proposed allocation of geographical areas should not require the NAACP to discontinue voter registration programs that were already taking place under the supervision of local NAACP branches.[84]

Wilkins's fears on this issue were not without foundation. Several branch officers had already complained that SNCC, CORE, or the SCLC were duplicating or even ignoring NAACP efforts in their communities, and the situation worsened as the newer groups intensified their voter registration efforts. Wilkins proposed that the SRC should disburse funds to established voter registration programs, such as the NAACP's, rather than wait for the results of new methods to find the most effective means of encouraging registration. "Diversionary efforts" that sidetracked registration campaigns should be discouraged, he argued. Small, local groups, such as voter leagues and churches, should not be granted funds directly, but only through national or regional agencies, which, in his opinion, would be better placed than the SRC to evaluate such groups.[85] That meant, of course, that the NAACP, with its "many years of experience," would be best placed to decide which local groups were deserving of VEP funds. Such a measure would also keep much of the community activity under the control of the NAACP. SNCC and CORE chose as their territory the most isolated rural areas of Mississippi. This infuriated Wilkins; he believed it was impossible to achieve any significant results in those communities and that any voter registration efforts were better concentrated in the metropolitan areas of the South.[86] In general, Branton and the SRC agreed to Wilkins's terms, and the program progressed reasonably smoothly, even though in the Association's view the project merely "augmented" existing NAACP voter registration efforts.[87] But the Association had no intention of subordinating its efforts to the broader VEP program. John Morsell told branch leaders that the Association would continue its normal program of activities, which would be supplemented by VEP funds.[88]

The bickering and infighting that began to emerge during the voter registration discussions became painfully obvious during the Albany, Georgia, campaign, launched in November 1961 when two SNCC workers, Charles Sherrod and Cordell Reagon, brought together a loose coalition of six local organizations, including members of the local NAACP youth branch. The Albany Movement, as the group became known, issued various demands to city leaders regarding such things as equal employment opportunities and an end to police brutality, but its principal goal was to desegregate municipal facilities. Dr. William Anderson, a local osteopath who had had little previous involvement with civil rights groups, was named president, and in that capacity he approached the local NAACP branch to secure its support. The local Association leaders, however, were reluctant to offer any help. The NAACP's state and regional officials, Vernon Jordan and Ruby Hurley, in an attempt to keep any activity in the city under the Association's control, argued that there was already a local NAACP branch and that another civil rights group was unnecessary. Unfortunately, the branch they were referring to was almost inactive, and Jordan was unable to stimulate any interest in reviving protest activity from its leaders, leaving the way clear for the Albany Movement.[89]

When Martin Luther King arrived in the city in December, the campaign took on a life of its own. Although negotiations were already under way before he arrived, King's presence emboldened Albany Movement leaders to press for a speedy concession from city officials. This only served to infuriate the officials, who rejected the demands. Tension escalated when over two hundred fifty demonstrators, including King, were arrested at a prayer march. Although King vowed to stay in prison through Christmas, Anderson was on the verge of a nervous collapse, and terms were agreed that allowed King and the others to be released from jail. With the demonstrations now halted, however, local officials swiftly disregarded the tenuous agreement, and the ebullience of the Movement gave way to disappointment. King returned to Albany in July 1962 to be sentenced. As expected, the SCLC's arrival revived enthusiasm for the protests. But the local police chief, Laurie Pritchett, had studied nonviolent tactics and made preparations for any jailed demonstrators to be sent to prisons across the state, and the protests gradually died away.

No group emerged from Albany cloaked in glory. It was the SCLC's first public failure, and SNCC activists had no hesitation in making fun of King's elevated position, while the NAACP concerned itself with protecting its own position and reputation. Reports to the Association's head office by Vernon Jordan resonate with suspicion about the motives of the other groups involved. According to Jordan, there was hostility between movement leaders and the SCLC, but the NAACP was also suspicious of SNCC, with local leaders advising a youth worker early on in the protests to avoid "getting involved with anything initiated by SNCC."[90] Nevertheless, while it may not have succeeded in winning concessions from the city government, the Albany Movement has been described as "crucial" to the development of the civil rights movement because it demonstrated that blacks could be mobilized on a large scale and because its mistakes provided valuable lessons for the future.[91]

The wave of direct-action protests caused an enormous increase in work for the NAACP's legal team and the Inc. Fund. Although the Fund had separated completely from its parent organization in 1956, the two were still linked in the minds of the public; but they had, in effect, become like competitive siblings. The explosion of protest activity had resulted in a significant increase in public donations to help support the protesters, but donors assumed the NAACP and the Inc. Fund were one and the same, and the Association soon began to see a deficit in its own books as donations that very probably were meant for the NAACP ended up instead with the LDF. According to an internal report, the NAACP was spending between $75,000 and $100,000 a year, or just under 10 percent of its income for 1961, out of its general budget to support legal activities, but without any increase in donations to support this work. The Inc. Fund, however, saw its income rise from $361,000 in 1959 to over $586,000 in 1961 without experiencing additional demands on its funds from other activities.[92]

Both organizations recognized the problems inherent in this confusing situation, but the organizations appeared to be divided, in process if not in purpose. A committee was set up to determine what form the Association's legal program should take and how it could and should work with the Inc. Fund, given that each organization shared the same goal—an end to racial discrimination. In its final report, the committee proposed that the NAACP's legal team direct its work toward civil rights legislation, legal attacks on the Association, and internal problems that arose between branches. The Inc. Fund, by contrast, should focus on a desegregation program. This division of labor was relatively straightforward, and Wilkins proceeded to issue a set of guidelines for branches on how to proceed with legal cases. Unfortunately, his memorandum was a masterpiece of bureaucratic opacity. Branch leaders were expected to extrapolate an effective legal strategy from instructions such as this: "When persons or groups on the local or state levels ask legal assistance from the local NAACP Branch or State Conference in a civil rights case differing from, or having implications beyond, the routine local cases customarily handled alone by the Branch or State Conference, the Branch or State Conference shall forward such a request in writing to the Secretary at the National Office."[93]

With no sign of a lull in activity, Wilkins escaped to Europe in the fall of 1962. He visited the continent several times during the 1960s, either for vacation or as a representative of the American government. On this particular trip, he was treated like an ambassador for civil rights. Wherever he appeared, in newspapers or on television, he explained a little of the history of the struggle for equality, how the NAACP was structured, and, most important for him, how its program differed from that of other groups. One of his interviews, with a French radio station, was broadcast several times because of the interest in the subject, much to the State Department's delight. The press attaché from the American Embassy in Paris wrote to thank Wilkins for his "reasoned optimism" in explaining the racial problem in the United States.[94] However, even as the attaché was congratulating Wilkins, events in Mississippi were unfolding that would prove that any optimism was unfounded.

The state's governor, Ross Barnett, had loudly and very publicly refused to comply with the Supreme Court's rulings on desegregating schools and colleges. His segregationist rhetoric inflamed public debate and raised the political temperature in a state that was already overheated about the "progress" of civil rights. The situation exploded when James Meredith, a twenty-nine-year-old Air Force veteran, attempted to register for classes at the University of Mississippi in the fall of 1962. When Meredith originally applied to the university his application was rejected with a series of blatant excuses. Meredith then reluctantly approached Medgar Evers and Inc. Fund lawyers for help in gaining admittance. When the federal courts finally supported his application, he attempted to register for classes. With this seemingly simple act the curtain was raised on what Inc. Fund lawyer Constance Baker Motley called "the last battle of the Civil War."[95]

The night before Meredith's enrollment Barnett spoke to the fired-up crowd at an Ole Miss football match. His emotional remarks about loving his state and its customs sent the crowd into a frenzy. When state troopers, who had been ordered to stay on site to keep control, were withdrawn on orders from a representative of the governor, contrary to promises made to President Kennedy, a riot ensued in which two people were killed and many injured. The following morning, protected by US marshals, Meredith picked his way through the debris to the admissions office and completed his registration. By the end of the week, more than 23,000 federal troops were stationed on the campus to restore order.[96] The riot coincided with the latest space launch, and the proximity of the two events prompted Wilkins to despair of the situation in Mississippi: "In the same week in which the United States launched its third astronaut into space, it had to use thousands of soldiers and hundreds of federal marshals to enable one Negro, James Meredith, to enter the University of Mississippi, in order to complete his education. A few short years ago, not many would have believed it was easier to send up a manned spacecraft than to guarantee an American citizen his right to attend his own state's university. But the facts are the facts."[97]

Meredith's admission was of enormous symbolic importance to black communities throughout Mississippi, but the episode badly damaged the Kennedy administration's credibility on civil rights, and it would take another show of almost fatal violence by southern whites to convince the president that he had to act decisively.[98] The civil rights issue put Kennedy in a quandary; blacks were disappointed and frustrated at the lack of executive action, while southern whites used what limited action there had been as evidence of left-wing liberalism.[99] But results in the congressional and gubernatorial elections in November 1962 showed that the battle lines were shifting. Voters in Georgia and South Carolina, on the one hand, elected racial moderates to govern their statehouses. Mississippi and Alabama, on the other, chose ardent segregationists. The Republican Party, which had historically considered the South as a lost cause, became increasingly conservative and began to make significant southern gains.

Kennedy had not abandoned civil rights entirely, however. In February 1963 he presented a special message to Congress in which he laid out his administration's accomplishments and a list of what remained to be done. Drawn up by Lee White, an assistant special counsel, in conjunction with the Justice Department, the list focused almost entirely on voting rights and was a long way from the Democrats' ambitious civil rights plank of 1960. Wilkins was not impressed and was quick to point out its flaws: "in many respects, President Kennedy's civil rights message to Congress is an admirable document. . . . However it offers no new proposal for dealing with the acute problem of discrimination in housing. Nor does it call for an effective deadline for school systems to achieve desegregation. Also lacking is a recommendation for a Federal FEP law with strong enforcement powers. These are the weakest aspects of Mr. Kennedy's message."[100] The continued lack of any political will to address these issues left Kennedy's commitment to civil rights open to question, regardless of any civil rights message he might send to Congress.[101]

Kennedy's tepid proposals became an unequivocal commitment

when the intractable force of southern racism confronted nonviolence in Birmingham, Alabama. Even measured against the appalling standards of other Dixie cities, Birmingham was in a class of its own. Long considered the most segregated city in the United States, the city had a particularly belligerent police chief, Eugene "Bull" Connor. Putting lessons learned in Albany, Georgia, into practice, King and his SCLC colleagues decided to wage war on Birmingham's segregated facilities. They relied on Connor's notorious hostility to desegregation to provoke him into an action that would, they hoped, ultimately benefit the movement.[102] Thousands of protestors joined King in Birmingham in April 1963 to prod the city's government into implementing a policy of desegregation. The city's intransigent police department responded with a ferocity that was entirely unexpected.[103] SCLC's goal of filling the city's jails was soon achieved, and the organization resorted to using children as protestors. Over a thousand schoolchildren took to the streets, where they were attacked by snarling police dogs and police wielding—and using—cattle prods and water cannons, at Connor's instruction. The sight of such tactics being used against such young protestors was almost too much for the country to stomach and illustrated more vividly than any speech, article, or congressional testimony the violent extent of southern racism.[104] Within a month, a settlement had been brokered between the protestors and Birmingham's political and business leaders to desegregate facilities and introduce equal hiring practices.

Wilkins was reluctant to concede the impact of Birmingham, even though it played a crucial part in persuading Kennedy to push forward legislation that a year later became the landmark Civil Rights Act.[105] Wilkins conceded that public outrage was a contributory factor in the introduction of the civil rights bill, but argued that the protests failed to influence any congressman from the areas in which the protests took place.[106] Instead, he attributed the combination of several episodes that took place over a series of months around the Birmingham protests as having equal weight. One of the protests that Wilkins credited as being an important factor in promoting executive action on civil rights was under way in Mississippi. While the Birmingham campaign garnered media attention both domestically and internationally, the NAACP's branch in Jackson, Mississippi, was waging its own protest. The Jackson movement began in late 1962 with a boycott of stores in the downtown area of the city. Despite calls for support, the NAACP's national office paid little attention until the success of the Birmingham campaign indicated that King might make Mississippi his next target.[107] The threat of the SCLC bandwagon rolling into Jackson suddenly galvanized the NAACP's national office into action. Gloster Current revealed a degree of panic in a memorandum to branches that urged them to step up direct-action protests. He identified Jackson as the likely target for the "next scene of attack by King forces" but argued that "whatever target is selected next, it will make it that much harder for the NAACP to carry on its work effectively."[108]

When protesters were brutally beaten and kicked while police stood by, many of Jackson's outraged black community joined the call for desegregation in the city. Faced with a potential disturbance on the scale of Birmingham, the mayor agreed to most of the blacks' demands, but quickly reneged on the agreement as soon as the trouble appeared to have passed. His duplicitous tactics brought hundreds of young blacks onto the streets, and around 450 young demonstrators were arrested during a demonstration, suddenly energizing both the movement and the NAACP's leadership.[109] Wilkins called on other branches to protest in support and, more importantly, raise money to fund bail and legal costs.[110] He then flew down to Jackson to speak at a mass meeting and join the protestors on the city's sidewalks.

Since his only arrest in the 1930s, Wilkins had avoided direct confrontation with the authorities. But he was now under pressure from NAACP members to roll up his sleeves and get involved in the fight on the street. A telegram from Eugene Reed to Wilkins at the end of May was just one of many urging him to go to Jackson and lead from the front line. If he was arrested, Reed suggested, so much the better, as it would force those who had been standing on the sidelines to take action. The likelihood that Wilkins would be arrested should he join the protests was a calculated risk, but one that promised to yield considerable favorable publicity. Nevertheless, he remained reluctant to put himself in that position, and did so only when Medgar Evers told the national office that King was threatening to come to Jackson if the NAACP did not take control of the protests.[111]

Once there, Wilkins gave a rousing speech to fire up the demonstrators, then joined Evers and the other protestors the following morning to picket a variety store in downtown Jackson. As anticipated, he was quickly arrested, and, along with Evers and Helen Wilcher, another protestor, indicted on a felony charge of restraint of trade. Wilkins had no intention of staying in jail and was quickly released on a $1,000 bond, but his arrest had a galvanizing effect on the NAACP's members and even on King himself who, on hearing of Wilkins's arrest, told his aides "We've baptized brother Wilkins."[112] L. H. Holman of the Chicago branch urged Wilkins to stay in Jackson now that the NAACP had "regained the initiative," while Percy Sutton, an influential politician in New York, wrote to say, "I couldn't have been more proud of you than I was when the news of your arrest in Jackson, Mississippi, flashed across the television screen on Saturday night. Even on 125th Street, here in Harlem, the Black Nationalists were saying on Sunday 'Sutton, your boy Wilkins, was in the thick of it—Boy that's the stuff.'"[113]

With momentum on their side, Wilkins, Current, and other NAACP leaders then took the unexpected and inexplicable decision to call a halt to the demonstrations and add more conservative blacks to the strategy committee, thereby curbing the energy of the movement and leading to a gulf between the local branch and its younger members.[114] John Dittmer offers several credible reasons for the decision: the debilitating cost of getting the demonstrators out of jail, political infighting between the national office and the Jackson movement's leaders, and the NAACP's general discomfort with direct action tactics.[115] But another interpretation of the decision might also be that Wilkins, ever conscious of the wider political ramifications of mass action at this time, was keen not to antagonize the Kennedys and risk the tenuous relationship he had built up with the administration by having his organization involved in such demonstrations.

Then, in early June, Alabama governor George Wallace blocked the entrance to the University of Alabama to prevent the enrollment of two black students. Kennedy used Wallace's actions as a public demonstration of the administration's willingness to tackle the race issue. He federalized the National Guard and forced Wallace to allow the students to enter, with none of the violence witnessed at Oxford. Kennedy chose this moment to finally address the nation on civil rights. Stating the case simply and unequivocally, Kennedy told the nation that it faced a moral crisis that required action on a national, state, local, and individual level. "We cannot say to ten percent of the population that you can't have that right; that your children cannot have the chance to develop whatever talents they have; that the only way that they are going to get their rights is to go into the streets and demonstrate. I think we owe them and we owe ourselves a better country than that." Finally, Kennedy gave Wilkins tangible hope that circumstances were changing when he announced that he planned to send legislation to Congress that would give black Americans the right to be served in public facilities.[116] Wilkins was delighted with Kennedy's forceful remarks and sent a congratulatory telegram immediately. "Your speech last night to the nation on the civil rights crisis was a clear, resolute exposition of basic Americanism and a call to all our citizens to rally in support of the high traditions of our nation's dedication to human rights. Thank you."[117]

The celebration was short-lived. Just hours after Kennedy delivered his speech, Medgar Evers was murdered as he arrived home from a meeting of the Jackson movement. Evers's death was a devastating blow to the Association and to Wilkins personally. Wilkins wrote later, "My eyes filled with tears. I had not felt such a rush of feeling since Earl's death. If there was moment in my life when I hated whites, that was it."[118] Evers had been a tireless and courageous field-worker, balancing the almost impossible demands of the NAACP's national office to retain control of civil rights activities in the state with the need to cooperate with other groups working in the state.[119] But all the goodwill and respect that Evers had earned was not enough to overcome the resentment that Wilkins felt toward other groups, especially the SCLC, in the days after Evers's death. Immediately following the murder, King announced the creation of a bail fund in Evers's name under the auspices of the Gandhi Society, the SCLC's legal arm. Wilkins was furious, and insisted that the fund be administered by the NAACP rather than the SCLC.[120] Wilkins's nephew Roger later recalled that his uncle was still smarting at Evers's funeral. "Can you imagine it?" he fumed. "Medgar was an NAACP man all the way, and King comes in and tries to take the money."[121]

Hostilities did not cease even at Evers's funeral. More than four thousand mourners, including Wilkins, Martin Luther King, and Ralph Bunche, braved temperatures of more than 100 degrees and packed the Masonic Temple in downtown Jackson to pay their respects. The swelter- ing temperature exacerbated the atmosphere in Jackson, which had been almost unbearably tense in the days between Evers's murder and his fu- neral; police and demonstrators had clashed several times. As the funeral cortege made its way toward the funeral home, followed by a crowd, which was by now about 5,000 strong, chaos erupted when a group be- gan chanting "We want the killer" and throwing bottles, provoking a stampede. Police responded by beating protestors with clubs and tried to disperse the crowd with dogs, inflaming the situation. Just when it looked as if events were about to take a turn for the worse, John Doar, an at- torney with the Justice Department, successfully defused the situation by stepping out from the barricades and, with his arms in the air, appealing directly to the protestors to calm down.[122]

In this overheated atmosphere, Wilkins's anger and grief led him to make a series of unusually combative public remarks about other groups during a speech to an NAACP branch in Alexandria, Virginia, a few days later. Although sometimes caustic in his correspondence and in person, he rarely let his temper show in public; but the speech in Alexandria proved to be one of those rare occasions. He turned the full extent of his rage onto other civil rights groups who "furnish the noise and get the public- ity while the NAACP furnishes the manpower and pays the bill."[123] He dismissed their dramatic tactics, briskly saying, "All the rest start a little and then rush off somewhere else. They are here today, gone tomorrow. There is only one organization that can handle a long sustained fight— the NAACP," and then warned, "Don't go giving them your money, when it should be given to us. Don't get so excited. To give them your money is like a Baptist giving money to the Presbyterian Church."[124]

Wilkins was unapologetic about the attack despite criticism from NAACP members. In response to some correspondents who disliked such public approbation, he said, "it is the NAACP which has maintained unity in spite of pettiness, provocation and open contempt and hostil- ity on the part of followers of, and workers in, CORE and SLCC."[125] Wilkins stopped short of overt criticism of leaders of the other groups and claimed to want no breach among the civil rights organizations, but in another scathing display of anger he wrote to an NAACP member, "We were at work when Negroes who now shovel out bushel baskets of money to a hypnotic handclap rhythm and white people who now write checks to salve their conscience could not find a lone dollar bill for the NAACP, battling for a place for the Negro when there was, literally, no place for him in the citizenship picture."[126] He remained unapologetic a year later when, during an interview with author Robert Penn Warren, Wilkins's anger was still evident: "it's a little tough to find yourself vilified and sneered at as a kind of a knitting old lady, over in a corner, while the revolution is being carried on by us strong men, and yet called upon to bear the financial burden."[127]

When Kennedy's civil rights bill was sent to Congress even Wilkins had to admit that the proposed legislation was the most comprehensive civil rights legislation ever proposed by an American president. Nevertheless, he argued, it still did not go far enough, not least because the legislation failed to include a provision to create a statutory Fair Employment Practices Committee. Even more galling was the "revised and truncated Part III of the 1957 civil rights bill," which in its new iteration was limited to the denial of civil rights in school cases rather than broader denials of rights.[128] Even in school cases, Wilkins complained that "it provides only for continued piecemeal action, school district by school district."[129]

Shortly after submitting the bill to Congress, Kennedy met with a group of civil rights leaders, including Wilkins, King, A. Philip Randolph, and Whitney Young, the new leader of the Urban League. He proposed that these leaders take on the task of persuading congressmen who were not yet committed to one position or another to pass the bill. But the group could not agree on tactics. King and some of the other leaders advocated using demonstrations to pressure Congress into passing the bill, while Wilkins and Young were reluctant to use direct-action tactics for fear of antagonizing congressmen and therefore jeopardizing the legislation. Instead, Wilkins worked with the LCCR in crafting a strategy that would identify those congressional votes that could be most important and then mobilize LCCR members to lobby the relevant congressmen. Wilkins was also on guard for any weakening of the bill by the time it reached the House. "If the bill at that time is as strong as we hope it will be, the job will be one of defeating weakening amendments. If the bill is weaker than the present Administration bill, the job will be one of strengthening it."[130]

To support the public accommodations portion of the bill, Wilkins appeared in front of the Senate Commerce Committee where he delivered one of the most impassioned addresses of his career. He told the committee, "While the Congress will be debating in the next week, Negro Americans throughout our country will be bruised in nearly every waking hour by differential treatment in, or exclusion from, public accommodations of every description. From the time they leave home in the morning, en route to school or to work, to shopping or visiting, until they return home at night, humiliation stalks them."[131]

The hearing took place at the height of the summer, and Wilkins described the journey a black family might make from Norfolk, Virginia, to the Gulf Coast of Mississippi. He described the decisions such a family would have to make during the journey: "How far do you drive each day? Where, and under what conditions can you and your family eat? Where can they use a rest room? Can you stop driving after a reasonable day behind the wheel or must you drive until you reach a city where relatives or friends will accommodate you and yours for the night? Will your children be denied a soft drink or an ice cream cone because they are not white?"[132]

Wilkins's role in public hearings was often to explain the historical context of the black experience and the importance of the civil rights movement in addressing injustice. In this instance, he emphasized the significance of the sit-in protests, citing the example of one of the first sit-in protestors, who was "a veteran in his country's non-segregated Air Force [who] after service overseas to spread and preserve democracy could be refused a cup of coffee and a piece of pie in his home state." Such treatment, he added, was "something he just could not take any longer." Wilkins exposed the absurd distinctions that Congress made in its treatment of its black citizens. "The Congress has legislated for the health and welfare of its livestock. Why does it balk at legislating for the welfare of its twenty million loyal Negro citizens? Are cows, hogs and sheep more valuable than human beings?"[133] He continued, "The players in this drama of frustration and indignity are not commas or semicolons in a legislative thesis; they are people, human beings, citizens of the United States of America."[134]

Wilkins's testimony was not entirely without humor. When Senator Strom Thurmond (D-SC) asked whether a woman's running a beauty parlor from her home would fall under the public accommodations law that Wilkins was demanding, Wilkins replied that he would not be inclined to fight his way in to be served in her parlor.[135] Such questions aside, however, Congress, like the White House, was preoccupied by the prospect of a proposed march on the capital, for which plans were already taking shape. When Senator Winston Prouty (R-VT) asked Wilkins to guarantee that the march would be nonviolent, he refused, saying that "even in New England, where self-control is a virtue of the people," no one could promise such a thing. Instead, he was "relying on the restraint of his people, which has been exemplary."[136]

In truth, Wilkins shared some of Prouty's wariness about the proposed march. He was initially hesitant to offer his support, arguing that such a protest would only be appropriate in the event of a filibuster and warned advocates of the march that the demonstration must have a specific objective.[137] The politically astute Wilkins must also have realized the risk the Kennedy administration had taken in introducing civil rights legislation in the year before a presidential election and feared that disturbances such as those seen in Birmingham could only damage the bill's chances of survival, particularly if those disturbances took place in the backyard of the White House.[138] But his complaints were primarily rhetorical: whatever his views, the Association had to be involved in any demonstration on the scale being discussed by the other groups if it was to continue to have any credibility or influence.

In early July, leaders of the major civil rights groups came together in New York for the first planning session of the proposed March on Washington for Jobs and Freedom. Attendees at the meeting later described Wilkins's powerful hold on the gathering. John Lewis of SNCC saw the meeting as a "real exercise in power and positioning and political rivalry."[139] On entering the meeting room, Wilkins tapped the shoulder of the more "junior" members or deputies that he did not want in attendance and insisted they leave.[140] Among those ejected were James Forman, Bayard Rustin, and Fred Shuttlesworth, each of whom, to the surprise of Lewis, acquiesced to the demand—a measure of Wilkins's standing among the attendees: even if Wilkins was disliked personally, they recognized the NAACP's importance to any civil rights endeavor.[141] Rustin had originally been proposed as the director of the march, but Wilkins exerted his authority on this decision too, insisting that Rustin's history of pacifism, his previous association with Communism, and his arrest for homosexual activity would all be unnecessary distractions for the press and critics of the march. A compromise was suggested: Randolph would be named director, but Rustin, as deputy director, would actually organize the event.

In an attempt to contain the various forces that could disrupt the march, the leaders drew up an agreement to define the proposed demonstration, stating, "We are going to Washington to demand that adequate and meaningful civil rights legislation be passed, and to call for training and work for all people, Negro and white." The leaders emphasized that any form of confrontation would have no place during the march and also warned that the demonstration had been carefully planned to prevent any disruptions. "Sit-ins (in Congress, the streets, in places of public accommodation etc) are not part of the March program for August 28. Persons wishing to engage in such actions are urged not to join the March."[142] It is not clear whether that document was ever issued as a public statement, but many of the points were contained in a statement issued by the leaders prior to the March: "It will be orderly but not subservient. It will be proud, but not arrogant. It will be non-violent but not timid. It will be unified in purpose and behavior, not splintered into groups and individual competitors. It will be outspoken, but not raucous."[143]

Having the demonstration be peaceful was by no means a foregone conclusion. If Wilkins was in any doubt that black Americans were becoming more militant, the Association's own members provided a reminder. The NAACP's annual convention opened in Chicago shortly after the official announcement of the March on Washington; there, Chicago's black community had, as elsewhere in the country, become exasperated with the pace of civil rights reform, and they were in no mood to be placated by political rhetoric.[144] To the embarrassment of the Association's leaders, at one meeting convention delegates booed two speakers, one of whom was Chicago's Mayor Richard Daley, who had inflamed members with an address to delegates earlier in the week in which he made remarks about "negro ghettoes" in Chicago.[145] In addition, members of the Revolutionary Action Movement (RAM) heckled speakers, and more than two hundred delegates walked out of a workshop led by James del Rio, a member of the Detroit branch who had recently criticized the Association's tactics.[146]

That the balance of power had shifted was evident when a resolution endorsing a broad program of direct-action activities was passed by the convention. Members wanted an acknowledgment by NAACP leadership that the Association's strategy would be broadened to include mass action as well as litigation. The resolution also tackled branches that resisted direct-action protests, stating that if a branch resisted or hindered direct action, an appeal could be requested of the committee branches, which would be expected to raise the appeal with the board of directors.[147] In addition, youth branches demanded, and were given, more autonomy and support when their proposals or ideas clashed with their local branch.[148]

Some of the NAACP's younger members were already tired of waiting for resolutions and were taking action. In St. Augustine, Florida, the local branch, led by Robert Hayling, a local dentist, had begun a campaign to desegregate the city's facilities. Protests intensified throughout the summer, with youth members picketing Woolworth's, McCrory's, and other stores that operated segregated lunch counters. When the demonstrators were arrested, four of the youths, aged fourteen to sixteen, were jailed and sentenced to schools for delinquents; but because the county had no juvenile detention facilities, the children were held in the local jail for some months before being released. Initially, the national office paid scant attention to the events in St. Augustine, but by September lunch counters in the city were on the brink of being desegregated and some employment opportunities were opening up for blacks, even though the Ku Klux Klan met every step of progress with violence. By early 1964, frustrated by the lack of response from federal authorities and the NAACP's national office, Hayling, who had resigned from the Association a few months before, approached the SCLC for help. King's group seized the opportunity to move into the city and build local support for its own organization. SCLC's subsequent campaign in St. Augustine left the NAACP on the periphery once more, bemoaning the attention paid to King.[149]

King was by this point the moral center of the civil rights movement and considered its leader by the public. His position in history was assured by his address at the March on Washington, which took place on August 28, 1963. Approximately 250,000 people gathered peacefully to participate in an event that has come to symbolize the apex of the civil rights movement in popular culture. One of the leaders almost did not speak at all. John Lewis, the head of SNCC, had prepared a combative speech that heavily criticized the pending legislation and, invoking the ghost of General Sherman, declared that SNCC and its followers would march through the south in pursuit of their own "scorched earth" policy. Worried that the speech would antagonize the Kennedy administration, a committee made up of Randolph, King, Rustin, leaders from SNCC and SCLC, and clerics persuaded a reluctant Lewis to tone down his words.

Wilkins, who was introduced by Randolph as the "acknowledged champion of civil rights in America," used his few minutes to prod the Kennedy administration and Congress into passing the pending legislation. "We have come asking the enactment of legislation that will affirm the rights of life, liberty and the pursuit of happiness and that will place the resources and the honor of the government of all the people behind the pledge of equality in the Declaration of Independence." He ended by paying tribute to W. E. B. Du Bois, who had died in Ghana the previous day. "It is incontrovertible that at the dawn of the twentieth century his was the voice that was calling to you to gather here today in this cause. If you want to read something that applies to 1963 go back and get a volume of *The Souls of Black Folk* by Du Bois published in 1903." He also called upon the crowd to "keep up the speaking by letters and telegrams and, wherever possible, by personal visit," but avoided any mention of applying pressure with more direct mass action.[150]

The day ended with King's soaring speech about his dreams for a free and color-blind society, which has come to be seen as one of his finest moments; and the March has become King's day in cultural memory. Nevertheless, the NAACP under Wilkins's leadership played a crucial role in ensuring that the march was a success. Once over his initial and rather belligerent reluctance, Wilkins did much to keep the theme of the march in focus. The Association had contributed $10,000 and the assistance of five full-time staff members in New York and Washington. Henry Lee Moon was responsible for public relations, while Gloster Current and John Morsell spent at least half their time on administration for the march.[151] Wilkins also mobilized the branches in support of the march, and members from across the country chartered trains and buses to the capital.

Immediately following the speeches, the civil rights leaders met with Kennedy, who congratulated them on the day's success. But Wilkins was not going to be deterred from the primary purpose of the event and told the president, "I feel it my lot, sir, in this afternoon of superlative oratory, to be the one to deal rather pedantically and pedestrianly with the hard business of legislation."[152] The group made a plea for a stronger FEPC and a provision in the bill to allow the Justice Department to intervene in discrimination cases. Kennedy, wary of losing Republican support, refused.[153] A few weeks later, while supporters were still basking in the success of the March on Washington, intractable whites in Alabama proved yet again that the administration could no longer afford the luxury of political bargaining for civil rights when a splinter group connected with the Ku Klux Klan set off a bomb under the Sixteenth Street church, killing four young girls—Cynthia Wesley, Denise McNair, Carole Robertson, and Addie Mae Collins—and injuring twenty other people.

On Capitol Hill, Congressman Emanuel Celler (D-NY) was emboldened enough by the Birmingham bombing to add strong new provisions to the bill under consideration in the House. The public accommodations portion was widened to include private businesses; a dramatically expanded Title III would allow the Justice Department to sue any infringement of civil rights; and the FEPC provision was strengthened.[154] While Celler's amendments were almost everything Wilkins and the other civil rights leaders could have wished for, they were an unpleasant surprise to Robert Kennedy. The attorney general had quietly been making deals with House Republicans on the basis of the notion that it was more important to craft a pragmatic bill that would be passed than a strong bill that would fail, and he began a campaign to dilute the stronger provisions.[155]

Wilkins sent a telegram to members of Congress, arguing that the compromises inflicted on the legislation during the committee stage had weakened an already "soft" bill and asserted that the Birmingham bombing was a "defiance of basic truth that Negro citizens are included under

United States constitutional guarantees." The proposed amendments, he argued, "agrees with bombers that the United States Department of Justice may not act on its own to uphold these guarantees." He ended the telegram on a defiant note, stating, "a vote for softened version in its present form is a vote for so little as to be of dubious value to Negro citizens or to its architects."[156]

Political imperatives, particularly the 1964 presidential election, drove the Kennedy administration to argue for a compromise bill that diluted some of Celler's stronger provisions. Robert Kennedy was particularly reluctant to allow the Title III provision to go through unchecked, and President Kennedy questioned whether the LCCR could deliver the necessary votes, thus raising the specter of complete failure. Presented with the choice of a weakened bill or no bill at all, Celler agreed to restore some of the original White House provisions, while Kennedy agreed to praise the new bill as being stronger than the one originally proposed by the administration. The FEPC and Title III provisions were deleted and only expanded public accommodations provisions were added to what was essentially the bill the Kennedys had originally suggested. After much political horse-trading, the administration and congressional leaders managed to gather the necessary votes to get the bill out of committee and onto the floor.[157]

As anticipated, President Kennedy argued that the amended bill was better than his original proposal and that it would stand a greater chance of passing successfully through Congress. Wilkins and other black leaders were bitterly disappointed.[158] Wilkins painted a bleak picture of the events that had taken place since the last civil rights bill was debated and despaired at having to fight for Title III yet again. "Even to the naked eye of a layman it is worse than it was in 1956. Yet the Kennedy Administration seems to be saying that the Justice Department powers deemed necessary in 1956, requested by the Eisenhower Administration and passed by the House of Representatives, are not necessary today." As for the FEPC provision, Wilkins argued that a black unemployment rate three times that of white workers, which he said was caused by "three factors, automation, racial hiring practices by employers and racially restrictive practices by some unions," made federal action on employment discrimination an urgent necessity.[159] Still, when the bill was reported out of the House on

November 20, even in its neutered state, it still offered the brightest hope for civil rights reform in history.

Three days later, Wilkins was working in his office in New York when he heard the news of President Kennedy's assassination. Despite his frustration at the political considerations that governed Kennedy's approach to civil rights and his frequent exasperation with the administration's reluctance to deal with the southern bloc in Congress, Wilkins believed that the president had understood the moral imperatives for civil rights legislation; and he, like almost every other American, was shaken by the young president's death. He noted, "Kennedy was concerned—and deeply so—that Negroes should enjoy their rights as citizens; he was for correcting patent, long-standing and openly admitted inequalities; and for the protection by the United States of the rights guaranteed to all citizens of the Constitution. But he never 'gave' the Negroes anything except two invaluable items: respect and recognition in the same measure and with the same warmth with which he bestowed these upon other Americans; and an opportunity to achieve in society where the normal competition was sharpened many times over by the factor of skin color."[160] There was little indication whether Kennedy's successor would be the movement's friend or foe.

5

All the Way with LBJ

President Kennedy's death left everything in limbo, and it was far from clear what Lyndon Johnson's sudden elevation to the Oval Office would mean for the pending legislation. Still, Wilkins tried to reassure NAACP members that the new president was a friend of black Americans. "As Vice-President," he asserted, "Mr. Johnson has given active personal and affirmative leadership to the equal-opportunity phase of the JFK program." For proof, Wilkins referred to a speech Johnson made on Memorial Day that year at Gettysburg, which was entirely devoted to a plea for equality for black Americans. "His speech at Gettysburg, PA last spring placed him irrevocably in the civil rights camp. No one as well aware of political implications as Lyndon B. Johnson would have made such a speech inadvertently. It is a fair and justified estimate that it represents our new President's personal conviction and his commitment to continued advancement in the crusade for racially unrestricted opportunity, dignity and justice."[1]

Johnson quickly began to court the main black leaders. He had made it clear to aides Bill Moyers and Jack Valenti that passage of Kennedy's civil rights legislation was a priority and that securing the support of Wilkins, Whitney Young, and Martin Luther King was essential in making that happen.[2] To make his determination clear, Johnson addressed a joint session of Congress five days after Kennedy's death and made a plea that was almost impossible to rebuff: "No oration or eulogy could more eloquently honor President Kennedy's memory than the earliest passage of the civil rights bill for which he fought so long. We have talked long enough in this country about equal rights. We have talked for one hundred years or more. It is time to now write the next chapter, and to write it in the books of law."[3]

Wilkins's initial reaction to Johnson's address was measured. "The whole message had a strong tone affirming basic Americanism," he stated. "It cannot but assure all our citizens that our country will move forward and that President Johnson is ready to lead the Congress and the people in any action in the national interest." Wilkins's caution was understandable, given Johnson's role in the passage of the 1957 civil rights bill and the tortuous route the present legislation had already taken to get through the House of Representatives. Wilkins's political pragmatism soon took over, however, and he followed his earlier remarks with a press statement in which he said, "Mr. Johnson would push for enactment of the Kennedy civil rights package because of his 'own conviction that it was essential and because of the political necessity' of it."[4] Wilkins was enthusiastic when talking about the speech to the press. He told the *New York Times* that the speech was a "rallying cry against bigotry and hate and violence" and said that it showed Johnson to be a "civil rights leader in his own right and not just a follower of President Kennedy." Johnson had, according to Wilkins, "left no doubt as to his recognition of the urgency of the civil rights issue or of his commitment of full support to the cause of equal rights for all Americans."[5]

White House advisers such as Lee White and Bill Moyers, some of whom had worked closely with civil rights leaders during the Kennedy administration, also recognized the need for urgent action, and they encouraged the president to meet with each of the black representatives as quickly as possible. Johnson originally wanted to invite the leaders to his ranch in Texas, arguing that entertaining such a group at his home would "be a pretty dramatic thing for the nation."[6] It certainly would have been a striking confirmation of his commitment to equal rights, but Johnson was eventually advised against doing so for fear of looking "phony."[7] Nevertheless, he did manage to make one public declaration when he intervened to add Wilkins and Whitney Young to the guest list for President Kennedy's funeral when he noticed they had not been invited.[8]

The unlikely political alliance between Wilkins and Johnson began to take shape on November 29, when Wilkins became the first civil rights leader to meet with the new president. The "dean" of the group, as Robert Caro called him, received the full "Johnson treatment," as the president assured Wilkins of his support for the pending civil rights bill but warned that he could not lobby for its passage.[9] The two men sat almost knee to knee as the president set to work persuading Wilkins of his sincerity in getting the civil rights bill passed. He warned Wilkins that the country's future depended on how civil rights activists managed the fight over the coming months and quietly told him, "I want that bill *passed*."[10] Wilkins later asked Johnson why he was waging such a determined fight for the bill. The president repeated King's words at the March on Washington: "Free at last, free at last. Thank God almighty, I'm free at last," which has been interpreted by one Johnson biographer as the comments of a man liberated from political considerations that had prevented him from taking action until that moment.[11]

The shared desire to see the civil rights bill passed forged a close working relationship between the two men that remained strong throughout Johnson's presidency. It helped that Wilkins was a moderate with a strong belief in the power of the legislative process, making him Johnson's natural confidant on civil rights issues.[12] Others in Johnson's administration shared the president's good opinion of Wilkins, including press secretary George Reedy, who advised Johnson that he should consider Wilkins "*the* Negro leader," echoing the consensus of opinion among administration officials about Wilkins's "judgment and sense of fair play."[13]

Johnson had emphasized to Wilkins the importance of enlisting the help of Republicans in both the House and Senate, but the administration knew that the civil rights groups would need to be bolstered by support from other organizations if their lobbying was to have any effect.[14] Lawrence O'Brien, an aide to Johnson, also suggested that Wilkins urge religious leaders in the LCCR to supplement the lobbying efforts of civil rights organizations. A call was sent to the National Council of Churches convention that was meeting in Philadelphia to request that members return home via Washington, where they could lobby their congressmen. Many answered the call to join NAACP members on Capitol Hill, which was soon awash in clerical collars.[15]

If Wilkins was initially skeptical about Johnson's motives, these early meetings reassured him that the civil rights movement had a friend, finally, in the White House.[16] Johnson's approach to civil rights has been described as a struggle among his conflicting feelings of compassion, pragmatism, and a quest for power. He had a reputation as a compassionate legislator during his time in Congress, but his personal convictions about social justice were often compromised by his ambition.[17] Even as he was directing the passage of the 1957 civil rights bill, Johnson assured many outraged constituents that reports of his support for the bill were "entirely unwarranted. I am unalterably opposed to it," telling his constituents that he had "always been opposed to forced integration of the races and I am still opposed. We must maintain the right of the states to deal with matters that are in their proper jurisdiction." These words would come back to haunt him as president.[18]

When Kennedy appointed Johnson as chairman of the President's Committee on Equal Employment Opportunity, it suggested to Wilkins that Johnson was more serious about civil rights issues than had previously been thought, although Wilkins did not know that Johnson was reluctant to assume the role, in part because the committee had so few resources it was almost ineffective. Nevertheless, the chairmanship brought Johnson into contact with a range of black leaders, many of whom were encouraged by his apparent sincerity in wanting to achieve equal opportunities for black Americans.[19] It was during this period that Wilkins felt it had become "possible for his [Johnson's] feelings [on race issues] and his future to coincide."

For Wilkins, access to the highest reaches of power was a satisfying recognition of his position—at least in his own eyes—as the foremost black leader in the country. Walter White had enjoyed the support of Eleanor Roosevelt, and through her gained limited access to President Roosevelt. White had also thrown his support behind Truman during the late 1940s and had been rewarded with some executive action on equal rights. However, neither White nor any other black leader had enjoyed the kind of collaborative relationship with a president that characterized Wilkins's and Johnson's interaction. Wilkins was ambivalent at best about most presidents before Johnson, judging them entirely on their commitment to civil rights. Johnson's commitment to pushing through Kennedy's civil rights program, however, meant that Wilkins soon became an enthusiastic ally. In the first three months of his presidency, Johnson called or met with Wilkins several times. During these meetings or calls, the president solicited Wilkins's advice on what he should say about civil rights in his first State of the Union message, gathered Wilkins's opinion on black appointees, and goaded Wilkins to seek Republican support for the civil rights bill.[20]

Recordings of telephone conversations between the two give a flavor of their relationship. During one telephone conversation early in his presidency, Johnson asked Wilkins for his opinion on a number of subjects related to civil rights, including the suitability of Spottswood Robinson and Leon Higginbotham for judicial appointments. Johnson asked whether Wilkins wanted the two appointed; if he didn't, Johnson would appoint someone else. In this case, Wilkins was effusive in his praise of both men, saying that he would consider the appointment of Higginbotham a personal favor, to which Johnson promised that the appointment "would be made in the next five minutes." True to his word, the president appointed him a judge to the Eastern District of Pennsylvania on the same day that he spoke to Wilkins.[21]

Ever the politician, Johnson hoped these conversations would help secure the good opinion of the black community, which in some areas of the country had become a powerful voting bloc. Wilkins was a valuable conduit to that constituency. The only other black leader who commanded Johnson's attention and favor to a similar degree was Whitney Young of the Urban League. Although much younger than Wilkins, Young shared his pragmatic approach and, like Wilkins, believed in using established power structures such as business and Congress, rather than direct action, to achieve equality; but the League's constituency was not as broad as the NAACP's, nor its activities as widespread. The relationship between Johnson and Wilkins therefore strengthened during the fight for the civil rights bill.

The original bill, sent to Congress in June 1963, contained provisions to fight discrimination in voting rights, public accommodations, and federally assisted programs; give more authority to the justice department to enforce the desegregation of public schools; establish a Community Relations Service and a statutory Commission on Equal Employment Opportunity; and continue the Civil Rights Commission. Even in the emotionally charged atmosphere that pervaded Washington in early 1964 it was clear that the stakes were dangerously high for both Wilkins and

Johnson. After early attempts by the Kennedy administration and Congress to dilute some of the provisions, Wilkins warned that failure to pass the bill would encourage many blacks to abandon any faith in the legislative process and resort to direct action to find relief.[22] If that happened, Wilkins would surely lose much of his authority, and the NAACP was likely to find its entire strategy questioned to an even greater degree by more militant groups who already saw little benefit in pursuing such a slow and uncertain plan. Johnson too had staked his political reputation on the passage of the bill.

Johnson had made it clear to Wilkins that this was not a fight he could wage alone, and he put increasing pressure on the NAACP to take up the most public parts of the battle. In a telephone call to Wilkins in January 1964 Johnson prodded him to "get working on this bill" as soon as possible, arguing that it was his responsibility to persuade Republican leaders to support the legislation. Johnson had long experience in navigating the personal politics involved in Congress and knew the sort of fight that lay ahead in persuading politicians to support the bill. "You can't make a southerner change his spots," he warned Wilkins. "If we lose this fight, Roy, we're going back ten years."[23] Nevertheless, despite his insistence that he could not get involved, Johnson could not resist directing Wilkins's strategy in addition to waging an intense lobbying effort of his own. He told Wilkins to focus on Senator Everett Dirksen (R-IL) in an effort to persuade him of the potential benefits of the bill for the Republican Party and assured Wilkins that he would have access to the White House whenever necessary, either in person or on the telephone.[24]

In much the same way as Johnson was able to make full use of his prodigious knowledge of Senate personalities and procedures to help ensure passage of the civil rights bill, Wilkins was able to make use of his knowledge of the membership of the NAACP and LCCR to exert pressure on Congress. At the time of Kennedy's death, the bill had stalled in the House Rules Committee. The LCCR had planned a campaign of rallies, demonstrations, and letter writing targeted at members of the committee over the Thanksgiving recess, but the events in Dallas postponed further activity.[25] However, with Johnson's very public endorsement of the legislation and his plea to enact the bill as part of Kennedy's legacy, the bill's progress finally began to gain traction. Johnson pressured his friends in Congress and in the media to call for a discharge petition, which would allow the bill to move out of the committee stage and onto the floor if 218 congressmen signed the petition. Emanuel Celler (D-NY) filed the discharge petition in early December and, after a slow start, support began to build. Once a majority in favor of the petition seemed clear, the committee's chairman, segregationist Howard Smith (D-VA), decided to forgo a humiliating defeat and allowed the bill to go through to a House vote.

Wilkins quickly rallied the troops. He announced in December 1963 that the NAACP would urge its members to vote against candidates who opposed the civil rights legislation.[26] He then summoned Association delegates to Washington before the House began to debate the bill in early February 1964. Clarence Mitchell assigned members drawn from LCCR organizations including the NAACP to watch four or five congressmen, who were potential supporters of the bill, from the balcony of the House. According to Mitchell's biographer, one of the aims of this tactic was to give the impression of a full gallery—and an interested electorate—to add pressure on lawmakers.[27] Members of LCCR organizations, nicknamed "gallery vultures," populated the House galleries throughout the debate, monitoring votes on amendments. House rules prohibited spectators from taking notes, so the "vultures" had to remember how the votes were cast and report their observations to LCCR organizers the following morning. They then returned to the galleries, while a second group of volunteers were stationed on every floor of the two House office buildings to ensure that friendly congressmen were on hand to vote.[28] After nine days of debate, the House passed the bill by a margin of 160 votes, and without the kind of compromise amendments that had weakened earlier civil rights acts. Arnold Aronson boasted to members that LCCR tactics had been credited both by friends and enemies of the bill with playing a major part in its passage.

To prepare for the Senate debate, Wilkins instructed NAACP branch presidents on lobbying tactics: "Name a special committee for letter writing. Ask them to call people, speak to people, write to people and get individuals to write the two Senators from your state . . . ask your youth members to ring doorbells and get people to pledge to write letters to the Senators. Keep a list. Keep score. Hold huddles. Compare notes."[29]

To bolster these lobbying efforts, the LCCR held a strategy meeting in Washington, DC, from which a five-point plan emerged. It consisted of proposals for a one-day conference, with voter registration committees to check on progress, a student assembly to encourage discussion of the bill, a day of protest to be held by the women of B'nai B'rith to urge their 200,000 members to telegram their senators, an interfaith meeting, and regular visits to senators by LCCR delegations.[30]

While Mitchell continued the association's lobbying effort on Capitol Hill, Wilkins traveled the country to garner support for the bill at rallies and on television, speaking to students, religious and civic groups, and local NAACP branches. Ensuring passage of the bill dominated much of his life for much of the first half of 1964; almost every speech he made and every appearance were devoted to stressing the importance of a successful resolution. Wilkins targeted senior senators to protest against amendments suggested by Senator Bourke Hickenlooper (R-IA). He met with former president Eisenhower to discuss the bill, and he also debated the legislation on television.[31]

The bill almost faltered in the final stages when it came up against the inevitable filibuster. Because of the potential of this tactic to scupper civil rights legislation, the NAACP had tried unsuccessfully for decades to either eradicate the filibuster or at least change the cloture rule to make it easier for filibusters to be halted. It was a measure of the opposition against the bill in some quarters that the filibuster on this occasion lasted for fifty-seven days—including Saturdays. Senator Robert Byrd (D-WV) was the last to speak, and he took full advantage, talking for over fourteen hours. The filibuster was finally brought to a close by a historic cloture vote. Although Wilkins, Mitchell, and the LCCR were tireless in their efforts to ensure that supporters of the bill were in the right place at the right time, at the very final stages it took the force of the White House to cajole those who were wavering. Hubert Humphrey spent the evening before the cloture vote calling Democratic senators who still had not committed themselves. It was expected that the vote would be very close, so every ally was crucial. The next morning Senator Clair Engle (D-CA), who was terminally ill and could only communicate his vote by pointing to his eye, was among those who ended the filibuster and passed the bill with a final tally of 71 votes to 29—four more than the minimum required. It was only the second successful cloture vote since 1927 and the first ever to stop a filibuster on a civil rights bill. The cloture vote caused almost as much celebration in the ranks of the LCCR as the passage of the final bill. "The strong margin by which the cloture petition passed is . . . a tribute to those in the Leadership Conference who helped marshal support for the move that finally broke the filibuster," Wilkins noted. He added that "the overwhelming nature of the victory has broad implications for the future of the Senate and may mark the first real break in southern domination of the body."[32]

The House passed the bill and its amendments at the end of June, and the Civil Rights Act was finally signed into law by Johnson during the early evening of July 2, 1964. Earlier that day, Johnson had called Wilkins to discuss the timing of the signing. The July Fourth holiday weekend was approaching, and the president was concerned that signing the bill before then would spark trouble in the South, although he also felt it should be signed as soon as possible. Wilkins urged the president to follow his instinct and sign the bill straight away, as any delay might be seen as hesitation by the administration about the act and its provisions. He also suggested that signing it immediately would be a gracious gesture to those Republican congressmen who had played a crucial role in its passage and were about to leave for their party convention. Within hours, Wilkins had flown down to Washington to join Clarence Mitchell, Joseph Rauh, Arnold Aronson, James Farmer, A. Philip Randolph, Martin Luther King, and over one hundred others in the East Room of the White House to watch Johnson sign the historic legislation.[33]

The NAACP declared the act on a par with the Emancipation Proclamation and the Declaration of Independence in importance, calling it "a measure by the people for the people."[34] In his annual report to the Board of Directors, Wilkins said it was "the final Congressional affirmation of the Negro's status and rights as a constitutional citizen . . . a Magna Carta for the race, [and] a splendid monument for the cause of human rights."[35] It was also an opportunity for congratulations within the NAACP. Mitchell was effusive in his praise of Wilkins's "statesmanlike and impressive leadership." He had been critical of the efforts of newer groups, such as SNCC and SCLC, and reiterated his belief that Wilkins's more conservative and measured approach was by far the most effective.

"You have found the way of consistent, effective, forward movement that will be long remembered when the history of this period is written by objective persons who want to tell the truth rather than by scribes who want salable [*sic*] instead of facts."[36]

Establishing a set of rights in the statute book was no guarantee that those laws would be respected or obeyed. But although Wilkins anticipated further courtroom battles to ensure the law's implementation, he rejected the idea of using demonstrations to force the issue. Mindful of antagonizing Johnson, and also aware of damaging the potential for future legislation if civil rights groups were too aggressive in testing compliance with the Civil Rights Act, he urged a cautious approach. "If you have to change spark plugs in your car, you don't use a sledge hammer," he warned. "We ought to be smart rather than loud in the manner we choose to implement the bill."[37] At the NAACP's annual convention in Washington in June 1964, Wilkins told delegates that the Association would maintain a "high degree of productive militancy without resort to 'adventurism.'"[38]

Once Johnson had signed the bill, the NAACP would have much work to do. Ensuring compliance with its provisions and monitoring implementation would require further, sustained efforts including, Wilkins said, "money and staff and a far-reaching program not solely of action, but of education and community projects."[39] But the Association had no time to prepare these efforts. Barely two weeks after the bill became law, riots broke out on northern streets. The threat of violence had hung in the air for some months but, as Johnson's conversation with Wilkins on the morning of July 2 illustrated, everyone had been looking in the wrong direction: the possibility that the tinder was as explosive in New York as in Alabama had barely been considered. A violent confrontation between police and local people began in Harlem when James Powell, a black teenager, was shot dead by an off-duty policeman. The unrest quickly spread to Bedford-Stuyvesant, Brooklyn, Rochester, and Jersey City. The speed with which these disturbances spread, bringing death and destruction in their wake, was terrifying. In Harlem, one person was killed, over one hundred people were injured, and hundreds were arrested. In Rochester, the toll was even worse: four people died and hundreds were hurt. By the time the riots ceased at the end of August, the cost of the destruction was estimated to be in the millions.[40]

In an attempt to defuse the tension, NAACP branch leaders in New York City and Brooklyn traveled through the affected areas with loud-speakers and sound trucks. The Brooklyn branch also distributed leaflets demanding, "Cool it baby!" and saying, "Violent demonstrations and looting hurt our cause—Think!"[41] But for Wilkins, the solution to the rioters' complaints was to be found in the ballot rather than bricks. He wrote a lengthy article in the *New York Times* shortly after the riots began. Although sympathetic to the plight of poor, urban blacks, he argued that political participation would have long-term benefits in their communities. "They know about it, and they use it, but not as effectively as the Irish, the Poles, the Italians and the Jews have used it . . . The ballot is no cure-all but it is a tool in a democratic society that no group, disadvantaged socially and economically, can afford to ignore."[42]

One *New York Times* correspondent challenged Wilkins's rejection of riots as a useful or persuasive political weapon, arguing that the riots that took place in the Harlem and Bedford-Stuyvesant areas of New York the previous month had in fact resulted in a volunteer program that gave 600 youths work, and in the appointment of the first black police captain to a Harlem precinct—a significant development when many of the disturbances were sparked by actual, or rumored, police violence. Wilkins, however, was not convinced. "Undoubtedly a violent outburst here and there has produced an infinitesimal gain in a highly localized area, but I hope Mr. Weiss [the author of the letter] is not advocating violence as a planned tactic. Observers of the present scene uniformly remark upon the microscopic 'improvement' in Harlem after the riot of 1943. One of the districts involved this year had only 20 percent of its Negro citizens registered to vote. Full registration might easily have produced a dozen Negro police captains stationed elsewhere than in Harlem and thousands of sound and continuing jobs, not 600 summer workers, as welcome and helpful as these are."[43]

Contributing to the tension was Barry Goldwater's arrival on the national stage. Goldwater was the likely Republican candidate for president, and his extremism put Wilkins in an awkward position. The NAACP was historically and assiduously bipartisan, but the senator's critical remarks about the civil rights bill, which he viewed as unwarranted federal intervention in the rights of both states and individuals, made it impossible for

Wilkins to be anything other than contemptuous in his comments about the Republican front-runner. While the civil rights bill was still being debated in Congress, Goldwater told an audience in New York City that the Republicans would "cool the fires of racial strife." Wilkins immediately issued a blistering attack on the candidate: "Your position is part of the cotton batting comfort accorded this regime of blood and death by those senators now blocking even a vote on a civil rights bill."[44]

Concern about Goldwater's remarks was such that NAACP delegates passed an extraordinary resolution at the Association's national convention at the end of June. The resolution—the first partisan resolution in the history of the NAACP—accused Goldwater of opportunism in his "self-serving statement" supporting equal rights, particularly in light of his lack of support for civil rights legislation, and called upon the Republican National Convention to deny him the nomination and instead nominate a candidate who "represents the Republican Party's philosophy of equal opportunities for all citizens."[45] Wilkins went further at a press conference the following month, in which, according to the *New York Times*, he departed "from the usual calm that characterizes his comments" and "said with heat: Whenever a candidate whose supporters are racists raises the question of racism, he invites the injection of racism into a campaign."[46]

Wilkins also warned the other civil rights leaders that more demonstrations could damage Johnson's chances at the polls. As the political convention season approached with no end in sight to the urban disturbances, he sent a telegram to black leaders, calling them to an urgent meeting to discuss the issue. "There is no safety in the assumption that Goldwater cannot win the election," he cautioned. "He can win it and he can be helped to win if the wrong moves are made. It is of highest importance we take council at earliest moment to ensure that without modifying any essential position we do nothing to produce votes for Goldwater. The promise of the Civil Rights Act of 1964 could well be diminished or nullified and a decade of increasingly violent and futile disorder ushered in if we do not play our hand coolly and intelligently."[47]

On July 29, Martin Luther King, James Farmer, Whitney Young, A. Philip Randolph, John Lewis, and Bayard Rustin met with Wilkins at NAACP headquarters in New York City to discuss the next steps. It is unclear whether Wilkins or Whitney Young first proposed the idea of a moratorium, but the previous evening Wilkins had spoken with President Johnson, who was concerned about the effect of the riots. Although the president did not explicitly request that the demonstrations be halted, he was clearly concerned about the effect on his presidential campaign. Wilkins told the president that a meeting with the other leaders was scheduled for the following day.[48] He promised to "attempt to get a statement agreed upon to call off demonstrations and concentrate on registration and voting." This suggests that there had been no prior discussion between the groups, and there was certainly no assumption that an agreement could be secured.

At the meeting, Wilkins proposed a moratorium on demonstrations until the elections had taken place in November, in the hope that this would dissipate tensions temporarily.[49] In advocating this, he was making a sharp reversal of his opinion of only a year before, when he had told convention delegates that blacks could not be expected to agree to Kennedy's request for a moratorium.[50] This time, however, he was emphatic in his belief that halting demonstrations during the election campaign would be vital if Goldwater—and the growing white backlash—was to be stopped. The proposal highlighted the fault lines that were now developing within the civil rights movement: Randolph, Rustin, Wilkins, and Young urged a moratorium; Lewis and Farmer firmly rejected the idea; while King, according to David Garrow, took the path of least resistance: in attempting to avoid confrontation with Wilkins, he found something to agree with from both sides.[51]

Lewis argued that the right to demonstrate should never be compromised for any reason, but he was also reluctant to be seen as favoring one party or candidate over another. In his report to the board of directors in September, Wilkins contended that Farmer and Lewis both agreed with the moratorium personally but that the internal politics of their respective organizations would not allow them to endorse it.[52] However, Farmer later said that he disagreed with the proposal because he thought the young activists in the movement would ridicule the decision, and its inevitable failure would show that the movement's leaders were unable to control its direction or its members.[53]

As a compromise, the resulting statement called for a "broad curtailment if not total moratorium, of all mass marches, mass picketing and mass demonstrations" until after the election in November. It was signed by Young, Wilkins, King, and Randolph, but not by Farmer and Lewis, who refused to put their names to the statement. Painting a bleak picture of what might happen should Goldwater be elected President, the statement said, "the present situation . . . presents such a serious threat to the implementation of the Civil Rights Act and to subsequent expansion of civil rights gains that we recommend a voluntary, temporary alteration in strategy and procedure."[54] The leaders proposed "a temporary change of emphasis and tactic, because we sincerely believe that the major energy of the civil rights forces should be used to encourage the Negro people, North and South, to register and to vote. The greatest need in this period is for political action."[55] A second statement, issued alongside the first, condemned the riots, drawing "a sharp distinction between the [rioting] and legitimate protest efforts by denied and desperate citizens seeking relief." It also, however, called for "more socially sensitive police action, for machinery for continuing communications and local civilian review."[56]

The refusal of Lewis and Farmer to sign the moratorium statement highlighted the growing difference between the groups about the best way to secure civil rights. When Lewis heard Wilkins's comments, he reportedly said he remained silent "in the interests of unity"; given King's reluctance to antagonize Wilkins, Lewis's inclination to do likewise would be understandable.[57] Tensions were running high within SNCC, Lewis's own organization, which was becoming increasingly radical as it intensified its voter registration efforts in Mississippi amid violence and fear and despite reports of discord between some of the black SNCC workers and white volunteers.[58] Farmer, too, was facing internal challenges at CORE: the previous year, at its national convention, a black chairman had been elected for the first time, and the mood inside his organization was shifting increasingly toward black nationalism.

As the rioting in the North died down, attention was drawn yet again to Mississippi. Two days after the Senate passed the Civil Rights Act, three CORE workers disappeared in Philadelphia, Mississippi. Two of the missing, Andrew Goodman and Michael Schwerner, were young white men from New York, while James Chaney was black and a native Mississippian. Schwerner and Chaney were CORE staff workers, while Goodman was a volunteer who had just arrived in the state. The three men were working in the region as part of the "Freedom Summer" voter registration project along with hundreds of college students, the majority of whom were white, middle class, and from the North and Midwest. The disappearance of the three quickly attracted national attention. After an extensive search the bodies of Goodman, Schwerner, and Chaney were found in early August. All three had been shot; James Chaney had, in addition, been brutally beaten.

Concern about the safety of blacks in Mississippi was so high that shortly before the CORE workers' disappearance, the NAACP had sent an investigative group to find out what conditions were like for civil rights workers in the state. The group found few "glimmers of light," and their report made depressing reading. Although the investigation simply confirmed what many already knew—that those involved in civil rights activity operated in a climate of fear and intimidation; employment discrimination was endemic; and the legal and judicial structure was so corrupt that murder, bombings, and violent attacks not only continued to go unpunished but were often conducted with the full knowledge and sometimes cooperation of the local police—the report provided useful evidence with which to lobby Congress. The Association urged the Department of Justice to investigate the abuse of authority by local and state officials and make recommendations to Congress for the passage of further legislation. The report also called on the Civil Rights Commission to hold public hearings in the state to examine charges of denial of equal protection of the law.[59]

Mississippi's reputation as the most dangerous state for civil rights activists had encouraged civil rights groups in early 1962 to unite under one umbrella organization, the Council of Federated Organizations (COFO), which would coordinate efforts by all the national, state, and local groups working to boost voter registration in the state. By the summer of 1964 this effort was primarily under the leadership of SNCC.[60] The NAACP disliked SNCC's expanding role in Mississippi. The Association was always reluctant to participate in any program or activity in which it was forced to share or cede control to another group, and having to work within the COFO structure became increasingly difficult for its branches. Local leaders argued that COFO's programs were undermining the NAACP's efforts in Mississippi, while the other groups accused Wilkins of controlling COFO's finances and therefore, by default, its activities.[61]

When COFO announced plans for a Freedom Summer, which would bring hundreds of Ivy League students to aid voter registration work in the state, Gloster Current warned Wilkins that it would likely create "considerable problems" for the organization. "The COFO project, if the Bill passes, could well bend our efforts to implement the Civil Rights Bill. Are we ready for an ideological revolution? Can we permit Aaron Henry to carry the banner alone in Mississippi under COFO with an inexperienced Field Secretary who still doesn't quite understand all the implications?"[62] There is no record of Wilkins's response to Current's questions, but there can be little doubt that he shared the opinion of his colleague. From the beginning of 1964, dissent had been brewing in the national office. Herbert Hill, the NAACP's labor secretary, described the NAACP's confusion during this period in an interview some years later with historian Simon Hall. Hill described the NAACP as simplistic in its view that American society could be changed through education and legislation and that the Association underestimated the country's attitude toward race. This lack of awareness meant that the NAACP "was significantly weakened" after the passage of the Civil Rights Act because it failed to make a "fundamental re-examination of the assumptions about race in American society and develop a significantly new program."[63]

James Booker, an old foe of Wilkins, reported in the *Amsterdam News* that some members of the board wanted to dismiss Wilkins and replace him with Franklin Williams, a former NAACP official on the West Coast who by this time was a member of the staff at the Peace Corps, and also suggested that there was a move to change the manner in which the president of the NAACP was elected.[64] Wilkins moved swiftly to dismiss Booker's assertions. In a letter to the executive staff criticizing the article, Wilkins made only an implicit reference to the suggestion that he could be replaced; instead, he took issue with Booker's suggestion that he was against change. However, Wilkins's statement dealt less with the specifics of Booker's claims than the fact that the article had been published at all, and Wilkins suspected the collusion of someone at the meeting, asserting, "The harm lies in the public discussion of it and the manner of that discussion—in this case a community column devoted to rumors, reports and tid-bits." He argued that public speculation "looses a chain reaction among employed staff and, by interaction, among our vast volunteer membership and officer corps. It has its effects, also, in the board itself."[65]

Another newspaper went even further than Booker. An article in the *New York Courier* headlined "The Revolt against Roy Wilkins" claimed that the "smoldering revolt against Roy Wilkins . . . broke out in the open at the January board meeting and bids fair to become more pronounced with the passage of time."[66] The article referred to arguments over a one-day boycott of New York schools proposed by a new coalition of local civil rights groups led by Reverend Milton Galamison, a pastor at one of the largest Presbyterian churches in New York and leader of an organization called the Citywide Committee for School Integration. Although some NAACP members were part of the loose coalition of those organizing the boycott, Wilkins refused to support it, repeating his argument that such protests could only be effective where "local conditions warranted."[67] Almost half of New York's schoolchildren stayed home for the first protest in February 1964, but subsequent demonstrations were less successful and the city's boycott movement quickly faded away—but not before it provided critics of Wilkins with ammunition.[68] As preparations for the boycott were under way, board members, frustrated at Wilkins's hesitation, questioned his leadership at the board's annual meeting shortly before the boycott took place. The press also devoted several articles to both the protest and its implications for black leadership in the city. One warned that "the profusion of civil rights organizations will produce so much confusion that the average Negro or white citizen will wander through this supermarket of philosophies—and buy nothing."[69] The *New York Courier* was quick to defend Wilkins, but feared that "The NAACP rebels . . . are biding their time until they have sufficiently embarrassed and discredited him to make his replacement seem warranted."[70]

Wilkins struggled to restore morale inside the organization, but succeeded only temporarily, as discontent rumbled on throughout the year. In October 1964, Eugene Reed, a dentist from Amityville, New York, called for a change in the composition of the NAACP's board of directors to "reflect more aggressive, grass-roots opinion."[71] Reed was joined by Jack Tanner, head of the NAACP's Northwest Conference of Branches, in a chorus of disapproval that followed Wilkins throughout 1964 and into the following year. Reed, Tanner, and their supporters publicly criticized him whenever possible, most often around the time of the Association's annual conference. Tanner, for example, told one newspaper that "the job of the NAACP is to intensify the heat on all fronts in all parts of the country and not to play around with the Government. There is growing sentiment that the organization is becoming inert."[72]

The Association's leadership was not unaware of the problems in the relationship between the national office and NAACP branches. Tensions had become apparent during 1963 when a consulting firm, Lennon/Rose from Chicago, had been hired to study the NAACP from national office to branch with the primary aim of helping the Association save money.[73] The study took four months to complete, with consultants visiting branches in twenty-two cities, and, although it was mainly supposed to be a cost-cutting exercise, the consultants also raised questions about the strategy, leadership, and personalities within the Association. Among the questions the consultants asked were whether the NAACP should be more militant, and whether its fund-raising methods were effective. Although the consultants did not officially ask questions about Wilkins, branch leaders were questioned closely about his management style, personality, and public image. This led Wilkins to accuse the survey of being little more than a "vendetta carried out by a 'faction' in the board."[74]

Althea Simmons, the NAACP's field secretary on the West Coast, sent Wilkins a summary of her conversation with Sam Rose, and her comments suggest that the consultants were less than convinced about Wilkins's leadership, even at the beginning of the survey.[75] Simmons reported that the consultant was "obviously fascinated with the factions within the National Board of Directors." Rose apparently told Simmons that the Chet Lewis faction should gain control because that group was willing to revitalize the association. (Lewis, leader of the Wichita, Kansas, NAACP branch, was one of the "Young Turks," a group of board members who wanted a more militant NAACP.) Rose also claimed, said Simmons, that Wilkins's "idiosyncrasies," such as "not wanting staff or branch people to meet him when he comes into town," were "hurting the Association." (Wilkins made a point of making his own way to NAACP branches and activities to maintain independence from any of the local

factions.)[76] The lack of press coverage given to Wilkins and the NAACP
was also questioned, despite Simmons's retort that the fact that Johnson called Wilkins before any other civil rights leader hardly suggested a
shortcoming in this regard. According to Simmons, Rose told her that
the NAACP was "the poorest run organization I have ever seen," that the
branch structure should be radically overhauled, and that younger people
should be brought in to run the organization "from the top right down
to the bottom."[77]

All participants were asked why the Association did not enjoy a larger membership relative to the total black population, and why only a
small number of members were actively engaged in implementing the
Association's programs at a local level. Simmons told Wilkins that during Rose's visit to the Los Angeles office the consultant raised several
questions about the process of taking instructions from a regional office
as well as the national office.[78] To address the situation, the consultants
recommended decentralizing the NAACP's regional framework. The Association operated regional offices for the Southeast, the West Coast, the
Southwest, the Tri-State Area, and the Midwest, but the structure could
be cumbersome. The West Coast region, for example, had, in addition to
a regional office, a field secretary, five area conferences, and a number of
branches throughout the state, with information and instructions coming
from all directions.[79]

Lennon/Rose's solution was for the Association to establish seven
regional offices, to which local branches would report, with the offices
situated in the largest cities in each region. Only issues that could not be
dealt with by the regional office would be sent up to head office. Within
each regional office, field directors and secretaries would deal with local
membership drives, fund-raising, and direct-action campaigns.[80] Reorga-
nizing the field structure in this way, the consultants argued, would eliminate the bottleneck of communication that existed between the national
office and branches. More important, by releasing national office staff
from day-to-day tasks that could and should be managed by regional
teams, more thought could be given to the development of programs.[81]
A lack of funds meant that the expansion of the Association's field staff
did not take place until the end of the decade, at which point its field
staff doubled in number to forty, many of whom focused on special-

ized issues, such as education and voter registration rather than general branch work.[82]

The final report concentrated mainly on organizational restructuring and logistical tinkering. To ease the management burdens on the secretary, the consultants proposed that his title be changed to executive director, which was more "descriptive of the responsibilities of the executive who is in fact to 'direct' the NAACP organization in the preparation and implementation of programs." In addition, the number of people reporting to that position should be reduced from twenty to just one: a newly created director of operations.[83] By creating an operational role, the consultants argued that Wilkins would have more time for public relations, strategy planning, and public appearances. The director of operations would be responsible for national programs involving labor, voting, education, housing, fund-raising, and youth activities.

The report appears to have been adopted with little dissent. Gloster Current approved of the multibranch idea but questioned the wisdom of closing some of the regional offices, particularly in areas such as Mississippi. Current was more concerned, however, with the distinctions that would be made between "line" and "staff" functions in the reorganization. His main complaint was that many of the roles that the consultants had identified as line positions, such as public relations, general counsel, and the directorship of the Washington bureau, were in fact staff positions, responsible for advisory and strategic decisions.[84] As one of those who would be "demoted" by reporting to the director of operations rather than to Wilkins, Current's remarks surely reflected a certain amount of self-interest. Nevertheless, he was right to question the wisdom of not only attaching too many responsibilities to one role, but also removing access to the final arbiter of strategy and tactics. In September 1964, the NAACP announced Wilkins's new title, John Morsell's appointment as director of operations, and Gloster Current's new role as director of branches and field administrator. New positions for fund-raising, office administration, and training were also announced, along with plans to open several new regional offices.[85]

The disparity between what was happening "on the ground" and the political considerations of the national office became more apparent during the 1964 Democratic National Convention in Atlantic City. A delegation from the Mississippi Freedom Democratic Party (MFDP), a group organized by COFO, arrived at the convention and challenged the party's establishment to allow it to be seated at the presidential nominating convention and replace the all-white delegation. The MFDP clearly had moral authority on its side, and its presence highlighted the blatant and illegal discrimination that prevented blacks from taking full part in the political process in Mississippi. Johnson was determined that the convention should pass without incident, but Wilkins warned the president that the discovery of the bodies of Goodman, Chaney, and Schwerner in Mississippi shortly before the convention began had "taken on a much more emotional load on the black side of the color line than it has before and there is simply nothing for any organization or body to do except endorse the proceedings." He then said that he "would be absolutely in an untenable position if I opposed the seating of the Freedom Party."[86]

Johnson engineered a compromise, whereby the MFDP was offered two seats at the convention as delegates "at-large," with the other delegates admitted as "honored guests," while the state's official delegation would be required to sign an oath of loyalty to the Democratic Party and its platform and to agree to revise its discriminatory rules in the selection of delegates.[87] This proposal was bitterly rejected by the MFDP, while the loyalty oath was too much for the Mississippi delegation, which walked out of the convention. Nevertheless, after much backroom trading, the oath was adopted by the convention at large, and it ensured that discrimination would be prohibited in choosing delegates to the 1968 Democratic convention.[88] John Lewis of SNCC wrote later, "It was a major letdown for hundreds and thousands of civil rights workers both black and white, young and old people alike who had given everything they had to prove that you could work through the system. They felt cheated. They felt robbed."[89]

Fannie Lou Hamer, one of the leaders of the MFDP, had given powerful and emotional testimony to the credentials committee about the violence and hardship she had endured simply for trying to register to vote. But, according to Hamer's biographer, once she had testified, Wilkins told Hamer that the members of the MFDP were all "just ignorant" and that, having made their point, should pack up and go home. Apparently, his remarks angered Hamer so much she canceled her membership to the NAACP and often said later, "There ain't nothing that I respect less than the NAACP."[90] Even if Wilkins was not as blunt as Hamer recollected, his patrician and hierarchical disposition suggests he may have been uncomfortable with Hamer's independence and the passionate dissent of this newcomer to the national stage. Also, given his jealous oversight of the NAACP's position, he would have resented the connection between SNCC and the MFDP and wanted to dissipate the other group's influence at the convention.

When the votes were counted in the November election, Johnson was returned to the White House with a landslide.[91] He was voted into office by a remarkable margin, winning just over 61 percent of the popular vote and 90 percent of Electoral College votes. Black voters had turned out to the polls in record numbers—around six million, according to NAACP estimates—and almost all those votes were cast for the Democrat, setting a pattern that has yet to be reversed in subsequent elections.[92] The Association claimed some credit for the large number of black voters and suggested that they had contributed significantly to the number of votes cast for Johnson and Humphrey.[93] But many at the national office were uneasy about supporting a candidate so unequivocally, and Gloster Current warned Wilkins of the dangers in aligning with one political party.[94]

Current's concern was echoed by some of Wilkins's detractors on the board, who used his closeness to the president as a reason for him to abdicate his role as executive secretary. Jack Tanner, one of the most militant "Young Turks," told an NAACP Area Conference that Wilkins "elected the President of the United States . . . when he declared a moratorium on demonstrations" and called on him to resign, arguing that his closeness to Johnson prevented him from challenging the White House into more dynamic action.[95] Wilkins responded by suggesting that signs of dissension within the organization were damaging to morale and hampered its ability to carry out the work necessary to implement the Civil Rights Act, arguing, "At the very time the NAACP should be in high gear, the Tanner speech is undermining our unity and diverting our energies. . . . Unless something is done, Mr. Tanner's speech and the follow-up at Denver is likely to guarantee, despite all efforts to the contrary, that the NAACP will be worse off at the end of 1965 than it was at the end of 1964. In other and plainer words, Mr. Tanner, whether he intends to or not, is wrecking the NAACP."[96]

Wilkins was now so closely linked to Johnson that shortly after the election it was rumored he had been offered a cabinet post. Speculation about a possible cabinet position for Wilkins first appeared in *Jet* magazine in November 1964; then, at the NAACP annual conference, Max Dean, a delegate from Flint, Michigan, repeated the rumor on the conference floor. The position was said to be part of a deal agreed with Johnson that the NAACP would not oppose the nomination of former Mississippi governor James Coleman to the Fifth Circuit Court of Appeals.[97] There is no evidence of such an offer or deal in the NAACP, Roy Wilkins, or Lyndon Johnson archives; nor is there any evidence in the telephone recordings Johnson made of his conversations. At one point in October 1965, when Johnson was considering appointing Robert Weaver to the cabinet, he did tell Wilkins that he was the person he would like to appoint; but he certainly made no offer, nor mentioned any previous offer. Wilkins firmly denied that such an offer had been made, assuring the NAACP's board, "My skills and heart are in the struggle for equality for my people through the NAACP. I have no intention of bowing out now when the Association's 55-year drive to wipe racial segregation from American life is so well on the way to realization."[98]

As soon as the election was over, the president called the black leaders and met with each one twice within two weeks. Prior to his second meeting with Wilkins, Johnson sought his opinion on who should be included in the new administration and also how communication with civil rights leaders could be simplified. "I want to use you as a critic to check it out and give me any conflicting ideas," he told Wilkins. Wilkins, ever cautious of ceding any power to other groups, told the president that a request was already being drafted for a conference and that "the move to hurry was to try to prevent any one person running to the president."[99] With such a strong electoral mandate, Johnson moved quickly to implement his domestic agenda, much of which fell under an umbrella of programs collectively known as the Great Society, a broad initiative that included civil rights legislation, employment training and community development programs, education legislation, and the great Medicare and Medicaid programs that provided medical care for the elderly and for welfare recipients. It was the most extensive federal program since the New Deal, and in creating it Johnson declared a "war on poverty." Louis Martin, a member of Johnson's administration, suggested that the Great Society would "lift the floor of our middle class and the ceiling for thousands of deprived and disillusioned Negroes. It is the hope for Negroes in America." Clarence Mitchell was less convinced, describing it as an "adequate blueprint for improving conditions" but was certain that its success would depend on action rather than promises.[100]

One of the main legislative ambitions on the civil rights agenda was to deal once and for all with the problems blacks faced in registering to vote, particularly in the South. Although the Civil Rights Acts of 1957, 1960, and 1964 had all made some attempt, they were not strong enough to counter southern resistance. Despite combined and individual voter registration drives by the NAACP, SCLC, SNCC, and CORE, blacks in the most belligerent southern states still had to undergo various tests expressly designed to ensure they would not qualify for the electoral register. The US Commission on Civil Rights, in its hearings on voter registration held in Jackson, Mississippi, found that the county registrars in the state continued to discriminate against blacks through such devices as the state poll tax and literacy tests.

Wilkins argued that the civil rights groups and the president had been hesitant in fighting for stronger voting rights provisions in the 1964 Civil Rights Act out of fear that the legislation would meet the fate of its 1957 predecessor. He also suggested that Johnson wanted to assess how the provisions of the act were implemented before embarking on another major legislative battle. Certainly, the president had made scant reference to voting rights in his 1965 State of the Union address, other than two lines promising to eradicate barriers to voting, and made no mention of the subject in his inaugural address, even though getting black Americans onto the electoral rolls was one of Johnson's primary motivations in driving through the 1957 Civil Rights Act and continued to be an objective of his administration, if not an immediate concern. However, as Wilkins said, "The South gave us no time for a breather."[101]

In January 1965, in an effort to galvanize support for voting rights, SCLC led a demonstration in Selma, Alabama. The city was the county seat of Dallas County, an area that provided an appalling and vivid illustration of the paucity of black registration in some parts of the South: at the time of the demonstrations, of the 9,530 citizens registered to vote, only 335 were black—just 2 percent of the eligible black population—in a county where blacks were in the majority.[102] The demonstrations continued throughout February despite the brutal actions of Jim Clark, the local sheriff, and his posse of state troopers and local police. When a state trooper fatally shot Jimmie Lee Jackson, a young black man who was protecting his mother from an assault by another trooper during a night march, a confrontation between the civil rights activists and Alabama's segregationist governor, George Wallace, appeared inevitable. SCLC announced that, in defiance of Wallace's orders to desist, a march would take place from Selma to Montgomery, a distance of fifty-four miles, on Sunday, March 7, a day that would quickly become known as "Bloody Sunday."

As the marchers crossed the Edmund Pettus Bridge on the outskirts of Selma—without Martin Luther King, who was preaching in Atlanta on this Sunday—they were met by dozens of armed troopers who used tear gas, clubs, and horses to subdue the marchers when they refused to disperse.[103] As the police charged at the protesters, one witness reported hearing a gunshot; then a cloud of tear gas was released, and police began beating the marchers with nightsticks.[104] The situation was further inflamed when a white activist and Unitarian minister, James Reeb, was beaten to death by a white mob in Selma while taking part in a second march two days later.

Johnson made full use of the horror by introducing voting rights legislation. The president called Wilkins the day before addressing a joint session of Congress and told him that he would propose "a voting rights law that would redeem the bloodshed of Selma—and make sure it didn't happen again."[105] Even before the third march had taken place, Johnson used the events at Selma as a moral challenge to Congress in his speech: "The Constitution says that no person shall be kept from voting because of his race or his color. We have all sworn an oath before God to support and to defend that Constitution. We must now act in obedience to that oath."[106]

To ensure that the bill would not languish at committee stage or become trapped by a filibuster, Johnson told the assembly,

This time, on this issue, there must be no delay, or no hesitation, or no compromise with our purpose. We cannot, we must not, refuse to protect the right of every American to vote in every election that he may desire to participate in. And we ought not, and we cannot, and we must not wait another eight months before we get a bill. We have already waited 100 years and more and the time for waiting is gone. What happened in Selma is part of a far larger movement which reaches into every section and state of America. It is the effort of American Negroes to secure for themselves the full blessings of American life. Their cause must be our cause too. Because it's not just Negroes, but really it's all of us, who must overcome the crippling legacy of bigotry and injustice. And we shall overcome.[107]

Wilkins called the speech "a moment at the summit in the life of our nation . . . I had waited all my life to hear a President of the United States talk that way. And, at that moment, I confess, I loved LBJ."[108]

Disgusted with the violent images from Selma that were displayed across the world's newspapers and televisions, thousands of people throughout the United States joined in protests, marches, rallies, and vigils to support the Alabama protesters. Wilkins joined the call for federal troops to support the marchers in Selma as they prepared a third and final attempt to cross the Edmund Pettus Bridge.[109] When a federal judge issued an injunction against the proposed march, Wilkins accused the government of being a "partner, even if temporarily, of the Wallace storm-trooper machine." Although Johnson's attorney general, Nicholas Katzenbach, claimed later that it was he rather than the president who was hesitant about sending in federal troops, the Alabama state guard, which had been federalized, was on hand to maintain order when the fifty-mile march to Montgomery finally began on March 21, this time with King leading the procession.[110]

Wilkins joined the marchers for the last four miles but chose to stand back and let those who had walked all the way from Selma lead the way into the capital. He then joined other civil rights leaders and celebrities to address thirty thousand people at the capitol building.[111] King spoke eloquently, promising that blacks "are on the move now and not even the marching of mighty armies can halt us," while the crowd enjoyed the warm spring weather. The event inspired Wilkins to unusually emotional rhetoric: "This historic march is one more evidence that in this first Emancipation year we have been busy building a house—not one made with hands. A house for our spirit, once bowed down, but now tall and free."[112] The event had a tragic conclusion, however, when a white woman from Detroit, Viola Liuzzo, was shot dead by Klansmen while giving a lift to Leroy Moton, a young black activist who had been helping Liuzzo transport protestors back to their homes and schools after the march. Liuzzo was a member of the Detroit branch of the NAACP, and her murder left Wilkins with a "poisonous anger." Nevertheless, he recognized that the deaths of Jimmie Lee Jackson, James Reeb, and Viola Liuzzo "dotted the final i's and crossed all the t's on the Voting Rights Act. With martyrs, Congress found the strength to move forward."[113]

With his stirring address, and the images of Selma still in the nation's consciousness, Johnson's instruction to his attorney general in drafting a voting rights act was simple: "I want you to write the goddamnedest toughest voting rights act that you can devise."[114] Katzenbach did exactly as ordered and submitted the boldest civil rights legislation since Reconstruction. The bill prohibited the use of discriminatory tests to prevent voter registration and applied to all elections. But it was boldest in its expansion of federal action to ensure voting rights. Among its revolutionary provisions was a "trigger" mechanism whereby the Department of Justice was authorized to send federal examiners into counties where the overall (black and white combined) registration or turnout for the 1964 presidential election fell below 50 percent of eligible voters. Any states or counties caught by the triggering mechanism would have to seek permission from the Justice Department prior to making changes to its voting laws. The Act would also suspend literacy tests and prohibit the use of a poll tax as a requirement to register to vote.[115]

Wilkins acknowledged that these far-reaching provisions went further than any previous legislation had on this issue, but he was still not satisfied and argued that the proposed bill was "not enough."[116] Speaking before the House Judiciary Committee in his capacity as chairman of the LCCR, and thus representing a broad coalition of groups that had far greater lobbying strength than the NAACP on its own, Wilkins asked that all poll taxes be abolished and that the trigger mechanism be amended to launch with a black registration rate of less than 25 percent rather than 50 percent of overall voters, in order to widen the area covered by federal examiners.[117]

The poll tax had always been a particularly contentious issue for the NAACP. Although the Twenty-Fourth Amendment, passed in January 1964, outlawed the tax for federal elections, Wilkins argued that some states and counties still used it as a barrier for local elections and that a provision to ban the tax for all elections should be incorporated in the legislation. However, as Manfred Berg points out, a federal law prohibiting the poll tax on a state and local level could be seen as "constitutionally suspect," and the Johnson administration was reluctant to fight this issue and risk damaging the bill's progress through Congress.[118] Lee White assured Wilkins that the Johnson administration's stance on the poll tax issue did not differ from that of the NAACP and that "the question is solely one of the best route to the objective." White went on to say that it would be a mistake, however, to insist on a complete ban on the poll tax, as it might delay "early passage of a thoroughly effective voting rights bill."[119]

Given the weight of public sentiment, and Johnson's very strong support, the Voting Rights Act was approved by 333 to 85 in the House and 77 to 19 in the Senate. Johnson signed it into law on August 6, 1965.[120] That the more sweeping provisions survived intact was cause for celebration, as was the fact that, for once, the final bill was even stronger than the legislation originally proposed to Congress. The LCCR noted that even if the final version did not contain an outright ban on the poll tax, "there is a provision that will ring the death knell for that shameful assessment."[121] That provision gave authority to the attorney general to bring a suit before the Supreme Court challenging the constitutionality of the poll tax. The Voting Rights Act was the culmination of a historic year for civil rights legislation, beginning with the Civil Rights Act of 1964. As historian C. Vann Woodward wrote in the *New York Times:* "It was as if the first Reconstruction had been endowed with the Fourteenth and Fifteenth Amendments, the Reconstruction Acts, the Freedmen's Bureau, the Civil Rights Acts and the Ku Klux Klan Act by one session of Congress."[122]

There is no doubt that without the moral imperative of Selma, the fight to enact such radical legislation would have been significantly harder. However, the role played by the LCCR, Wilkins, Mitchell, and the

NAACP was important in ensuring that the legislation was not diluted. True, the political climate had become so much more conducive to the idea of federal action on civil rights that Katzenbach later minimized the role the LCCR played in the passage of the Voting Rights Act, arguing that the LCCR was "not so badly needed for this bill and thus had little effect on its outcome."[123] However, Katzenbach's comments underestimate the legacy of the LCCR's efforts in 1964 in helping to forge—and support—a coalition that could defeat the many obstacles put in the way of civil rights legislation by southern foes and their allies, and that established a legislative path that eased the way of the 1965 bill. And Lee White thanked Wilkins for the "excellent work being done by the Leadership Conference on Civil Rights in securing support for the voting rights legislation."[124]

The Voting Rights Act eliminated the most egregious examples of discriminatory actions that prevented black registration and clearly contributed to a significant rise in black voter registration. By 1969, according to Steven Lawson, approximately three-fifths of eligible black voters in the South had registered to vote. Even intractable Mississippi recorded an impressive increase in the number of black voters: the figure shot up to almost 60 percent in 1968 from a lowly 6.7 percent in 1964. Of equal importance was the effect on the number of blacks holding public office: by 1975 over twenty cities, including Detroit, Raleigh, Wichita, Newark, and Tallahassee, had black mayors, and there was a significant increase in the number of black officials serving on city councils.[125] The Act marked a moment where, as Wilkins described, "the civil rights movement seemed to be at the very apex of its power." Unfortunately, the factions and infighting among the civil rights groups was destroying the coalition, as whispers and rumors of backstabbing, power-grabbing, and other manifestations of discord grew louder.

One of the more damning rumors was that, in a meeting with Cartha DeLoach, the head of the crime records division of the Federal Bureau of Investigation (FBI), Wilkins had offered to encourage Martin Luther King to retire from the movement. However, there is scant evidence of such an offer. Much of the ammunition for these allegations stems from a meeting with Wilkins and DeLoach at the end of 1964, when a row had erupted between J. Edgar Hoover, the FBI's director, and Martin

Luther King. Hoover had called the civil rights leader "the most notorious liar in the country" in response to accusations King allegedly made concerning the FBI's failure to respond to complaints made to its agents in Albany, Georgia. King responded with dismay at Hoover's remarks and denied he had made the specific allegation, but emphasized the Bureau's ineffectiveness in protecting civil rights workers and investigating crimes perpetrated against them.

Through its extensive and intrusive surveillance of King, the Bureau had acquired evidence of King's affairs, and Hoover was threatening to make the evidence public, which could prove a disaster at a time when the momentum for even more powerful civil rights legislation was stronger than it had ever been. DeLoach claimed that during a meeting, which Wilkins had called to discuss the possible exposure of King's infidelities by the FBI, the NAACP leader said he "personally did not mind seeing King ruined," but that if these affairs were exposed, the civil rights movement would be damaged, probably beyond repair.[126] While Wilkins was certainly ambitious and disliked King, it seems unlikely that he would have suggested anything as potentially disastrous to the movement as attempting to oust the SCLC leader; and DeLoach's reports, which are often factually inaccurate, provide sketchy evidence. If anything, they reinforce Wilkins's defense. David Garrow and Kenneth O'Reilly are among those scholars who doubt DeLoach's account, arguing that Wilkins's version of events was closer to the truth, not least because nothing further was done about Wilkins's alleged offer.[127]

Johnson's advisers were well aware of the competition between the civil rights leaders, and particularly between King and Wilkins, but they were keen that Wilkins's position not be damaged. According to Steven Lawson, Katzenbach recommended that the president not attend a banquet in King's honor at the end of 1964 because of the "power struggle" in which, the aides claimed, King and Wilkins were said to be embroiled. The attorney general warned Johnson that his attendance might "elevate King" over Wilkins, who was drawn ever closer to the Johnson administration.[128] Indeed, in April 1965 the State Department asked Wilkins to undertake a series of engagements in Paris, Berlin, and London on the subject of race relations. During the trip Wilkins spoke to students, officials, and local media on America's progress in civil rights. On May

Day, he delivered a message from Johnson to a crowd estimated at about 400,000 in Berlin. Tailoring his comments to the international audience, which may not have been well informed about the inequalities in schools, jobs, housing, and voting rights, Wilkins repeated several salient and shocking statistics. But he also described what he saw as a crucial philosophical shift at work in the United States. He shaped his address by emphasizing three broad areas: the role of government, the assistance of white Americans, and "the relatively untold story" of black Americans in the fight for full equality, using his favorite device of mixing historical and contemporary examples to make his points.

Wilkins was a firm believer in the American way of life. He could recite a litany of appalling and egregious acts visited upon black Americans, and yet, to the State Department's relief, still speak with genuine faith and optimism about the steps his country was taking to address discrimination. Quoting from Johnson's speech to Congress earlier in 1965, Wilkins told his European audiences that, "the US government is dealing out in the open, all errors and all successes in full view of the world—with the delicate and emotional and ages-old problem of race and color." Wilkins was unable to resist some rhetorical flourishes however, ending with: "I suggest that this often shocking, often heartbreaking and always thrilling struggle of the black American and of his country should compel the attention and active interest of all men everywhere who dream of a formula for a world of men upright, in both body and spirit, in the dignity of freedom."[129] Not surprisingly, his trip was regarded as a great success by State Department officials, who felt that Wilkins had done much to put "alarming headlines into a better perspective" and helped to "clarify a facet of life . . . which has engendered much criticism" of the United States.[130] Still, given Wilkins's resentment of Martin Luther King—who had visited Berlin six months before Wilkins—he must have been less than pleased with the comment of *BZ*, a German newspaper, that "after the man of sensational actions and headlines, the man of persistent, detailed work came to Berlin."[131]

Shortly after Wilkins's return from Europe, his dream of freedom took one step closer to reality when, on June 4, 1965, President Johnson gave the commencement address at Howard University. The speech, which would come to be viewed as one of the president's finest, leaped ahead of the familiar commitment to ensuring equal rights. Instead, Johnson laid the foundation for affirmative action and changed the framework of the establishment's debate about what would be necessary to secure true equality, by acknowledging that freedom of opportunity was not enough to remedy the inequalities suffered by generations of black Americans.

Wilkins was prepared for Johnson's comments because shortly before making the speech, Johnson had called Wilkins to talk about an "all-out assault on the problems of race." It was a surprising subject for discussion, even for a president who had already demonstrated more commitment to the plight of black Americans than any since Lincoln; and the Howard speech drew fulsome praise from Wilkins, who was awarded an honorary degree from the university that same day.[132] In half an hour, Johnson laid out a new national plan of action for civil rights. He acknowledged that taking down what he called the "barriers to freedom" could not resolve centuries of discrimination and listed a number of statistics that illustrated the wide economic gap between blacks and whites. A large part of the reason for this gap, he argued, was the disintegration of the black family: "For this, most of all, white America must accept responsibility. It flows from centuries of oppression and persecution of the Negro man. It flows from the long years of degradation and discrimination, which have attacked his dignity and assaulted his ability to produce for his family."[133] To address these problems and help strengthen the family unit Johnson announced that he would hold a conference to develop to "help the American Negro fulfill the rights which, after the long time of injustice, he is finally about to secure."[134] In practical terms, this meant equal employment opportunities, improved housing and neighborhoods, equal access to education, and better welfare and social programs that supported the sick and the needy.

The Howard speech provided the theme of the NAACP's annual conference in Denver, which took place at the end of June 1965. Wilkins told delegates that the president "took the civil rights crusade beyond the opportunity stage."[135] Many delegates, however, expressed dissatisfaction with the Johnson administration, particularly over the rise in black unemployment and the perceived inadequacies of Title VII, the fair employment provision of the Civil Rights Act, which went into effect in June 1965. The NAACP's labor secretary, Herbert Hill, was among the most publicly critical of the Johnson administration's antipoverty program, arguing, "We must shed the illusion that there is a war against poverty. There is merely a BB shot against poverty."[136] Hill claimed that his view was shared by "many of the more than two thousand delegates at the NAACP convention [who] have a 'feeling of disillusionment' with the poverty program and therefore have their doubts about Title VII."[137] There was certainly much work to be done. Unemployment figures released by the Bureau of Labor Statistics around the time of the convention showed that nonwhite unemployment rates had increased by almost double in comparison with white rates between 1947 and 1962. Although those figures preceded the civil rights legislation, they nevertheless painted a bleak picture about the inequalities the act would have to address.[138]

Johnson's speech at Howard University relied heavily on a report by Daniel Patrick Moynihan, the assistant secretary of Labor for Policy Planning and Research.[139] The study, which still provokes controversy, examined the alleged collapse of the black family and its effect on the economic problems of black society. Moynihan argued that irreparable harm was being done to the black community by prolonged high unemployment and the absence of a stable family structure, which perpetuated a cycle of poverty. Moynihan's emphasis on the disintegration of the black family in the ghetto, the prevalence of female-headed households, and the correlation he found between those factors and the decline in household income attracted accusations of racism later in 1965. His report, although initially well received, proved increasingly controversial over the next six months, in large part because the Watts riots shifted the parameters of debate on the subject of black urban poverty and scared the Johnson administration and some white liberals who had thus far supported the movement. (As James Patterson points out, however, much of the debate surrounding Moynihan's report failed to accurately report his emphasis on unemployment as the primary cause of the plight of urban blacks.)[140]

Unlike some of his peers, including Whitney Young, Wilkins supported much of what Moynihan said; and, when a damning critique of the report by William Ryan, a white psychologist and civil rights activist, was published in *The Crisis,* Wilkins wrote to Moynihan, saying, "My opinion of the Ryan piece and of similar reasoning is well known to my immediate associate here . . . It is a silly and sinister distortion to classify as racist this inevitable discussion of a recognized phase of our so-called race problem."[141] As Moynihan later argued, "For just the reason that things were going so well, this was also the moment of maximum danger." By this he meant that, with all the attention focused on the South, little was being done, or recognized, about the scale and depth of problems facing blacks in the North and that trouble, as Moynihan said, "was in the offing."[142] Wilkins, in retrospect, agreed. "The day the President signed the Voting Rights Act, it looked as if we were bringing to an end all the years of oppression. The truth was that we were just beginning a new ordeal."[143] While the legal framework supporting segregation and disfranchisement had finally been dismantled, the picture for many black Americans was as bleak, if not bleaker, as it had ever been. The disparity between black and white unemployment, income, and education had increased since the *Brown* ruling had promised a brave new world of integration. Blacks held only 15 percent of professional, managerial, clerical, or sales positions compared with 44 percent of whites.[144]

One scholar, Thomas Pettigrew, a research psychologist who studied racism and intergroup relations, estimated in a report published in 1965 that, if one considered employment gains made by black Americans in the ten years between 1950 and 1960, it would take until 1992 for blacks to reach a proportional representation among clerical workers, until 2017 for professional positions, and until 2730 for business managers and proprietors.[145] Pettigrew attributed this disparity to several factors: the disproportionate number of black workers affected by technological innovations in manufacturing; the exclusion of black workers from labor organizations in key industries; discrimination in training programs and apprenticeships; and the high levels of unemployment among the young in the ghettos. These factors helped identify what came to be known as "institutional racism," by which organizations built in discriminatory practices that prevented access by minority groups to, for example, bank loans or employment training.[146] Unlike individual racism, which was obvious and, by the mid-1960s, becoming socially unacceptable, institutional racism was, and is, systemic, often subtle, and embedded within an organization's practices—a problem that would require a sustained and sophisticated approach to tackle.[147]

One aspect of life for black Americans that caused frustration, resentment, and anger was the attitude of law enforcement officials. Whether north, south, east, or west, blacks had to contend with brutality, bullying, and intimidation from the very group that was supposed to protect and serve. While terrible living conditions, economic hardship, and the absence of opportunities for advancement created the tinder, an incident involving the police often provided the spark for violence, particularly in urban communities. This proved to be the case just five days after the Voting Rights Act was signed, when a seemingly minor dispute between two young black men and a highway patrolman in the Watts area of Los Angeles provoked four days of devastating riots across approximately forty-five miles of the city. At least thirty-four people were killed and four thousand were arrested, with property in the area sustaining many millions of dollars' worth of damage. The riots were widely condemned by government officials, the media, and the general public.[148] However, Watts's impact on the civil rights movement was even more devastating than the smoldering rubble of ruined shops and houses. The NAACP dispatched several local officials, including Leonard Carter, the NAACP's field director in California; Edward Warren, president of the Association's Watts branch; and Norman Houston, president of the Los Angeles branch. Despite earning praise from city officials for playing a part in restoring order, in reality they could do little.[149] The riots were the dramatic—and highly visible—antithesis of nonviolent direct action and a clear sign that a sea change in the movement was under way. As Moynihan said, Watts "threw the civil rights movement entirely off balance."[150]

Wilkins was horrified by the riots and condemned the violence, saying, "Rioting and looting must be put down with whatever force is required. This is the first necessity toward any resolution of the problem involved."[151] But he then examined the causes, not least the historical legacy of white racism. "The blind craziness of the roving Negro mobs," he stated, "was created by the blind craziness of white people over, at least, the past hundred years."[152] He cited the passage of California's Proposition 14, which repealed the state's fair housing law, as an important contributory factor. Wilkins recognized that the Watts riots would force the civil rights movement to juggle two battles: on the one hand, they needed to ensure enforcement and compliance of federal civil rights legislation in the stubborn South; on the other, they had to find a solution to alleviate the problems of the ghettos in the North and West. Unfortunately, Wilkins later confessed, "No one was really prepared with a strategy or workable program," including the NAACP.[153]

Roy Wilkins and his sister Armeda, circa 1904. (Courtesy of the Humphrey School of Public Affairs, University of Minnesota)

(Above) Wilkins's home on 906 Galtier Street, St. Paul, Minnesota. (Courtesy of the Humphrey School of Public Affairs, University of Minnesota) *(Below)* Wilkins and his high school baseball team. (Courtesy of the Humphrey School of Public Affairs, University of Minnesota)

Roy Wilkins at around fifteen years of age. (Courtesy of the Humphrey School of
Public Affairs, University of Minnesota)

(Above) Mechanic Arts High School Bicycle Club. (Courtesy of the Humphrey School of Public Affairs, University of Minnesota) *(Below)* Working as a dining car waiter on the Northern Pacific's North Coast Limited. (Library of Congress)

Wilkins in workman's disguise during the 1932 Mississippi levee investigation. (Library of Congress)

Displaying a hangman's noose sent to the NAACP's national headquarters from Florida, circa 1959. (Library of Congress)

Roy Wilkins and Medgar Evers picketing a Woolworth's department store in Jackson, Mississippi, June 1963. (Bettmann/CORBIS)

Roy Wilkins with Joseph Rauh (far left), Whitney Young (second from left), A. Philip Randolph (second from right), and Walter Reuther (far right) of the United Automobile Workers at the March on Washington, August 1963. (Library of Congress)

Wilkins rests during a meeting at the White House, January 1964. (LBJ Library; photo by Yoichi Okamoto)

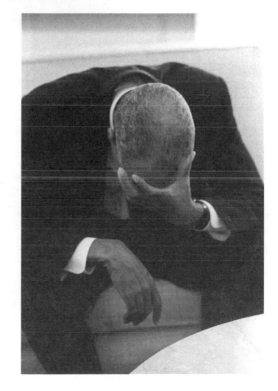

Wilkins and President Lyndon Johnson, August 1965. (LBJ Library; photo by Yoichi Okamoto)

Meeting of the Special Advisory Commission on Civil Disorders, July 1967. Left to right: Roy Wilkins, Governor Otto Kerner (chairman), President Lyndon B. Johnson. (LBJ Library; photo by Yoichi Okamoto)

6

A Crisis of Victory

The passage of the Voting Rights Act coincided with Wilkins's tenth anniversary as head of the NAACP. Under his watch the Association's general income had tripled; membership had increased from 240,000 at the end of 1954 to 455,150 ten years later, with a high point of over half a million members in 1963; circulation of *The Crisis* had risen by 200 percent; and the staff had expanded from 68 to 125.[1] The Association had seen the passage of momentous pieces of civil rights legislation, survived the best efforts of white resistance to wipe out the Association in the South, and also—so far—the challenges posed by the SCLC, SNCC, CORE, and other groups. But it almost seemed as if the Association's best days might be behind it. Despite its success, it was still in a precarious financial position, there was concern about the decline in membership, and the organization's direction was in a state of flux.

The decline in membership had serious financial implications and demanded urgent attention. Wilkins blamed the fall in membership numbers on changes to its fund-raising program, where less emphasis was being placed on door-to-door solicitations, but he also argued that a "mistaken belief that the war against racial discrimination is over and everyone can relax" was exacerbating the problem.[2] Membership levels had fluctuated dramatically over the years, making it difficult to make long-term financial and strategic plans. The Association was almost always in a precarious financial position; but because it was wary of increasing membership fees, revenue from memberships was never going to be sufficient to cover the organization's operating costs unless it increased its base by a significant number. Even following 1963's record membership levels, the NAACP

ended the year with a deficit of approximately $300,000. Life member-
ships, which cost $500, helped to some degree, but in the mid-1960s
these made up only about 3 percent of total membership.

The split with the Inc. Fund had also taken its toll on funding at
a time when the legal implications of many direct-action protests put
significant pressure on the Association's coffers. In addition, neither contributions to the NAACP nor many of the expenses incurred in its work
were tax deductible, thus adding still more pressure on an already strain-
ing system. To address these problems, general counsel Robert Carter
proposed a new entity to the Internal Revenue Service (IRS) that would
have tax-deductible status and therefore be much more attractive to foundations, corporations, and large-scale philanthropic donors. Following
the IRS's approval, the Special Contribution Fund (SCF) was created in
1964 to allow tax-deductible contributions to the NAACP to be made
through the SCF. Donations to the fund could be used for litigation (including bail bonds), voter registration, and public information programs.
In fact, the only elements in the NAACP's program that could not be
funded through SCF contributions were the Association's lobbying activities. Applying lessons learned from the painful split from the Inc. Fund,
Wilkins ensured that the SCF was entirely controlled by the NAACP's
board and executive director.

Income from the Special Contribution Fund, which became fully
operational in 1965, contributed around one-third of the Association's
budget in its first year. Appealing to large corporate donors and philanthropic foundations was a departure for Wilkins, who disliked fund-raising outside of the Association's membership—possibly as a result of the
NAACP's past experience of working with donor organizations, where
money was given under certain terms and conditions that sometimes did
not fit with the Association's way of working or its broader goals. Nevertheless, even without much effort from Wilkins, the SCF's tax-deductible
status began to attract large, regular donations from individuals and corporations. Foundations too began to dig into their pockets. In 1967, for
example, the Ford Foundation donated $300,000, which allowed the
NAACP to expand some of its most important programs.[3]

There were plenty of demands on this new influx of cash. The complexity of the problems requiring the NAACP's attention, not least bail-

ing out protestors in Mississippi, demanded significantly more funds than were available in its accounts: the NAACP estimated it would need a budget of at least $1.5 million in 1965 in order to maintain operations at existing levels.[4] The SCF helped to some extent in that the additional funds allowed the Association to expand its field staff, more than a third of whom were occupied in specialized work, such as education workshops, leadership training, and youth work, rather than general branch work, which made much better use of the Association's extensive branch structure and, in fact, belatedly followed the recommendations of the Lennon/Rose survey carried out in 1963.[5]

The long, hot summers of 1964 and 1965 were stark reminders that the Civil Rights and Voting Rights Acts, momentous as they were, would do little to address, at least in the short term, many of the problems facing black Americans. For Wilkins, there were worrying signs that the president was distancing himself from the civil rights issue. Johnson was frustrated by what he saw as ingratitude from the black community and encouraged Wilkins to do what he could to call for a concerted effort to bring a halt to the demonstrations and disturbances.[6] Even without the riots and demonstrations, however, the war in Vietnam was claiming much of his attention. Wilkins, for his part, was slow to recognize the growing disquiet about US involvement in Vietnam among his own constituency. Rumblings began in April 1965, when the NAACP branch in Flint, Michigan, drew up a resolution urging President Johnson to find a peaceful solution to the conflict in Vietnam and withdraw American troops from the country. The branch criticized the United States's self-appointed role of "international policeman" and issued a sly aside that decisions were being taken by a still unrepresentative Congress.[7] The resolution drew a swift and stern rebuke from the NAACP head office. John Morsell warned branch leaders in no uncertain terms that the officers concerned could not be "unaware of the controversial nature" of their position and that they had no right to promote this view as an NAACP policy without the approval of the NAACP convention. Gloster Current went as far as to revive old fears of Communist infiltration when he suggested that the Flint resolution was prompted by a left-wing element and warned against branches becoming involved in "left-wing shenanigans."[8]

Although the Flint resolution was an early indication of unhappiness about the Vietnam War among NAACP members, even at that stage it represented the strength of members' feeling in other branches. The national office received numerous letters of protest from the general public, NAACP members, and branch leaders asking what the Association was going to do about the war and what was believed to be a disproportionate number of black Americans who were being drafted and killed, which the Department of Defense claimed was due to the higher proportion of black soldiers serving in combat units. Wary of losing the support of the president by criticizing US policy in Vietnam, Wilkins refused to condemn the war and avoided any attempt to link the growing peace movement with the civil rights movement. By August 1965, however, Wilkins could no longer ignore the dissent. He told White House aide Bill Moyers that he was spending a considerable amount of time in "keeping the 'peace in Vietnam movement' from becoming too big a factor in the civil rights movement."[9]

In an attempt to halt the protest, he hid behind bureaucratic loopholes. When a resolution about the war in Vietnam was passed during the NAACP's 1965 convention, Wilkins refused to consider any resolution on the issue because the NAACP was a civil rights organization. He then issued a statement saying that, "in the absence of an authorizing resolution, units of the Association may not participate in the anti-war demonstrations." He could not, of course, limit individual participation, but any members who participated in peace demonstrations in their own right were prohibited from implying any Association support.[10] Nevertheless, a growing number of members disagreed with his view and rejected his refusal to see any connection between Vietnam and the wider civil rights issue. Still, the NAACP's leaders were not about to lose any bargaining chips by getting involved in the unfamiliar and murky world of international politics.[11] Wilkins believed that the political bartering system was crucial to achieving legislative goals, and the recent riots had exasperated the president and eroded support among white voters. With midterm elections approaching, Johnson needed to retain that white support, and, as Whitney Young told Martin Luther King, "Johnson needs a consensus . . . if we are not with him on Vietnam, then he is not going to be with us on civil rights."[12] It was an unsavory deal. Historian Manfred Berg uses the harshest terms to describe Wilkins's stance: "In essence, the NAACP secretary was demanding that black men fight and die in Vietnam so that civil rights leaders could put their 'loyalty, heroic service and sacrifice . . . on the bargaining table.'"[13]

The NAACP was not the only organization to be shaken by antiwar sentiment among its members. Opposition to Johnson's foreign policy was also forcing the various organizations within the fragile civil rights coalition apart. In January 1966, Sammy Younge, a US Navy veteran and SNCC worker in Alabama, was murdered for attempting to use a whites-only restroom. In response, SNCC issued a statement that accused the American government of bearing responsibility for Younge's death as well as the deaths of people in Vietnam because, in the case of the former, it failed to uphold American law and, in the latter, it was pursuing a policy of aggression that violated international law. To the Johnson administration's fury, SNCC called on eligible Americans to resist the draft and instead work in the civil rights movement or human rights organizations.[14]

Wilkins was quick to disassociate the NAACP from the SNCC statement. In his weekly newspaper column, he said that the statement had been made on behalf of a single organization and should not be considered representative of the rest of the movement, or of the opinion of the majority of black Americans.[15] Wilkins asserted that the weight of public opinion was for military intervention in Vietnam, pointing to strong popular support by black and white Americans shown in opinion polls—and ballot boxes—for Johnson and his Vietnam policy.[16] This was true—for a time. Shortly before the 1966 midterm elections Johnson saw his approval ratings leap by ten points, to 56 percent, despite or possibly because of an intensification of bombing in Vietnam following a concerted campaign to defend his foreign policy. But public opinion, and certainly that of the NAACP's members, was turning against the war.[17]

Adding to Wilkins's fury were comments from SNCC's leaders questioning the value of the legislative victories of the civil rights movement. Certainly, the complexities of the problems in urban ghettos demanded a new response from civil rights leaders. Daniel Patrick Moynihan summed up the problem: "They [black Americans] now have enforced legal rights as never in their history, but they remain terribly weak in economic and social terms—a situation that is, if anything, more conspicuous in the face of a booming, full-employment economy now entering its seventh year of unbroken expansion."[18] The economic questions raised by the urban riots presented the NAACP with a challenge of staggering complexity. The NAACP had always tackled employment and economic issues primarily in terms of discrimination and legislative redress; but, as August Meier and John Bracey argue, the Association's traditional activities were not adequate to deal with the consequences of centuries of economic inequality and racial oppression.[19] Herbert Hill was as effective in his area, labor relations, as Clarence Mitchell was on Capitol Hill and had done much to tackle employment discrimination and put pressure on labor unions into opening up their chapters to black members.[20] However, the NAACP did not have a clear and comprehensive strategy for expanding employment; indeed, the civil rights movement could do little to reform the economy in the absence of government intervention.

President Johnson's announcement in early 1966 that his administration would continue to fund his Great Society programs while at the same time fund the escalating war in Vietnam was a relief to the Association, but civil rights began to decline in importance for the administration. Nevertheless, in April 1966 the president sent a new civil rights bill up to Capitol Hill. The bill aimed to ban discrimination in the sale and renting of houses—an issue of enormous importance to blacks across the United States. It also would mandate an end to discrimination in the selection of federal and state juries and allow the attorney general to initiate suits to force the desegregation of public facilities. The new bill was a sign that the administration had not completely abandoned civil rights and that it acknowledged there was still much work to be done.

Shortly after the proposed legislation was sent to Congress, the White House conference on civil rights finally took place. The violence in Watts and the backlash against Moynihan's report had prompted the president to postpone the grand civil rights conference that he had first promised in his Howard University commencement address the previous year. In the months leading up to the conference, Wilkins had attended several planning meetings. These meetings were marked by heated discussions about everything from the program to the invitation list. Over the course of the planning sessions, the emphasis of the conference changed. A businessman, Ben Heineman, rather than a civil rights leader or politician, was appointed conference chairman; and of the 2,500 attendees at the

conference, there were more business leaders and local government officials than national politicians or representatives from civil rights groups.[21]
The White House was determined to avoid the kinds of confrontations
and challenges seen in the planning meetings, with the result that there
was less substantive discussion than many observers wanted. Nevertheless, according to a historian of the conference, the event marked a frag-
mentation of the liberal coalition behind Johnson's Great Society and the
political impetus behind integration.[22]

SNCC was not represented at the conference, which it had boycotted
in protest of Johnson's policy in Vietnam at the instigation of its militant
new leader, Stokely Carmichael, who had recently ousted John Lewis as
the head of the organization and who represented the ideological shift
toward separatism within SNCC.[23] Wilkins was confronted with this new
philosophy barely two weeks after the White House conference. Once
again, Mississippi provided the battleground. In January 1966, Vernon
Dahmer, a former president of the Hattiesburg branch of the NAACP,
was murdered when a petrol bomb was thrown into his home in retaliation for his promise that he would receive poll tax payments at his grocery
store and pass them on to local officials as part of the voter registration
process. As a protest against violence of this kind, James Meredith—who
had had an ambivalent relationship with the NAACP since his attempt
to enroll at the University of Mississippi in October 1962—began a
220-mile "march against fear" from Memphis, Tennessee, to Jackson,
Mississippi, to challenge the pervasive atmosphere of fear among black
Mississippians.[24] Neither the NAACP nor any other civil rights group had
any involvement in Meredith's action, which was foolhardy, confused,
and courageous; but on the second day of his march, when he was shot
and injured by a sniper, Wilkins and other leaders rushed to his bedside
in a Memphis hospital.

Gathered around Meredith's hospital bed were Wilkins, King, Carmichael, Whitney Young, and Floyd McKissick, James Farmer's more radical
successor at CORE, who conferred about how to best to continue Meredith's protest. Wilkins argued that the march should be a show of support for the 1966 civil rights bill that was then working its way through
Congress. Carmichael differed in almost every way from leaders like
Wilkins and Young and was in no mood to defer to them. Not surprising-

ly, Wilkins was vehemently opposed to using the march for any criticism of Johnson and was more than willing to withdraw the NAACP's support from the march if there was no assurance that it would not be a forum for attacks on the president.[25] He was also disturbed at SNCC's insistence that white participation be drastically reduced and that a Louisiana-based group known as the Deacons for Defense and Justice be used to protect marchers along the route.[26] The Deacons advocated armed self-defense, and SNCC's insistence on their participation was a clear rejection of the philosophy of nonviolence. Nevertheless, King agreed to march with SNCC. Wilkins and Carmichael exchanged angry words that ended with the SNCC leader suggesting that it was time for Wilkins to retire and write his memoirs.[27]

Carmichael later admitted that his aim was to alienate Wilkins and Young to the point of dissuading them not to take part in the march and to isolate them from the rest of the group. King's participation, by contrast, was vital, in part because of the media attention he attracted but mainly because Carmichael hoped that King's involvement would pull him inevitably to the left of the movement.[28] King's increasing identification with the peace movement was already having that effect; but, thanks to the Meredith march, the contradictory aims of the left and right wings of the movement, which had previously been able to coexist, were forced irreparably apart. The arguments across Meredith's hospital bed destroyed any possibility of compromise and forced SNCC and the NAACP in particular to take diametrically opposed views on separatism and, increasingly, on whether to fall in step behind the president's foreign policy in Vietnam.

Before the march resumed SNCC and CORE released a manifesto that set out the parameters by which the march would be conducted. The march would be a "massive public indictment and protest of the failure of American society, the government of the United States, and the state of Mississippi to deliver equal rights." To obtain those rights, the signatories called upon the president to take action on several counts: to send voting examiners into the Deep South states; to order the Justice Department, the FBI, and US marshals to enforce existing laws to protect civil rights activists; to strengthen the 1966 civil rights bill to include the automatic application of the jury provision; and to fund an "adequate budget and program" to improve the lot of blacks living in northern ghettoes.[29] Wilkins and Young both refused to sign the document.

In a statement Wilkins drafted but never issued, he reiterated that the march should have primarily been a show of support for pending civil rights legislation and voter registration. However, as SNCC's demands echoed those of the NAACP, Wilkins's reaction can only be attributed to his personal animosity toward Carmichael and his rejection of what he viewed as criticism of President Johnson inherent in the manifesto. An initial draft of the NAACP's recusal, in which Wilkins stated, "We cannot be a party to a personal attack when the target should be the sprawling bureaucracy of government itself," certainly supports that supposition. Wilkins's fury at the contretemps with Carmichael led him to complain of the difficulties in cooperating with other civil rights groups. "The whole business showed the NAACP again how difficult it is to have genuine co-operation, on an equal responsibility basis, with groups that do not have the same commitments and which may very well be pursuing certain goals that have nothing to do with civil rights at all." In the statement that was finally released to the press, Wilkins's comments were far more tempered, shifting the emphasis onto the supposed lack of clarity around the objectives of the march. However, he took the opportunity to disparage the concept of black separatism, stating, "the first draft [of the manifesto] properly indicated the weak enforcement of the new civil rights laws, but did not specify school integration or the wiping out of employment discrimination. These two items involve integration, and one organization already has announced that it was through with integration."[30]

Although Wilkins publicly offered lukewarm support of Meredith's objectives, he abhorred Carmichael's separatist rhetoric. He had rejected Marcus Garvey's espousal of black nationalism years before, and his views had not softened in the intervening years: Wilkins firmly believed that black Americans should demand—and receive—full equality within American society, not outside. Still, Wilkins knew that it would be almost impossible for the NAACP not to participate in the march. He conceded in a statement to members that those who wished to take part in the march were free to do so. "Such a matter concerns a man and his deep personal feelings and the decision must be a personal one," he noted, leaving the unfortunate branch officers to interpret what exactly that might mean. He was no less ambivalent in a press release, stating that the NAACP supported the objectives of the march "as set forth by James Meredith" while making no mention of the new objectives set out by Carmichael.[31]

Wilkins used his newspaper column to further distance himself and the Association from the march and its new aims. "Meredith wanted to persuade people to use the ballot. Instead, 'tough talk' is being used. Meredith wanted to take a little time so that all could move forward together. Instead, such movement as is taking place is separate and suspicious."[32] When, at the conclusion of the march in Jackson, SNCC and CORE banned Charles Evers from addressing the final rally, Wilkins was incensed: "Apparently his signature on the 'manifesto' was more important than his brother's life blood for a cause about which others were yelling slogans and delivering orations."[33] Wilkins's fury had not dissipated in the brief period between the end of the march and the NAACP's annual convention. In a memorandum to delegates he complained of a litany of financial exploitation and deceit inflicted upon the NAACP by other groups.[34] But he reserved the full force of his anger for a denunciation of both the rhetoric and the philosophy of Black Power.

Carmichael had first used the slogan "Black Power" publicly at a meeting in Greenwood, Mississippi, toward the end of the "Meredith March" in late June 1966. It had an immediate and electrifying impact on the civil rights movement and redefined the public vocabulary of race relations.[35] It also demanded a new response from Wilkins, and his reaction has become one of the defining features of his leadership. Prior to Carmichael's remarks at Greenwood, Wilkins had planned to use his speech at the NAACP's annual conference to talk about poverty programs, but the debate about Black Power provoked him into taking a different line. He used his address to make his views clear: "In the transition period of the civil rights movement 1966 is developing into a critical year . . . For the first time since several organizations began to function, where only two had functioned before, there emerges what seems to be a difference in goals."

He then went on to define in the harshest, most uncompromising way his views on Black Power. "No matter how endlessly they try to explain it, the term 'Black Power' means anti-white power. In a racially

pluralistic society, the concept, the formation and the exercise of an eth-
nically-tagged power means opposition to other ethnic powers, just as
the term 'white supremacy' means subjection of all non-white people. In
the black-white relationship, it has to mean that every other ethnic power
is the rival and the antagonist of 'Black Power.' It has to mean 'going-
it-alone.' It has to mean separatism." And separatism, Wilkins argued,
offered little to the disadvantaged but the chance to "shrivel and die. . . .
It is a reverse Mississippi, a reverse Hitler, a reverse Ku Klux Klan. Black
Power . . . can mean in the end only black death."[36]

His speech was the clearest explanation of the philosophy that had
guided his work in the Association for almost forty years. He told delegates, "The end was always to be the inclusion of the Negro American, without racial discrimination, as a full-fledged equal in all phases
of American citizenship. The targets were the barriers, crude or subtle,
which blocked the attainment of that goal."[37] As part of that ambition,
Wilkins promised that the focus of the NAACP's program would be the
"power and majesty of the ballot," fair employment, the elimination of
residential segregation, and the desegregation of public education. He
made it clear that the Association was not going to be persuaded to join
the more militant groups in "fancy capers for the sake of capers . . . in this
unsettled time when shifts are the order of the day and when change is in
the air, we can sail our NAACP ship 'steady as she goes,' with more drive
to the turbines, more skill at the wheel."[38]

A series of polls published during this period serve the claims of both
the Black Power activists, who were vociferous in their disdain of what
they considered to be the malleable commitment of white liberals involved in the civil rights movement, and Wilkins's eagerness to disassociate the mainstream movement from proponents of Black Power and
later from the antiwar protests on the grounds that militant activism was
driving away white support. It was clear that by late 1966 the tide of
public opinion was turning away from civil rights demonstrations. One
survey reported that 85 percent of whites felt that demonstrations were
damaging the black cause. In the same survey, when whites were asked
whether, if they were in the same position as blacks, they would feel justified in demonstrating, 53 percent said yes in 1963, compared with 37
percent who disagreed. By 1966, the figures were almost reversed, with

50 percent saying demonstrations would not be justified and 37 percent suggesting they would.[39]

When the 1966 civil rights bill failed to pass, Wilkins laid the blame for its defeat squarely on Black Power rhetoric and the ghetto riots.[40] He particularly resented accusations that the NAACP pandered to white supporters or was out of touch with the majority of blacks. One particularly stinging rebuke came from James Meredith. Although Meredith was no follower of any particular philosophy, his views commanded the attention of the press. In an article for the *Saturday Evening Post,* Meredith called the Association "the 20th-century house Negro" for every American president and added, with a particularly vicious sideswipe, "It does not command the emotions or respect of most younger Negroes, and the older Negro is becoming more and more disenchanted."[41]

Even more damning, Meredith drew a clear distinction between the civil rights movement, which he described as a collaboration of both upper- and middle-class blacks and white liberals, of which the NAACP was a part, and the "Negro movement," which he argued was represented by a pride in black culture and traditions and with which the NAACP was most definitely not connected.[42] Wilkins was quick to refute Meredith's accusation that the NAACP was simply a "house Negro" for the Oval Office by citing its differences with every president since the Association's formation in 1909. He also challenged Meredith's assertion that the NAACP was not a mass Negro organization by citing the number of black office holders within the organization and the number of grassroots branches it could lay claim to.[43] The new generation of activists argued that Wilkins and his ilk had squandered their political capital on civic rights at the expense of economic advancement, and for that group Wilkins represented an unacceptable accommodation to the white power structure.

A poll of blacks living in urban ghettoes—the constituency that had yet to see the benefits from legal and legislative successes—highlights Wilkins's irrelevance to this group. Researchers asked 496 black men who were arrested during the 1967 riot in Detroit to list their favorite black leaders. Martin Luther King led the poll by a wide margin, followed some way behind by Stokely Carmichael, with Adam Clayton Powell, Muhammad Ali, and Malcolm X sharing lower ratings. Roy Wilkins was not mentioned at all. Prisoners in Detroit might not have formed any part of Wilkins's support base, but the results suggest how removed he was from the urban working class despite a network of NAACP branches that was almost unmatched by any other group.[44] The Association was active—often militantly so—in many urban areas outside the South. Nevertheless, Wilkins always appeared to be more uncomfortable dealing with the unemployed of the Detroit, for example, than with the unemployed of rural Mississippi.

The political will to tackle the problems of racism waned as riots wreaked havoc in thirty-eight cities from Philadelphia to San Francisco during the summers of 1966 and 1967. Wilkins issued an "alert" to branches in an attempt to quell the riots during the summer of 1967: "Don't just be against riots; be active in preventing them." He then listed several things people could do, such as lobbying local political leaders to demand jobs, particularly for black youths; more play areas and community activities; and better policing. "Talk Turkey, yes," Wilkins urged. "But do turkey, too. Keep the Summer (and fall) cool."[45] Because of the correlation between poor housing and urban violence, Wilkins had warned the government that it faced a tough choice about either enforcing a nondiscriminatory housing policy or facing more violence in the ghettoes when the provision dealing with housing discrimination was diluted as the 1966 civil rights bill worked its way through Congress. He later recalled, "The federal, state and local governments were mincing and maneuvering as the Senate had done over the 1966 Civil Rights Bill, and the separatists and firebrands were practicing the most impassioned kind of racial brinkmanship. The climate was more dangerous than I had ever seen it."[46] In the face of high black unemployment, housing discrimination, and continued police brutality, Wilkins warned, "Real trouble could erupt at any time. Negroes are determined to use any feasible weapon to halt the murders."[47]

By this time, Wilkins was being attacked from within his organization as well as from outside. The Young Turks, a group that had already caused dissension among the board in 1964 and 1965, saw an opportunity finally to get rid of Wilkins and replace him with a younger, more dynamic leader. Jack Tanner, described by one reporter as the "sultan of the Young Turks," had begun his campaign against Wilkins in 1964, and he made a blatant call for Wilkins to step down in a speech to the NAACP Area Conference in California in 1965, which Wilkins managed to deflect by engaging the support of senior board members, such as Bishop Stephen Spottswood. Tanner took up the fight again in 1966. In an attempt to demonstrate the isolation of Wilkins and the NAACP's leadership, he argued that part of the NAACP's annual convention, ideally a board meeting, should take place in Watts and be open to any who might wish to attend. Wilkins and Spottswood swiftly dismissed the suggestion with the argument that Tanner's changes would be a logistical nightmare and would be of only symbolic importance.[48] At the convention, Tanner also attacked the complexity of the process by which board members were elected, arguing that it was designed to thwart dissension. Even worse, he apparently described the convention as "LBJ controlled" and called upon members to make use of Black Power to advance their own interests.[49]

Tanner failed to generate much response among the NAACP's members, who were, on the whole, moderate and inclined to favor stability over revolution. Nevertheless, the media attention paid to Tanner's comments compounded a growing impression that the civil rights coalition, and the NAACP itself, was in chaos. Although Wilkins denied a permanent split within the movement, it was evident that the coalition was disintegrating. When Wilkins appeared on *Meet the Press* with Carmichael and Young in August 1966, journalist Carl Rowan asked whether there was a "crisis of leadership" within the movement, in which "a host of warring civil rights groups [were] each pursuing its own special interest." Wilkins dismissed any hint of discord, suggesting that differences of opinion were inevitable and that he did not foresee any split in the movement.[50] But the argument about Black Power had forced each group into taking a position to the political left or right even within their own organizations.

The Johnson administration became increasingly concerned at the growing rift. The president's Special Counsel, Harry McPherson, said the movement was facing a crossroads: one road would lead to violence and suppression while the other route, although uncertain, involved working within the system. The fact that McPherson was unable to define the purpose of the less militant route indicates how quickly and how far the more militant groups had redefined the parameters of the movement.

This, McPherson pointed out, placed Johnson in an uncomfortable position in his support for civil rights: "The very fact that you have led the way toward first-class citizenship for the Negro, that you are identified with his cause, means that to some extent, your stock rises and falls with the movement's."[51] But within the Johnson administration, consensus on how to deal with the rising anger of black Americans was hard to find. Attorney General Nicholas Katzenbach disagreed with McPherson's suggestion that Johnson should meet both established and new black leaders, arguing that "whatever appeal the extreme groups have is based upon arguments that the older leaders are the pacific captives of the administration-establishment and are thus not sufficiently militant." He also questioned McPherson's suggestion that the president meet with younger leaders. Katzenbach argued that the NAACP and SCLC could set up "militant but peaceful" groups of young people to compete with SNCC, saying, "If some of the Young Turks in the NAACP were to join in a new youth organization, it might take considerable pressure off of Roy Wilkins in the immediate future."[52]

The violence became personal for Wilkins when a conspiracy by an extreme militant black group, the Revolutionary Action Movement (RAM), to assassinate Wilkins and Young was uncovered by New York police. It is difficult to establish how serious a threat this was. Wilkins himself appears to have been unperturbed. Speaking at a news conference he said, "Apparently anyone who doesn't believe in machine guns is an Uncle Tom. I would like to find out why killing me would help their cause. I'm a harmless guy and I can't see why anyone would want to kill me. Assassinations don't solve anything. It's kind of a silly approach."[53] He had been less sanguine about the prospects of his safety a few months earlier, when he was scheduled to speak in several towns across Mississippi in late 1966. Just before he left, he placed a case in a drawer at his house to be opened only if he did not return from Mississippi. The case presumably contained money to help Mrs. Wilkins through a period of probate, as well as a note to be given to his wife in private.[54]

Forcing the breach even wider was the debate between those who advocated merging the peace and civil rights movements and those, like Wilkins, who were firmly against any such thing. In April 1967 Martin Luther King gave an impassioned and powerful speech in New York City in which he made a clear moral case for merging the two issues. First, he recalled the optimistic prospects offered by Johnson's poverty program; but then came Vietnam.[55] King echoed arguments made about black participation in earlier conflicts, saying, "We were taking the black young men who had been crippled by our society and sending them eight thousand miles away to guarantee liberties in Southeast Asia which they had not found in southwest Georgia and East Harlem." King called on the government to declare a unilateral cease-fire to open the way for a negotiated peace. He also called upon religious leaders to protest the war through words and actions, and, in the case of ministers of draft age, through choosing to become conscientious objectors. "Every man of humane convictions must decide on the protest that best suits his convictions," King asserted, "but we must all protest."[56]

In his weekly newspaper column, Wilkins took issue with King's words. He argued that the SCLC leader's views were not representative of most black Americans, who, he said, were interested more in solving problems in their own country. He rejected the idea that the rising cost of the war in Asia meant that civil rights programs would or should be put aside and pointed to the experience in World War II, when much the same argument was made but black patriotism was rewarded by the desegregation of the armed forces and the creation of the FEPC.[57] While Wilkins's argument was weak, and there was some evidence that black Americans were ambiguous about American involvement in Vietnam, a Harris poll taken in May 1967 showed that around 25 percent of blacks agreed with King's stand on Vietnam.[58] This was hardly a groundswell in public opinion, but it was a significant minority and could be seen as a sign of growing support in light of the short amount of time that had elapsed since King's speech and the survey's being taken. Papers in the NAACP archives suggest a significant increase in interest on the part of NAACP members about the Association's stance on the Vietnam War.

King's remarks forced the NAACP into finally declaring its position on Vietnam. For the most part, the Association simply reiterated the "separate issues" doctrine that Wilkins had spoken of before; but as hard as the NAACP defended its separate issues argument, it was difficult to ignore the growing public anger at the discriminatory way black soldiers were treated at every level.[59] Black Americans were severely underrepresented on draft boards, with black members making up just over 1 percent of local draft boards and none in most of the southern states—a situation the Association tried to remedy with lawsuits in Mississippi and South Carolina.[60] Black inductees rarely qualified for college or occupational deferments and, in 1966, a significantly higher rate of white inductees failed medicals than black, although this disparity shrank by 1969. Project 100,000, a Great Society initiative introduced in 1966, which aimed to enroll 100,000 men who, because of physical or educational limitations, would not qualify for service under existing rules, attracted an influx of black inductees. This raised the proportion of blacks in the military from around 9 percent in 1964 to just under 12 percent by 1972, a larger proportion of which served in combat units. There was also a perception that there were a greater number of black casualties, which was certainly true in the early stages in the conflict. Black soldiers accounted for almost 20 percent of all combated-related deaths in Vietnam between 1961 and 1966, but in the later stages of the war that figure fell to around 12 percent.[61]

The division within what was left of the civil rights coalition was summed up in a report by Gloster Current in April 1967. "The extremists will stop at nothing to create havoc and confusion and involve Negroes, perhaps in rioting to create the impression that Negroes are tired of money being siphoned off for war purposes," wrote Current. Recognizing the political disparities now at work within the civil rights movement, Current told Wilkins, "Whether we wish to acknowledge it or not, we have a resurgence of the left such as we have not had since World War II. NAACP branches are going to be invaded and urged to get aboard the peace movement." In response, he suggested, the NAACP should "mount an offensive to give the American people the facts and to urge youth and Negroes in the communities to pay no attention to the fools. There ought to be an off-the-record meeting of the Negro press and key well chosen Negro leaders to decide how to deal with what seems to be in the offing."[62]

7

The Survivor

Wilkins was tiring of the fight. The continued unrest in the ghettoes, the foiled RAM plan to assassinate him, and the aggressive rhetoric left him feeling "violence well[ing] up around all of us."[1] He was now in his late sixties and had suffered with ill health intermittently for the past thirty years. Nevertheless, he still refused to consider retirement; he had resisted several internal attempts to remove him and had survived most of his detractors in other groups. But with no succession plan in place, questions were beginning to be raised about who should succeed Wilkins and what the NAACP's direction should be in the coming decade, a decade in which the next steps were far from clear.

His position as the establishment's favorite civil rights leader was cemented when Johnson asked him to sit on a presidential commission. Disturbed by yet more violence in the summer of 1967, Johnson established the National Advisory Commission on Civil Disorders to answer three questions: "What happened? Why did it happen? And, what can be done to prevent it happening again and again?"[2] Illinois governor Otto Kerner chaired the commission, and the president asked Wilkins to join the panel, which was made up of four congressmen; the police chief of Atlanta, Georgia; the mayor of New York; a businessman; a union leader; and the commissioner of commerce for Kentucky. All were considered moderates on civil rights; they were also all white. Wilkins was, in addition to being the only black person on the panel, the only one who had been actively involved in the civil rights struggle. As such, according to Nathaniel Jones, who was assistant general counsel for the Commission and later the NAACP's general counsel, Wilkins supplied a necessary firsthand perspective on the history and the realities of the black experience.[3]

The moderate composition of the group initially attracted criticism, particularly from the more militant wing of the civil rights movement, which doubted that a committee made up of these establishment figures could emerge with any recommendations of substance. But the panelists were appalled at what they discovered, and when the commission presented its report at the beginning of March 1968 it delivered a damning indictment of American society.[4] "Our nation is moving toward two societies, one black, one white—separate and unequal," a state of affairs for which the Kerner Commission blamed white society. "What white Americans have never fully understood—but what the Negro can never forget—is that white society is deeply implicated in the ghetto. White institutions created it, white institutions maintain it and white society condones it."[5] The commission's many recommendations included a stronger welfare system to help support black families in the poorest areas, the creation of two million new jobs, vocational training for the long-term unemployed, and the construction of six million affordable homes within five years.[6]

Civil rights leaders across the spectrum praised the commission's findings. Even CORE's Floyd McKissick was delighted. "We're on our way to reaching the moment of truth. It's the first time whites have said: 'We're racists.' Now's the time to seek some common truths." He also said that CORE considered the report to be such "an important moment in the history of this country, whites finally admitting racism, that we will have a full written response whereby there can commence a type of dialogue that never existed here before." Martin Luther King called the report's recommendations "timely" and congratulated Wilkins personally by saying that the pronouncement on white racism was "an important confession of a harsh truth."[7]

Unfortunately, there was silence from the White House. Johnson saw the Kerner report as a direct repudiation of his attempts to address the problems facing black Americans and was furious at the commission's findings.[8] He initially refused to receive a copy, and said publicly that he agreed with only some of its proposals, claiming that it needed more financial detail. For example, although no costs were listed in the report,

White House aides estimated that the proposal to create two million jobs would alone require an increase in the federal budget of approximately $6 billion, while enhancing Social Security along the lines recommended by the Kerner panel would require an extra $7–9 billion.[9] When Johnson remained silent, Joseph Califano, Johnson's senior domestic aide, urged the president to speak about the commission to show that he was serious about its conclusions and that he was not going to ignore the report.[10] Wilkins refused to be drawn into criticizing the president; he simply expressed regret that the president did not accept the report. But Johnson's implicit rejection of the commission's findings rendered the report almost useless.

On April 4, 1968, barely a month after the publication of the Kerner report, Martin Luther King was murdered in Memphis. Wilkins immediately issued a statement saying the Association was in "a state of shock" and, like many others, was "angry and bewildered." He suggested that a fitting legacy would be to speed up action on civil rights.[11] Stokely Carmichael, however, predicted more violence, pointing out, with some truth, that King was "the one man of our race that this country's older generations, the militants and the revolutionaries and the masses of black people would still listen to."[12] As news of King's death spread, riots broke out in more than one hundred cities across the country. The Army was called out to restore order in Chicago and Washington, while the National Guard was dispatched to police dozens of other cities. Wilkins attempted to calm the situation, saying, "If those blacks who are really angry will stop and think for 24 hours . . . violence would have been the last thing King would have wanted." But it was too late. By the end of the month, the riots had brought about the deaths of over forty people, caused over $45 million of damage, made nearly 5,000 people homeless, and put tens of thousands of troops on the streets of American cities.[13]

Several summers fueled by anger, impatience, and the increasing militancy of young activists had changed the face of the civil rights movement, and the NAACP was struggling to both understand and satisfy the new demands. Six weeks before King's death, Wilkins convened a small conference in New York City, attended by twenty-two distinguished black academics, journalists, businesspeople, and politicians to discuss the new landscape and the NAACP's position within it. It was not simply a matter of working out what the Association could or should do to help solve the problems that had given rise to such violent and bitter frustration or the rise of black militancy, but also how the NAACP fitted into a world where, at least financially, the government was the biggest organization now active in civil rights and foundations and businesses were developing their own civil rights initiatives. Conference participants were asked for their opinions on how the Association's program could be "sharpened up" to meet current and future needs.

Over two days in late February, the participants discussed the Association's internal structure, its programs, government activity in the civil rights area, and urban unrest. They arrived at an unequivocal conclusion: the NAACP must shift its concentration from the courts and Congress and instead become closer to the "the troops" on the ground. Rather than being a civil rights organization, the Association should become a "leadership organization" with a broader focus on alleviating the economic problems of urban blacks, while at the same time maintaining a civil rights role in rural areas of the South, "where it continues to be relevant."[14] Critics had long made similar observations about the NAACP, and the proposals from the February conference, if taken to heart, would require a fundamental change in the Association's strategy. But the acknowledgment that its current model was inadequate signaled a new awareness that change was needed. Wilkins could take some comfort in the passage of the 1968 Civil Rights Act, also known as the Fair Housing Act, which contained fair housing provisions that had been removed from the civil rights bill that had failed to pass Congress in 1966.[15] But even with several pieces of momentous legislation on the books, the moderate civil rights leaders were under pressure from newer recruits who were attracted by the militant rhetoric.[16]

By 1968 Black Power was stirring up even the NAACP's members. The Association's annual convention, under the theme of "Building and Using Power in the Ghetto," in Atlantic City in June of that year was the most disorderly in its history, taking place amid threats of protests, demonstrations, and even a rumor that Wilkins and the president of the local branch would be shot on the opening evening. On the penultimate day, the breach between the old guard and the Young Turks that had been brewing for some time broke to the surface when hundreds of delegates walked out of the convention hall in protest when a resolution to create an autonomous youth division was rejected.[17]

The Young Turks had been baiting Wilkins and the NAACP's board of directors for five years, prodding them, without much success, to re-create the Association as a more democratic, mass organization. Shortly before the convention, they formed the National Committee to Revital-ize the NAACP, which proposed a radical separatist agenda and, even more controversially, questioned whether the NAACP's goal of racial integration was still relevant.[18] Protestors disrupted the final day's pro-ceedings by sitting in aisles, shouting Black Power slogans, and holding placards with words such as "Uncle Tom"—all of which was captured by the camera crews filming the convention for the television news. But, although the group attracted much attention, they never managed to win enough support either among the NAACP's members or its board of directors; and, after an hour of disruption, a majority of delegates halted further debate on Black Power by voting to impose a limit on debates on that subject and also on antiwar resolutions.[19]

After this debacle, there were fears that the rift, if left unchecked, could damage the Association beyond repair. During the previous three years, some changes had already been made in the NAACP's activities to increase the focus on urban needs. For example, branches were encour-aged to develop community action projects to help develop leaders in in-ner city ghettoes, and black businesses were encouraged to pool resources so that they could qualify for federal contracts. In addition, shortly after the convention a home loan program was announced, with the aim of increasing the financing of home and business mortgages to urban blacks, along with the establishment of information centers in the ghettoes to help residents with a wide range of housing issues.[20] The Association also gradually shifted more resources from the South to the North so that eventually the allocation was evenly divided between the two areas.[21] Also, in June 1968 four additional youth members, elected by their peers, were added to the board of directors; and the number of white directors de-clined by almost half during the decade.[22]

Similar breaches were appearing in other groups, particularly CORE, which was going through a leadership battle and a financial crisis. Still, Wilkins was keen to maintain a semblance of unity with other groups and accepted an invitation to speak at CORE's annual conference in July 1968. His reception at the convention was polite but not warm and, because of the possibility of violence, dozens of security guards were placed in the hall and around the speaker. Wilkins was never going to agree with the group's separatist agenda, saying it would be "like asking a sprinkling Methodist to submit to a total immersion," but he did acknowledge that the NAACP and CORE shared some common goals, most notably in attacking economic problems and building strong black communities.[23]

Nevertheless, Wilkins increasingly found himself at odds with the rest of the movement. By the time party conventions took place—the Democrats in Chicago and the Republicans in Miami—at the height of summer 1968, the atmosphere, Wilkins recalled, was like "a season in the bunker."[24] When violence broke out in Chicago during the convention, exacerbated by the aggressive tactics of the local police in trying to quash any demonstrations, Wilkins condemned the protestors rather than the police, although the latter outnumbered the demonstrators by more than two to one. His rejection of Black Power, his continued ties to an unpopular president, and his refusal to join those who argued that the peace and civil rights movement should be united into a single protest group earned him sharp criticism from many quarters. Even the president recognized his predicament and offered to help by suggesting that Wilkins publicly call him a "sonofabitch" on the grounds that it would improve his position.[25]

In October, Wilkins and his wife left for a European vacation, but on his return, as his ship docked back in New York, he was immediately thrown into one of the most serious controversies that had faced the NAACP for some years. Lewis Steel, a young lawyer who worked with Robert Carter as part of the NAACP's legal team, had written an article for the *New York Times* magazine entitled "Nine Men in Black Who Think White." In the piece, Steel argued that the Supreme Court was far from being the champion of civil rights that a ruling such as *Brown* would suggest. Rather, he charged, the Court had been guilty of striking down only the "symbols of racism" while leaving the "ingrained practices" intact. He argued that the Court had frequently subordinated racial equality to white America's "fear of rapid change." Steel dismissed the *Brown* ruling as an instance of the Court's catching up with postwar changes rather than leading the way toward an equal society, and he accused the Court of being patronizing and overly cautious, even timid, in dismantling statutes the judiciary branch had itself put in place that prevented black Americans from enjoying full equality.[26]

Shortly before publication of his article, Steel showed proofs of it to Robert Carter, who in turn showed them to Henry Lee Moon and asked him to order dozens of reprints for distribution to branches. Unfortunately, some members of the NAACP's board of directors, who were meeting in New York the day after the article appeared, did not share Moon and Carter's good opinion of the article. In fact, they argued that it was a repudiation of everything the NAACP had achieved. Worse, as the author was identified as a member of the Association's legal staff, they feared it might appear that Steel's views were those of the NAACP. Therefore, they felt, swift retribution was required. The board voted to fire Steel, effective immediately, in what the Association's general counsel described as a "star-chamber proceeding" without consultation with Carter, Wilkins, or Steel himself, who was given no opportunity to explain or defend his actions. Carter immediately demanded that Steel be reinstated within the week or he would resign in protest. When the board either would not or could not rescind the dismissal (it was claimed that Carter had not allowed time for all board members to respond), and also refused to hold a meeting to discuss the matter, Carter accordingly submitted his resignation two weeks after the article was published, along with six members of his team. So began a very public and bitter exchange with the Association. The public feud was bad enough, but the mass departure of its entire legal staff was a potential disaster and left the NAACP with the worrying prospect of having a legal department but no lawyers.[27]

Wilkins sailed into New York harbor shortly after the row erupted and, although he thought the board had acted precipitously, he supported the decision anyway, consistently claiming that he had no power to overturn a board action. He could, however, have done far more to dispel some of the acrimony between the various parties. Despite the arbitrary action of the board, he offered no support to Carter and his team and brokered no peace among the warring factions. The folly of this became clear as the row quickly developed into a much broader debate about the NAACP's internal operations. The board's undemocratic behavior sat badly with many of the Association's branches, as well as with more than a few board members, many of whom were appalled at the board's reaction, which they viewed as a stifling of criticism and dissent. The chairman of the West Coast region went so far as to instruct the branches in his area to withhold funds and reports until the situation had been "corrected." As Wilkins told the board, the national office was "operating under considerable tension" because of the dispute. Matters took a turn for the worse, if that was possible, at the end of November, when Wilkins was served with a court order filed by three New York area branch presidents and a board member. This moved the row into the courtroom.

Steel's article also exposed a growing divide within the national office between the old guard, who believed in the NAACP's traditional methods, and those, often but not always younger, who saw the urban riots as an indictment of those methods. When Wilkins discovered that only two of the staff lawyers, Carter and Steel, either were or had been members of the Association, and that in fact one of the lawyers had refused to join the NAACP, he used the information to support his claim that the legal staff was "an almost completely indifferent or even hostile segment of the national office staff." Carter's team, meanwhile, had become closely involved in cases that challenged the "entire political and economic system of the oppression of black people," including the appeal of Martin Sostre, a radical black activist who had been falsely accused of drugs and arson charges and sentenced to forty-one years in prison, and whom the lawyers considered a political prisoner.[28] In a statement released alongside the resignations, the attorneys claimed that the board had fired Steel in an attempt to "check the moves of the legal team" in taking cases such as Sostre's, and Carter later claimed that Steel's firing was actually aimed at gaining control of the general counsel's office.[29] Nathaniel Jones, who became general counsel shortly after Carter's departure, said later, "It was a long time before the toxins in the air cleared."

The turbulent year of 1968 drew to a dispiriting close with Richard Nixon's election to the White House. Although Nixon had often supported civil rights, Wilkins feared that the Republican's victory presaged a return to the "atmosphere of the Eisenhower administration."[30] Johnson's support of civil rights had, as Johnson had correctly anticipated, fractured Democratic loyalty in the South, leaving a gap that the

Republicans were quick to fill. By campaigning on a states' rights and law-and-order platform, Nixon successfully wooed Strom Thurmond, the segregationist senator and former leader of the Dixiecrat faction of the Democratic Party who had transferred his allegiance to the GOP in 1964, and secured Thurmond's backing for his nomination at the party convention. During the campaign, Nixon proposed a program of "black capitalism," involving federal loans and aid to help black businesses, but made it clear that, if elected, his administration would not follow Johnson's example of investing billions of dollars in the cities.

Nixon invited Wilkins to the inauguration, but the NAACP leader chose to watch the ceremony on television. However, he grudgingly accepted an invitation to dinner at the White House shortly afterward, during which the president asked Wilkins to tell him if he did "anything wrong" on civil rights.[31] In the following months, Wilkins took the president at his word and proceeded to chide the Nixon administration at every opportunity. Wilkins met with the president shortly after his inauguration to discuss school integration and discrimination in federal contracts, employment, and housing. He publicly chastised Nixon for not moving quickly enough on several civil rights issues, and it did not take long for the already tenuous relationship to degenerate. When it appeared that the president was easing the deadline for school districts to integrate, Wilkins, his voice shaking with anger, told delegates at the NAACP's annual conference in Jackson, Mississippi, "It's almost enough to make one vomit."[32]

School integration was a particularly contentious issue. Fifteen years after the Warren Court handed down its judgment, compliance with the *Brown* ruling was still patchy. However, while the Nixon administration was hesitant at best to insist that states speed up the integration process, the Supreme Court issued several decisions that forced the issue. In 1968, in *Green v. County School Board of New Kent County*, the Court rejected the "freedom of choice" plan, by which pupils could in theory choose which school they wished to attend in their district, and ordered a "root and branch" effort to desegregate schools and gave school districts a number of factors by which they could ensure a racial balance in schools.[33] The following year, in *Alexander v. Holmes County Board of Education,* the Court ordered school districts to eliminate separate school systems immediately. The NAACP called the *Alexander* ruling "a death sentence for 'all deliberate speed.'"[34] Nixon encouraged compliance but refused to withhold federal funds from school districts and made reassuring comments to southern districts that his administration would not force integration. Nevertheless, with these unequivocal Supreme Court decisions, progress on school desegregation suddenly picked up pace. Within a year of the *Alexander* ruling, the percentage of black students enrolled in majority-white schools had risen to 33.1 percent, up from 23.4 percent in the 1968–1969 school year.[35]

The Supreme Court reaffirmed its support to speed up school desegregation in its ruling in *Swann v. Charlotte-Mecklenburg Board of Education* in 1971, which held that busing children across a school district was an appropriate remedy for de facto segregation, where schools remained racially imbalanced because of residential factors.[36] However, the seemingly endless round of school desegregation battles were leading many in the black community to question whether integration was necessary, or even desirable. In Atlanta, for example, in 1973, a city where black pupils made up around 80 percent of the public school population, over two-thirds of the city's schools remained segregated, albeit in some instances through choice. The failure of school integration in that city prompted the local NAACP branch to abandon its demand for a racially balanced school system. It settled instead for an agreement that no public school would have less than 30 percent black students. The branch also agreed that black teachers would be appointed to administrative posts in the school system, including the position of superintendent. The settlement infuriated Wilkins, who called it a "second Atlanta compromise," and he promptly suspended the branch for going against the Association's integrationist policy.[37] The move by the Atlanta branch, which was not alone in taking a pragmatic approach, could have instigated a debate within the NAACP about its position on integration; but Wilkins did not encourage any such discussion, arguably to the cost of the organization.

The action by the Atlanta branch was a progression of a debate that had begun to some extent in 1969, when the argument for or against black separatism had moved to college campuses. Demands by some black students for all-black courses and dormitories in California prompted a typically dismissive response from Wilkins. Drawing on the experiences of older African Americans, who had had segregation involuntarily imposed on them and were dealing with the legacy of that entrenched discrimination, he argued, "Racial segregation can be the means of plunging their race back behind the barbed wire of restriction, inferiority, persecution and death to both the spirit and the body. The black youth of today owe it to themselves to study the appalling effects of segregation. When one asks for a little bit of it in order to go off in a corner and counsel together, one asks for the whole lot."[38]

However, as Yohuru Williams argues, by the late 1960s, Wilkins's views on Black Power were in fact becoming more complex and nuanced. He would never advocate the idea of separatism, but saw some common ground in the economic and community programs established by groups such as the Black Panthers. He suggested an "exploratory conference" with the Panthers in the summer of 1969 to try and develop "some sort of strategy that will be effective even if used in only a few areas."[39] Wilkins was careful to emphasize that the invitation was a private suggestion and not formally endorsed by the NAACP, but he was keen to maintain some communication with the group. This discussion, unfortunately, never took place; but by the end of the year Wilkins found himself more involved with—and more sympathetic toward—the Black Panthers than any conference would have allowed.

Just before dawn on the morning of December 4, 1969, police raided an apartment occupied by Fred Hampton, chairman of the Illinois branch of the Black Panthers, and Mark Clark, another local Panther leader. In the gun battle that followed, Hampton and Clark were killed, four other occupants were seriously injured, and two policemen were wounded. The killings were widely condemned at home and abroad, but black Americans, for whom this attack was just the latest, and most bloody, in a series of brutal attempts by law enforcement officials to subdue black protest, were particularly angry. It was later discovered that out of almost one hundred shots fired, just one came from the occupants of the apartment. Hampton had been shot twice in the head at point-blank range, despite being unarmed and already wounded. Four days later, police in Los Angeles used similar tactics when more than 350 officers, including members of the newly formed paramilitary Special Weapons and Tactics (SWAT) team, descended on the local Black Panther headquarters in the early hours, hoping to take the occupants by surprise. However, the Chicago raid had put everyone on high alert and, although no one expected a full-scale paramilitary assault, the eleven Panthers inside the building were armed and ready to defend themselves. In the four-hour gun battle that followed it is remarkable that there were no fatalities and only eight injuries.[40]

Attacks like those in Chicago and Los Angeles prompted many questions about the legality of the police action. The Justice Department announced it would set up a task force to investigate the Chicago shootings, alongside an "unofficial" panel announced by six black congressmen and a small independent panel that was asked by his family to conduct a separate autopsy on Hampton. Many were skeptical, however, that an official investigation would be objective, and there was a disturbing sense that young blacks in particular distrusted the democratic process. In response to this, Wilkins and former attorney general Ramsey Clark formed an independent commission to look into the deaths of Fred Hampton and Mark Clark.

It took three years to complete the commission's investigation. The final report, *Search and Destroy,* published in 1973, managed to be both damning and inconclusive. The commission had no legal standing and therefore it avoided explicit accusations of guilt, but found that there was probable cause to believe that the attack on Hampton and Clark's apartment in Chicago "involved criminal acts on the part of the planners of the raid." The commission concluded that the raid violated the Fourth Amendment's guarantee against unreasonable search and seizures as well as several statutes of the United States Code. But, the report argued, the failure of the various grand juries that had been established to investigate the incident, and had consistently refused to return any indictments against the officials involved in the raid, meant the justice system had also failed Hampton and Clark.[41]

Part of the reason that the commission took so long to produce its final report was that it was privately financed including funds from the NAACP. Unfortunately, just as the commission began its investigation, the NAACP was facing perhaps the most serious financial crisis in its history. Money had always been tight, but adding to the pressure was its legal defense of twenty students in California who had been charged with approximately 2,000 disorderly conduct charges and a lawsuit brought by business owners in Port Gibson, Mississippi, for damages of $3.5 million from the loss of trade as a result of a boycott. The lawsuit tied up the Association's finances as it worked its way through the courts (it would not be resolved within Wilkins's lifetime) and prompted the organization to institute a number of cost-cutting measures to try and meet the increased financial burden. The membership fee was doubled, to $4, and this was partly responsible for the 100,000 drop in membership during 1970.[42]

The last weeks of the 1960s were difficult personally, as well as professionally, for Wilkins. In December 1969, he was diagnosed with a form of intestinal cancer, and although the prognosis was good and the treatment successful, his illness prevented him from taking part in several important meetings, including those of a presidential advisory committee to review and develop plans for an all-volunteer army to which he had been appointed earlier in the year. By this time, John Morsell had taken on more and more of the administrative and day-to-day running of the NAACP's operations, and it is his name, rather than Wilkins's, that frequently appears in the minutes of commissions and committees and on correspondence to and from NAACP members.

This second brush with cancer, twenty-five years after the first, led Wilkins to consider retirement. He put aside thoughts of stepping down, however, when, despite his disdain of the Nixon administration, he was asked to take up the role of elder statesman again. In addition to representing the United States at the first United Nations International Conference on Human Rights, in Tehran in the spring of 1968, Wilkins led a US delegation to Monrovia in 1972 and visited Italy and Germany to assess whether the military's desegregation policy was being successfully implemented. Shortly before traveling to Liberia, he visited South Africa, where his remarks at a press conference in Johannesburg caused some controversy when it appeared that he was opposed to a withdrawal of American businesses from South Africa.

Rumors and speculation about Wilkins's retirement had increased as he approached and then turned seventy in 1971, but they intensified in 1974, when chairman of the board of directors Stephen Spottswood died suddenly and was replaced by Margaret Bush Wilson, an attorney from St. Louis, who fully intended to persuade Wilkins to retire.[43] His other great ally, Arthur Spingarn, had died in 1971, and by the time Wilson took over many board members were equally keen to see a change of guard. Several journalists refer to Wilkins's increasingly halting speech during this period, some going so far as to suggest that it could indicate a neurological condition.[44] If that was the case, Wilkins had no intention of either admitting to it or giving in to it and, to the detriment of the organization he had served for so many decades, still refused to step down. Shortly before the 1976 annual convention began, he wrote to the board to say that he had discovered plans that he would be forced to retire at the end of the year. This, he argued, would break an agreement made in November of the previous year that he would retire in July 1977, and, although he described relations between himself and the board as "cordial," he also claimed that there was a "nudge" toward his retirement that had been "almost constant" since Spottswood's death.[45]

In an unusual move for one as reserved as Wilkins, he used his keynote address to the 1976 annual convention in Memphis to drum up support from the Association's members to lobby the board to allow him to stay on until the following year. The man who had so jealously guarded the NAACP's reputation—and his own privacy—suddenly accused some members of the NAACP's board of waging "a campaign of vilification" against him. His voice sometimes faltering, Wilkins claimed that he had been accused of dishonesty and feebleness. Aiming his attack at Margaret Bush Wilson, he said, "I suppose I should laugh when a woman who shows no knowledge of good administrative practices refers to my administration of the affairs of the NAACP as 'horrendous.' But how does one laugh when his heart is breaking?" He then said he had been encouraged by members to postpone his retirement until after the annual convention of 1977, which was scheduled to take place in St. Louis, his hometown, where, he told delegates, his parents had migrated to, where he was born, where his mother had died, and where his wife, Aminda, had been born. If the board did not allow him to do this and fired him, Wilkins said, he would call upon the members to let him represent them directly, presumably meaning outside the framework of the NAACP.[46]

The speech was extraordinary—not simply because Wilkins chose such a public forum but also for his apparent disloyalty to the Association he had led for so many years. Delegates were stunned and board members furious; one even accused Wilkins of killing the Association.[47] But the battle was not simply about an elderly leader refusing to leave the stage; it was also about the balance—or possibly imbalance—of power between the executive secretary and the board of directors. In theory, the board set policy and strategy and was the highest authority in the organization. In reality, however, since James Weldon Johnson's time, the power lay with the executive secretary (or executive director, as the role had been renamed). With a new executive director and a new chair of the board there was an opportunity to dilute the executive director's role, which Gilbert Jonas, head of the NAACP's national development program during this period, said had been protected by a board of directors that Wilkins had shaped over the years to echo his philosophy.[48]

The board claimed that Wilkins had originally agreed, in writing, to the publicly announced retirement date, but he countered this with a claim that any such document must have been altered, deliberately or otherwise, and certainly did not have his agreement. His emotional appeal in Memphis then placed the board in a difficult position and left little choice but to defer a decision to the next board meeting, due to take place in New York in early September. The dispute threatened to divide the organization. The crisis was averted when it was agreed that Wilkins be allowed to retire the following year, at the St. Louis convention, but that in the meantime he would hand over most of his administrative duties to Gloster Current and assistant director Mildred Roxburgh, ostensibly to allow Wilkins to concentrate on urgent issues, such as the Port Gibson lawsuit, which still hung over the Association. The solution suited both parties: Wilkins remained on the payroll until his retirement and maintained an emeritus position within the organization, while the board established itself as the authority of the NAACP. However, despite the hasty fix, no succession plan had been put in place, so the prospect for upheaval was still enormous.

The continuity of the NAACP's executive structure had been remarkable. There had only been three secretaries since 1920. Walter White succeeded James Weldon Johnson in 1931. Wilkins, of course, became secretary in 1955 following White's death and so provided an essential link in a chain that had been in place for almost sixty years, with all of the institutional memory and organizational culture such continuity carries.

However, Wilkins had spent many years jealously protecting his position from both internal and external challengers and appears to have given little or no thought to a life outside the NAACP and also no consideration about who might lead the organization when he was longer able to do so. John Morsell, the deputy director of the NAACP and Wilkins's right-hand man, might have been thought of as a logical successor—he was a highly skilled administrator and brought intellectual weight to the national office—but he lacked Wilkins's political touch and his ability to engage with the Association's members.[49] Morsell had taken on an increasing amount of executive responsibility and, given his closeness to Wilkins, would have continued leading the NAACP in much the same way. But Morsell died of cancer in 1974, leaving an enormous gap in the national office.

A "search and screening" committee had been appointed in January 1976 and was meeting even while the rumpus between Wilkins and the board continued. The committee took its commission seriously: Montague Cobb, its chairman, found analogies in the Bible, the works of Shakespeare and Robert Browning, and the lives of Christopher Columbus, Abraham Lincoln, and Galileo to illustrate the heavy responsibility in finding a suitable candidate for "one of the most challenging posts in the nation."[50] Nevertheless, the committee rose to the challenge and over the year carried out a thorough selection process, and by the end of July, sixteen candidates had been interviewed for the role. Three months later, that list had been cut down to five finalists, from which a final candidate was selected by secret ballot. Benjamin Hooks, a lawyer from Memphis who was the first black member of the Federal Communications Commission, was named as Wilkins's successor in November 1976 and took office on January 1, 1977.

Faced with a financial disaster after the Association was ordered to pay $1.25 million as part of the Port Gibson settlement, a huge fundraising drive had been launched, which had raised $1.8 million. Thus, at the annual meeting in January 1977, the outgoing executive director could, for once, announce a budget surplus. After such a bruising retirement battle, Wilkins's last year with the NAACP was spent being lauded and celebrated by members across the country. As Wilkins had insisted, his forty-six-year career with the NAACP ended at its annual convention in St. Louis where, unlike the previous year's gathering, the air was heavy with warm farewells and nostalgia, although Benjamin Hooks must have been less than pleased with Wilkins's promise to reporters that he would remain as a consultant and "hold Mr. Hooks's hand."[51] The celebrations began with a standing ovation on the opening night and ended with "Roy Wilkins Night," when various dignitaries paid effusive and emotional tributes to him. One board member even broke down in tears when offering her eulogy to the "Rock of Roy."[52]

Divisions and feuds were temporarily put aside as Wilkins basked in the praise, but could not temper his tendency to have the last word. In his address to delegates, he urged members to continue the fight for full integration and warned that the Association was becoming a "board-oriented organization, with a staff that does not seem to know whether it is headed right or headed wrong." It was vital, he said, that the executive director be "a strong leader, supported by an able board, which will set policy, advise and consent. Otherwise, he will be merely a hound dog for the people who run the NAACP."[53] Unfortunately, it was argued in some quarters that his refusal to retire sooner had allowed board chairman Margaret Bush Wilson to assume more power and therefore weaken the position of executive secretary.

Shortly before his retirement Wilkins was profiled by *New York* magazine, and his comments went some way to reflecting the philosophy that had governed his leadership at the NAACP. In the article, the young reporter, Orde Coombs, described an elderly and faltering man, defensive and tired at times, but with the occasional spark of an old civil rights fighter. Coombs challenged Wilkins on why he had refused to step down for so long. Wilkins refused to be baited and said that he was waiting to hand over the reins to "some young person whose competence I admired," implying that very few fit that criterion. Coombs then asked Wilkins to explain why his ambitions for a post-Wilkins NAACP remained relatively humble (a continuation of its programs, upgraded schools, open housing, and jobs). His response serves almost as a eulogy for his own philosophy, which to all intents and purposes was the same as the NAACP's: "We don't like to make a noise just for the sake of doing so, and that's why we have always attracted responsible Negroes. We have always had a theme, and that theme never has changed. We wanted integration without compromise from the state, and we still want it now. Our dreams never change." Nevertheless, something of the old campaigner rose up when he was asked what message he would like to give young blacks as he left the arena. "Protest," said Wilkins. "Never accept the status quo. Never accept injustice. Protest. Protest. Protest."[54]

For a man who had committed so much of his life and energy to an issue as consuming as the fight for equality, opportunity, and dignity, retirement would always have been difficult, and the nature of his last year at the NAACP left Wilkins bitter. A profile in the *Los Angeles Times* published the month after his final convention painted a bleak, sad picture of an embattled and lost Wilkins, a man who had cultivated an aura of isolation so successfully that it "was now more complete than he intended."[55] He worked on his autobiography with journalist Tom Mathews, which he said would keep him out of mischief in retirement, and continued writing his newspaper column until May 1980, during which time he offered opinions on subjects ranging from the television series *Roots* to the unhelpful rhetoric of Ronald Reagan. His last column was a response to a riot that had exploded in Miami when policemen accused of beating a black man to death were acquitted. He argued that the violence was the inevitable product of years of broken promises and "a disaffection with the American system" that had taken place after the racial progress of the 1960s had been wiped out by economic retrenchment in the following decade, leaving blacks "on a conveyor belt in reverse, going nowhere fast." The only way forward, he wrote, was through "jobs, education, decent housing and fair administration of the law" rather than violence, which would wipe out the residue of any progress.[56]

A year after leaving the NAACP Wilkins had to defend himself against accusations by the *Washington Post* that he had collaborated with the FBI to discredit Martin Luther King, a claim that was vehemently denied by Wilkins and disputed by SCLC leaders. The *Post* reported that "a black leader" had cooperated with the FBI to discredit King. Although it was assumed that this "black leader" was Wilkins, it eventually turned out to be someone unrelated to the civil rights leadership. Two years before the *Post*'s article appeared, Wilkins told a Senate Intelligence Committee hearing that he had simply warned the FBI that its determination to remove King from the public eye would damage the civil rights movement. Other civil rights leaders, including Jesse Jackson, who had been a close associate of King's, and Hosea Williams, the executive director of SCLC, spoke out in Wilkins's defense, pointing the finger instead at old FBI tactics of divide and rule. By this time, however, Wilkins was either unwilling or unable to defend himself publicly, and it was left to his wife, Aminda, to deliver a statement that called the report "pure fantasy and a damn lie."[57]

His health was already failing when he left the NAACP; after that, it declined quickly. In the spring of 1979 Wilkins collapsed near Madison Square Garden in New York City and was hospitalized for two weeks, during which time he was fitted with a pacemaker. He became increasingly frail, and by the time he traveled to Washington in March 1981 to present the Smithsonian Institution with his personal collection of memorabilia from the civil rights movement a stroke had left him unable to speak or walk. It would be the last time Wilkins was seen in public. He was admitted to New York Medical Center in August, again with heart problems, but his condition deteriorated and he died of kidney failure on September 8, 1981. Even in death, however, he was still able to provoke: his funeral was held in a predominantly white church, which caused some of the black clergymen in attendance to complain quietly, unlike a group of pickets outside the church, who were angry that Wilkins had been buried by a white funeral home rather than a black one. Wilkins was buried as he lived—preaching integration to the last.

Conclusion

The obituaries and eulogies that appeared after Wilkins's death spoke of his steady leadership; his quiet, calm, and reasoned persona; and his long dedication to the cause. Some made reference to his productive working relationship with President Johnson. Others referred to his early journalism and his arrest in 1932 as evidence that this urbane, reserved man had, at one point in his life, borne some of the marks of the firebrand activist. Of course there were the inevitable comparisons with Martin Luther King. One editorialist said that King was the heart of the movement, while Wilkins was its mind; another offered a similar observation when talking about the March on Washington, saying that although "the day belonged to the dreams of Martin Luther King, Jr., the agenda belonged to Roy Wilkins." Joseph Rauh, who worked with Wilkins at the LCCR, encapsulated the difference between the two leaders most succinctly: "I guess you can say Martin was the front man who changed public opinion. But Roy was the one who was able to use that shift in public opinion to bring about legislation and legal rulings that benefited blacks, as well as any number of other people. . . . Roy wasn't the . . . one out front. He was the one in the back who got things done."[1]

Unlike Martin Luther King, for example, Roy Wilkins was not sustained by a deep religious or philosophical belief, nor was he wedded to any particular political principle. His single guiding conviction was simply that integration was right and it was achievable, and his dedication to that conviction was all encompassing. The tools he had most faith in to achieve that aim—litigation and lobbying—demanded patience and tenacity as well as an instinct for politics and a willingness to play the long game. Wilkins was far more comfortable walking the corridors of power than demonstrating on sidewalks. In his view, the path to securing equal rights led from the White House at one end of Pennsylvania Avenue to Capitol Hill at the other, rather than the streets of Selma or Birmingham. Wilkins had a politician's grasp of congressional procedure, and he was able to judge which members of Congress were open to persuasion, which were vulnerable at an election, whose seats were safe enough to allow them some latitude, and which were beyond any coaxing. Working in collaboration with Clarence Mitchell, head of the NAACP's Washington Bureau, and Arnold Aronson, the secretary of the LCCR, the coalition devised a series of lobbying strategies that relied on a detailed knowledge of the intricacies of congressional power. He could exercise this knowledge within the LCCR with the support of a powerful and broad coalition.

Wilkins found his natural home at the LCCR: if he was a bureaucrat at the NAACP, the LCCR allowed him to be a strategist. The LCCR liberated Wilkins from the constraints and rules of the NAACP. The agenda of the LCCR was very specific: to secure civil rights legislation. It required no resolutions, no votes by members, and no approval by any board of directors; and the coalition reinforced Wilkins's belief that strength in numbers was of crucial importance in securing societal change. In fact, Wilkins often appeared more comfortable leading the LCCR than the NAACP. But the alliance with the LCCR also had benefits for the NAACP. August Meier and John Bracey, whose studies of the Association remain among the most comprehensive, argued that the NAACP's leadership of the LCCR marked a "radical transformation" of the Association's lobbying efforts, that it moved from a strategy that made use of personal contacts to one that mobilized the available resources of the many groups and organizations that participated in the LCCR's programs.[2] While Wilkins was reluctant to collaborate with other civil rights groups unless the NAACP was able to control the program, the LCCR allowed him to forge a broad alliance of sympathetic groups that supported the Association's goals and had no wish to dominate its program. It is understandable, then, that Wilkins was one of the driving forces behind the LCCR, and through his leadership the organization was able to gather together a powerful lobby of diverse groups, that collaborated to bring significant pressure on Congress to pass civil rights legislation.

If navigating the white power structure was his greatest skill, what was Wilkins's greatest failure? His nephew, Roger Wilkins, suggests that it was his failure to engage young people. This was borne out time and again throughout Wilkins's career, despite several instances early on, where he had attempted to persuade the NAACP's leadership to expand its youth activities. The Association certainly did not ignore the potential offered by younger members. It established its youth department in 1934, with a national officer to direct its activities. Those activities, however, were rarely developed specifically to attract young people; they were often simply adjuncts of adult programs. This remained the case even when direct-action protests, for which youth members provided much of the energy, began in 1960.

While Wilkins was difficult, complex, and often petty and demanding with colleagues and peers, the NAACP's members loved him. Perhaps this was so because, despite being a national figure, he appeared to lead a life that would be familiar to many middle-class black Americans. His salary was never large enough to allow a lavish lifestyle and, despite his fondness for sports cars and first-class travel, he lived modestly in an apartment in Queens, New York, and he made sure to maintain close contact with the membership. Until the late 1960s much of his time was spent traveling to branches across the country to meet with, cajole, and encourage members to do their duty by the Association, and when he died they turned out in the thousands to attend memorial services at branches from Memphis to Pasadena. They knew he was never going to waver in his commitment to integration—even when some may have wished otherwise.

Wilkins was a "long distance runner" for civil rights rather than a sprinter. Like the organization he led, he took the long view and waged a patient, sustained war against racism in the face of a social movement. Although Wilkins was hierarchical, conservative, and, at times, obstructive, he maintained two organizations that were important in translating the passion and anger seen on the streets of Montgomery, Jackson, and Birmingham into legislative victories that would confirm equal rights. It was all too clear that legislation or a favorable legal ruling on its own was no guarantee of compliance or acceptance, so the emotional and moral force of protestors such as the Freedom Riders, sit-in students, the Little Rock Nine, and those courageous marchers who walked across the Edmund Pettus Bridge provided the necessary leverage to hasten the pace of change and create an environment where that change became possible.

Wilkins, from his position as head of the NAACP and LCCR, was able to help craft legislation to act as a bulwark against the regressive forces that attempted to turn back the clock. The Voting Rights Act is one of the clearest examples of his success: the "preclearance" clause of the Act, which requires those counties that were most egregious in their attempts to prevent black voter registration to obtain Department of Justice approval of any changes to their electoral rules, is still in place. Attempts to impose stringent new registration rules for the elections in November 2012, while not necessarily based on race, can be challenged because of the Voting Rights Act. That this statute is on the books is thanks in part to Wilkins and his colleagues.

Maybe Wilkins's greatest legacy is the survival of the NAACP. Of the many groups that emerged during the civil rights movement, SNCC and the Black Panther Party no longer exist, and although SCLC and CORE are still active they are shadows of their earlier incarnations; only the Urban League could now be described as a peer. While the mere survival of the NAACP is not necessarily a tribute to Wilkins's strategic skills—organizational survival is a hallmark of both large corporations and political parties, whose fortunes rise and fall, often regardless of who is in charge—the NAACP, which celebrated its centenary in February 2009, is still organizationally strong and, after a period of upheaval, now appears to have a stable executive team in place. Wilkins might find some of the Association's activities—litigation, education, civic engagement, and youth programs—familiar; but its reach has in recent years expanded to include issues such as climate change and anti-obesity initiatives, and its membership has diversified from those working in and with local branches to online activists. Nevertheless, as Wilkins told delegates in his last speech to an NAACP annual convention in St. Paul, "There is unfinished business for us to take care of."

Acknowledgments

This book is the result of an idle question that occurred to me while I was completing my master's degree and simply would not be stilled: Why did the NAACP disappear from the narrative of the civil rights movement after such stunning victories as *Brown v. Board of Education*? Of course, it did not entirely disappear; but I was intrigued that the organization that had been home to Ella Baker, W. E. B. Du Bois, Medgar Evers, Charles Houston, Thurgood Marshall, and so many other dedicated, courageous individuals was now judged by a consensus of historical opinion to be, at best, old-fashioned and irrelevant. Once I had completed my degree, I began investigating civil rights history and eventually came across Roy Wilkins; and so began what finally became this book.

Writing is a solitary exercise; but, as with most endeavors, I have relied on the help of others to bring it to fruition. In particular, I am grateful for the patience, guidance, and knowledge of Professor Adam Fairclough, who wholeheartedly embraced my rather vague proposal for the doctorate that provided the basis for this book. He provoked, prompted, and guided me through the complexities of the civil rights movement, and I am eternally grateful that a scholar of his reputation was willing to give a rather unconventional student the opportunity to indulge her conviction that there must be something more to say about Roy Wilkins than simply that he was the bureaucrat of the civil rights movement. I have also been fortunate beyond all reason to have the help and guidance of Professor Brian Ward, who first became acquainted with an earlier version of this work while sitting on my PhD defense committee. He has since been an invaluable source of common sense and humor as the transformation from doctoral dissertation to published book took place.

Arriving at the University Press of Kentucky was also a moment of great fortune. My heartfelt thanks go to all the team, from design and marketing to editorial. The help and advice I received from Anne Dean

Watkins, Bailey Johnson, Donna Bouvier, and particularly Steven Lawson eased me through the tortuous process of creating a book. I am particularly grateful to Professor Lawson for his perception and his careful, detailed, and considered comments. I hope the result lives up to his expectations and repays his efforts. Thanks must go too to the patient readers for their invaluable comments. I am grateful that they were not only willing to give up their time to read the manuscript at various stages but also for their comments and suggestions. Again, I hope this book repays their diligence.

This book relies heavily on the magnificent archives available in American libraries, especially the Library of Congress, which houses the enormous NAACP archives as well as the papers of Roy Wilkins, Arthur Spingarn, and Thurgood Marshall, and so was fundamental to my research. It was always comforting to see familiar faces behind the desk of the manuscript reading room whenever I was lucky enough to be able to visit, and I am eternally grateful for the help of the staff in that great library. Thanks are due too to the staff of the Lyndon B. Johnson Library in Austin, Texas; the Moorland-Spingarn Research Center at Howard University; University of Cambridge Library; the British Library; the Beinecke Rare Book and Manuscript Library at Yale University; the Roosevelt Study Center, Middelburg, the Netherlands; Michael Popadiuk at the St. Paul city government; and Julie Lund of the Humphrey Institute at the University of Minnesota, who was generous both with her time and by providing photographs of Roy Wilkins. I am grateful for financial assistance from the Roosevelt Study Center, the Lyndon B. Johnson Presidential Library, and the British Association for American Studies. Thank you to these institutions for their generous grants, which allowed me to complete research that may not otherwise have been possible. Thanks also to Judge Nathaniel Jones, Jack Greenberg, and particularly Roger Wilkins for sharing their reminiscences and memories of Roy Wilkins.

A project that has taken as long as this book relies heavily on the goodwill of friends and family, and I have prevailed on both, testing the limits of their love and patience. My greatest debt is to them—particularly to my parents, Peter and Shirley Ryan; my sister, Nikki; and my dear friends Gary Bass, Roseanne Bonnano, Victoria Burnett, Diane and John Cain, Celia and Peter David, Celina Dunlop, Louise Fawkner-Corbett,

Daniel and Gaby Franklin, Veronica Hale, Nicola Heywood, Pat Kliman, Laura McHale, Robin and Noelle Parr, Sumaya Partner, Avril and Peter Riddell, Jill Robinson, Gillian Tong, Cheryl and Mike Whitbread, and Jane Williams. Over the years they have offered hospitality, a soothing glass of wine, cheerleading, broad shoulders, and a willingness to prod me through those last few pages. Thank you.

Notes

Introduction

1. See, for example, Carolyn Wedin, *Inheritors of the Spirit: Mary White Ovington and the Founding of the NAACP* (New York: John Wiley, 1998); Kenneth Robert Janken, *White: The Biography of Walter White, Mr. NAACP* (New York: New Press, 2003); B. Joyce Ross, *J. E. Spingarn and the Rise of the NAACP* (New York: Atheneum, 1972); and Denton L. Watson, *The Lion in the Lobby: Clarence Mitchell Jr.'s Struggle for the Passage of Civil Rights Laws* (New York: Morrow, 1990). Mark Tushnet offers the perspective of a legal scholar in *Making Civil Rights Law: Thurgood Marshall and the Supreme Court, 1936–1961* (New York: Oxford University Press, 1994), while Juan Williams offers a more biographical study in *Thurgood Marshall: American Revolutionary* (New York: Times Books, 1998). Charles Houston, the architect of the NAACP's highly successful legal department has been similarly—and surprisingly—neglected. Genna Rae McNeil's *Groundwork: Charles Hamilton Houston and the Struggle for Civil Rights* (Philadelphia: University of Pennsylvania Press, 1983) remains the definitive biography, although McNeil's book is now joined by *Charles H. Houston: An Interdisciplinary Study of Civil Rights Leadership*, a collection of essays exploring Houston's life and work edited by James L. Conyers (Lanham, MD: Lexington Books, 2012). See also David Levering Lewis's masterful two-volume biography of W. E. B. Du Bois, *W. E. B. Du Bois, 1868–1919: Biography of a Race* (New York: Henry Holt, 1993) and *W. E. B. Du Bois: The Fight for Equality and the American Century, 1919–1963* (New York: Henry Holt, 2000). The NAACP's legal department has deservedly been the subject of several books: Manfred Berg, *The Ticket to Freedom: The NAACP and the Struggle for Black Political Integration* (Gainesville: University of Florida Press, 2005); Darlene Clark Hine, *Black Victory: The Rise and Fall of the White Primary in Texas* (Columbia: University of Missouri Press, 2003); Mark Tushnet, *Making Civil Rights Law: Thurgood Marshall and the Supreme Court, 1936–1961* (New York: Oxford University Press, 1994) and *The NAACP's Legal Strategy against Segregated Education, 1925–1950* (Chapel Hill: University of North Carolina Press, 2005); Clement Vose, *Caucasians Only: The Supreme Court, the NAACP, and the Restrictive Covenant Cases* (Berkeley: University of California Press, 1959); and Robert L. Zangrando, *The NAACP Crusade against Lynching* (Philadelphia:

Temple University Press, 1980). Still, it is surprising that historians of the civil rights movement have not paid more attention to such an important organization. See Patricia Sullivan, *Lift Every Voice: The NAACP and the Making of the Civil Rights Movement* (New York: New Press, 2009) for the first and, so far, only comprehensive scholarly history of the NAACP. Former NAACP fund-raiser Gilbert Jonas offers a perspective from inside the national office in *Freedom's Sword: The NAACP and the Struggle against Racism in America, 1909–1969* (New York: Routledge, 2005). Charles Flint Kellogg embarked on a multivolume history of the Association but published only the first volume, *NAACP: A History of the National Association for the Advancement of Colored People* (Baltimore: John Hopkins University Press, 1967). Poet Langston Hughes was commissioned by the Association to write *Fight for Freedom: The Story of the NAACP* (New York: Berkley Publishing, 1962). There are also several regional studies of NAACP activity. See Lee Sartain, *Borders of Equality: The NAACP and the Baltimore Civil Rights Struggle, 1914–1970* (Jackson: University Press of Mississippi, 2013) and Christopher Robert Reid, *The Chicago NAACP and the Rise of Black Professional Leadership, 1910–1966* (Bloomington: Indiana University Press, 1997). A timely examination of the NAACP's youth branches can be found in Thomas Bynum's *NAACP Youth and the Fight for Black Freedom, 1936–1965* (Knoxville: University of Tennessee Press, 2013).

2. Of Wilkins's peers, Martin Luther King has, of course, been the subject of the most intense and thorough scholarly examination. Among the most comprehensive of the many books about King are Taylor Branch's trilogy: *Parting the Waters: America in the King Years, 1954–1963* (New York: Touchstone Books, 1988), *Pillar of Fire: America in the King Years, 1963–1965* (New York: Simon & Schuster, 1998), and *At Canaan's Edge: America in the King Years, 1965–1968* (New York: Simon & Schuster, 2006). See also David Garrow, *Bearing the Cross: Martin Luther King, Jr., and the Southern Christian Leadership Conference* (New York: Quill, 1986) and *The FBI and Martin Luther King* (New York: W. W. Norton, 1981); Adam Fairclough, *To Redeem the Soul of America: The Southern Christian Leadership Conference and Martin Luther King, Jr.* (Athens: University of Georgia Press, 2001). For other civil rights leaders, see Nancy J. Weiss, *Whitney M. Young Jr. and the Struggle for Civil Rights* (Princeton: Princeton University Press, 1989); Paula F. Pfeffer, *A. Philip Randolph, Pioneer of the Civil Rights Movement* (Baton Rouge: Louisiana State University Press, 1990); Manning Marable, *Malcolm X: A Life of Reinvention* (New York: Viking, 2011); and Barbara Ransby, *Ella Baker and the Black Freedom Movement: A Radical Democratic Vision* (Chapel Hill: University of North Carolina Press, 2003). For firsthand accounts from leaders of the civil rights movement, see John Lewis with Michael D'Orso, *Walking with the Wind: A Memoir of the Movement* (New York: Harcourt Brace & Co., 1998); James Forman, *The Making of Black Revolutionaries* (Seattle: University of Washington Press, 1997); and James Farmer,

Lay Bare the Heart: An Autobiography of the Civil Rights Movement (Fort Worth: Texas Christian University Press, 1985).

3. *Plessy v. Ferguson,* 163 U.S. 537 (1896).

4. The most detailed study of the LCCR so far can be found in the autobiography of a former director of the LCCR: Marvin Caplan, *Farther Along: A Civil Rights Memoir* (Baton Rouge: Louisiana State University Press, 1999).

1. The Family Firm

1. Roy Wilkins with Tom Mathews, *Standing Fast: The Autobiography of Roy Wilkins* (Boston: Da Capo Press, 1994), 10–19; Edward Weiland, "No, I Never Wanted to Be White," *Long Island Sunday Press,* May 26, 1963, NAACP Papers, Part 3, Box 116, Library of Congress, Washington, DC (hereafter referred to as LOC). Details of Wilkins's early life are also drawn from the transcript of his reminiscences for the Columbia Oral History Project: Roy Wilkins, interview by William Ingersoll, New York City, 1960; Albin Krebs, "Roy Wilkins, 50-Year Veteran of Civil Rights Fight, Is Dead," *New York Times,* September 9, 1981; Cleophus Charles, "Roy Wilkins, the NAACP, and the Early Struggle for Civil Rights: Towards the Biography of a Man and a Movement in Microcosm, 1901–1939" (PhD diss., Cornell University, 1981); George R. Metcalf, *Black Profiles* (New York: McGraw-Hill, 1971), 85–111.

2. Wilkins with Mathews, *Standing Fast,* 20.

3. Wilkins, Columbia oral history transcript, 3.

4. Charles, "Roy Wilkins," 221.

5. Judge Nathaniel Jones, interview by author, December 15, 2007.

6. Gilbert Jonas, *Freedom's Sword: The NAACP and the Struggle against Racism in America, 1909–1969* (New York: Routledge, 2005), 345.

7. Letter, Roy Wilkins to Walter White, July 25, 1931, NAACP Papers, Part 1, Reel 13, LOC. The city of St. Paul produced a short but engaging film about Wilkins's childhood in the city, which is available on YouTube: http://youtu.be/NIjO5205HSY.

8. Wilkins with Mathews, *Standing Fast,* 44; Roy Wilkins, "Minnesota: Seat of Satisfaction," *The Messenger* 6, no. 5 (May 1924), reprinted in Tom Lutz and Susanna Ashton, eds., *These "Colored" United States: African American Essays from the 1920s* (New Brunswick: Rutgers University Press, 1996), 167–173.

9. Gene Grove, "Roy Wilkins Columnist," *Tuesday* magazine, July 1966, Roy Wilkins Papers, LOC.

10. Wilkins, Columbia oral history transcript, 29; Metcalf, *Black Profiles,* 87.

11. Wilkins with Mathews, *Standing Fast,* 75.

12. Marvel Jackson Cooke was interviewed by Kathleen Currie on November 3, 1989, in Harlem, New York, as part of the Washington Press Club Foundation's oral history project, Women in Journalism. http://www.wpcf.org/marvel-

cooke. David Levering Lewis writes that Jackson was "profanely grateful" for the broken engagement. David Levering Lewis, *W. E. B Du Bois: The Fight for Equality and the American Century, 1919–1963* (New York: Henry Holt, 2000), 186.

13. Charles, "Roy Wilkins," 301–302.

14. Wilkins with Mathews, *Standing Fast,* 98.

15. Metcalf, *Black Profiles,* 88.

16. Wilkins with Mathews, *Standing Fast,* 116.

17. Kenneth Robert Jankin, *White: The Biography of Walter White, Mr. NAACP* (New York: New Press, 2003), 162–165; Patricia Sullivan, *Lift Every Voice: The NAACP and the Making of the Civil Rights Movement* (New York: New Press, 2009), 151–152; Lewis, *Du Bois: The Fight for Equality,* 293.

18. Memo to the Board of Directors from W. E. B. Du Bois, Herbert J. Seligmann, William Pickens, Robert M. Bagnall, Roy Wilkins, December 1931, NAACP Papers, Part 1, Box 11, Reel 8, LOC; also W. E. B. Du Bois Papers, Reel 35, Roosevelt Study Center, Middelburg, The Netherlands (hereafter RSC).

19. Ibid.

20. Letter, Roy Wilkins to Walter White, December 12, 1931, Arthur Spingarn Papers, Reel 7, LOC.

21. Charles, "Roy Wilkins," 317.

22. Report, "Investigation of Labor Camps in Federal Flood Control Operations by the National Association for the Advancement of Colored People," August 1932, NAACP Papers, Part 1, Box C438, LOC.

23. According to the Census Report for 1931, the average hourly rate for road construction workers in the South was between 22 and 25 cents.

24. Wilkins, Columbia oral history transcript, 46. Press release, "NAACP Levee Camp Investigators Jailed and Threatened in Mississippi," January 13, 1933, NAACP Papers, Part 1, Box C438, LOC.

25. Press release, "Levee Camp Workers to Get Higher Pay, Shorter Hours," October 8, 1933, NAACP Papers, Part 1, Box C438, LOC.

26. See Dan Carter, *Scottsboro: A Tragedy of the American South* (Baton Rouge: Louisiana State University Press, 1995); James Goodman, *Stories of Scottsboro* (New York: Vintage, 1994); and James Miller, *Remembering Scottsboro: The Legacy of an Infamous Trial* (Princeton: Princeton University Press, 2009).

27. Janken, *White,* 152; Wilkins with Mathews, *Standing Fast,* 158.

28. Carter, *Scottsboro,* 376.

29. August Meier and John H Bracey, "The NAACP as a Reform Movement, 1909–1965," *Journal of Southern History* 59 (February 1993): 16.

30. Genna Rae McNeil, *Groundwork: Charles Hamilton Houston and the Struggle for Civil Rights* (Philadelphia: University of Pennsylvania Press, 1983), 120; minutes, Board of Directors meeting, January 4, 1932, Arthur Spingarn Papers, Reel 36, LOC; letter, William L. Patterson, National Secretary, International Labor Defense, June 1, 1933; letter, Roy Wilkins to William L. Patterson,

June 13, 1933, NAACP Papers; letter, Roy Wilkins to William L. Patterson, July 13, 1933; memorandum, Roy Wilkins to unnamed recipient (s), November 3, 1933; all from NAACP Papers, Part 1, Box C402, LOC.

31. Nancy J. Weiss, *Farewell to the Party of Lincoln: Black Politics in the Age of FDR* (Princeton: Princeton University Press, 1983), 56.

32. Sullivan, *Lift Every Voice,* 193; Harvard Sitkoff, *A New Deal for Blacks* (New York: Oxford University Press, 1978), 48; Weiss, *Farewell to the Party of Lincoln,* 68.

33. B. Joyce Ross, *J. E. Spingarn and the Rise of the NAACP* (New York: Atheneum, 1972), 199–201. Ross also describes in detail the internecine bickering and political fighting that took place between Du Bois, White, Spingarn, and, to a lesser degree, Wilkins and Streator, 198–216.

34. Memorandum, Roy Wilkins to members of the NAACP's budget committee, December 8, 1933, NAACP Papers, Part 1, Box F4, LOC; letter, Arthur Spingarn to Richetta Randolph, April 13, 1934, NAACP Papers, Part 1, Box C287, LOC; letter, Walter White to Arthur Spingarn, April 17, 1934, LOC.

35. Letter, W. E. B. Du Bois to the Board of Directors, June 26, 1934, NAACP Papers, Part 1, Box C287, LOC.

36. Letter, Roy Wilkins to Daisy Lampkin, August 8, 1934, NAACP Papers, Part 1, Box A29, LOC.

37. Memorandum, Roy Wilkins to Dr. Abram L. Harris, Chairman, Committee on Program and Policy of the NAACP, September 6, 1934, James Weldon Johnson Papers, Box 24, Folder 544, Beinecke Rare Book and Manuscript Library, Yale University.

38. Letter, Carl Van Vechten to Walter White, September 28, 1934, NAACP Papers, Part 1, Box F4, LOC.

39. Letter, Walter White to Charles Houston, August 7, 1934, NAACP Papers, Part 1, Box A29, LOC.

40. The Harris report is discussed in detail in Ross, *J. E. Spingarn,* 218–242; Janken, *White,* 192–197; Sitkoff, *A New Deal for Blacks,* 253–256; and Manfred Berg, *The Ticket to Freedom: The NAACP and the Struggle for Black Political Integration* (Gainesville: University of Florida Press, 2005); see also memorandum, Roy Wilkins to Abram Harris, September 6, 1934, NAACP Papers, Part 1, Box A29, LOC.

41. Letter, Roy Wilkins to Charles Houston, July 8, 1935, NAACP Papers, Part 1, Reel 13, LOC.

42. Editorial, "Union Labor Again," *The Crisis,* October 1934, 300 (NAACP Papers, Part 1, C436, LOC). The craft structure was the organization of a labor union on the basis of the specific skills of its members—for example, carpenters, electricians, or engineers. Such a structure allowed for the easy exclusion of less skilled workers from becoming members. For a relatively contemporary examination of the racial policies of the major unions toward black workers, see Herbert R. Northrup, "Organized Labor and Negro Workers," *Journal of Political*

Economy (June 1943), 206–221, reprinted in Bernard Sternsher, ed., *The Negro in Depression and War* (Chicago: Quadrangle Books, 1969), 127–149.

43. McNeil, *Groundwork*, 116–118; Mark Tushnet, *Making Civil Rights Law: Thurgood Marshall and the Supreme Court, 1936–1961* (New York: Oxford University Press, 1994), 13; Mark Robert Schneider, *We Return Fighting: The Civil Rights Movement in the Jazz Age* (Boston: Northeastern University Press, 2001), 342.

44. Two landmark victories in the 1930s led the way to *Brown: Pearson v. Murray*, 169 MD 478 (1936), which resulted in the desegregation of the University of Maryland's law school; and *Missouri ex rel Gaines v. Canada*, 305 U.S. 337 (1938), in which admission was ordered by the Supreme Court for a black student who wished to register at the University of Missouri law school.

45. Wilkins with Mathews, *Standing Fast*, 162.

46. Diary, January–February 1935, Roy Wilkins Papers, Box 76, LOC.

47. Sullivan, *Lift Every Voice*, 217–218.

48. Erik S. Gellman, *Death Blow to Jim Crow: The National Negro Congress and the Rise of Militant Civil Rights* (Chapel Hill: University of North Carolina Press, 2012), 120–121; Sullivan, *Lift Every Voice*, 220–221; Wilkins with Mathews, *Standing Fast*, 161.

49. Wilkins quoted in Berg, *Ticket to Freedom*, 98.

50. Wilkins with Mathews, *Standing Fast*, 174–176; Roger Wilkins, *A Man's Life: An Autobiography* (Woodbridge, CT: Ox Bow Press, 1991), 16–17.

51. The committee was known as COFEP for the first two years of its existence. The history of the FEPC is examined most extensively in Merl E. Reed, *Seedtime for the Civil Rights Movement* (Baton Rouge: Louisiana State University Press, 1991).

52. Albert P. Blaustein and Robert L. Zangrando, eds., *Civil Rights and the American Negro* (New York: Washington Square Press, 1968), 358.

53. August Meier and Elliott Rudwick, *From Plantation to Ghetto*, rev. ed. (New York: Hill and Wang, 1970), 252.

54. Sitkoff, *A New Deal*, 316.

55. Wilkins, Columbia oral history transcript, 82.

56. Letter, Roy Wilkins to Walter White, September 25, 1941, Papers of the NAACP, Part 17, Reel 29, University of Cambridge Library (hereafter UCL).

57. Letter, Walter White to Roy Wilkins, September 27, 1941, Papers of the NAACP, Part 17, Reel 29, UCL.

58. "An Appraisal of Branch Work and Methods," Ella Baker, Daisy Lampkin, Madison Jones, and Frederic Morrow (undated but circa Autumn 1941), Papers of the NAACP, Reel 40, UCL.

59. Ibid.

60. Memorandum from Roy Wilkins to Walter White, March 7, 1946, Roy Wilkins Papers, Box 36, LOC.

61. Sullivan, *Lift Every Voice,* 265; Barbara Ransby, *Ella Baker and the Black Freedom Movement: A Radical Democratic Vision* (Chapel Hill: University of North Carolina Press, 2003), 140–141. See also Merline Pitre and Bruce A. Glasrud, eds., *Southern Black Women in the Modern Civil Rights Movement* (College Station: Texas A&M University Press, 2013) for a view of NAACP grassroots activity in the southern states.

62. Janken, *White,* 265; Sullivan, *Lift Every Voice,* 263.

63. Neil A. Wynn, *The African American Experience during World War II* (Lanham, MD: Rowman & Littlefield, 2010), 26.

2. Treading Water

1. NAACP Annual Report, 1946, NAACP Papers, Part 2, Box A60, LOC; NAACP Annual Report, 1943, NAACP Papers, Part 2, Box K1, LOC.

2. Adam Fairclough, *Better Day Coming: Blacks and Equality, 1890–2000* (London: Penguin Books, 2001), 184.

3. Roy Wilkins with Tom Mathews, *Standing Fast: The Autobiography of Roy Wilkins* (Boston: Da Capo Press, 1994), 189. Although Wilkins doesn't specify a year when citing these membership figures, in 1948 the NAACP's total membership had reached almost half a million and it had 1,575 branches, youth councils, and college chapters. NAACP Annual Report, 1948, NAACP Papers, Part 2, Box K1, LOC.

4. Memorandum, Roy Wilkins to Walter White, November 13, 1945, Roy Wilkins Papers, Box 2, LOC.

5. Memorandum, Roy Wilkins to Walter White, September 8, 1945; memorandum, Roy Wilkins to Walter White, March 7, 1946; both from Roy Wilkins Papers, Box 2, LOC.

6. Letter, Ella Baker to Walter White, May 14, 1946, NAACP Papers, Part 2, Box A573, LOC.

7. Memorandum, Roy Wilkins to Walter White, March 7, 1946, Roy Wilkins Papers, Box 2, LOC.

8. Letter, Roy Wilkins to Daisy Lampkin, September 28, 1943, NAACP Papers, Part 2, Box A613, LOC.

9. Ibid. Wilkins made similar complaints directly to White, citing in particular the Secretary's frequent travels and his reluctance to give Wilkins more responsibility. Memorandum, Roy Wilkins to Walter White, July 19, 1943, Papers of the NAACP, Part 17, Reel 25, UCL.

10. Carol Anderson, *Eyes Off the Prize: The United Nations and the African American Struggle for Human Rights, 1944–1955* (Cambridge: Cambridge University Press, 2003), 143.

11. Draft memorandum, unsent, Roy Wilkins to Walter White, September 8, 1945, Roy Wilkins Papers, Box 2, LOC.

12. Wilkins with Mathews, *Standing Fast*, 191.

13. Carolyn Wedin, *Inheritors of the Spirit: Mary White Ovington and the Founding of the NAACP* (New York: John Wiley, 1998), 290.

14. The two cases eventually reached the Supreme Court in 1948 and 1950 respectively. See *Sipuel v. Board of Regents of Univ. of Okla.*, 332 U.S. 631 (1948) and *Sweatt v. Painter*, 339 U.S. 629 (1950).

15. The cases were *McGhee v. Sipes, Shelley v. Kraemer, Hurd v. Hodge,* and *Urciolo v Hodge.* The Supreme Court heard the cases, led by *Shelley v. Kraemer* (334 U.S. 1) in 1948, and held that racially based restrictive covenants violated the Fourteenth Amendment and were therefore unconstitutional and could not be enforced by courts.

16. Address, President Truman to the NAACP annual convention, June 28, 1947, http://millercenter.org/scripps/archive/speeches/detail/3345. Wilkins with Mathews, *Standing Fast*, 198–199; Patricia Sullivan, *Lift Every Voice: The NAACP and the Making of the Civil Rights Movement* (New York: New Press, 2009), 345.

17. Transcript, Truman's Address before a Joint Session of Congress, March 12, 1947, Truman Doctrine, Avalon Project, Yale University, http://avalon.law.yale.edu/20th_century/trudoc.asp.

18. Penny von Eschen, *Race against Empire* (Ithaca: Cornell University Press, 2001), 116.

19. Mary L. Dudziak, "Desegregation as a Cold War Imperative," *Stanford Law Review* 41 (November 1988): 62–63.

20. Resolutions adopted by the Fortieth Annual Convention of the NAACP, Los Angeles, California, July 16, 1949, NAACP Papers, Part 2, Box A38, LOC. The obstructive tactic known as the filibuster makes use of the privilege that allows a senator or series of senators to speak for as long as they wish, on any subject. It can continue until the other side compromises or concedes; if neither occurs, a filibuster can only be stopped by a cloture vote passed by three-fifths of the Senate.

21. Letter, Roy Wilkins to Daisy Lampkin, January 26, 1950, NAACP Papers, Part 2, Box A187, LOC.

22. Memorandum, W. E. B. Du Bois to the Secretary and Board of Directors of the NAACP, September 7, 1948, Arthur Spingarn Papers, Reel 17, LOC; David Levering Lewis, *W. E. B. Du Bois: The Fight for Equality and the American Century, 1919–1963* (New York: Henry Holt, 2000), 533–534; Sullivan, *Lift Every Voice*, 367–368; Kenneth Robert Janken, *White: The Biography of Walter White, Mr. NAACP* (New York: New Press, 2003), 308–309.

23. Memorandum, Walter White to W. E. B. Du Bois, September 13, 1948, Arthur Spingarn Papers, Reel 17, LOC; Anderson, *Eyes Off the Prize*, 143.

24. "Racial Unit Scored as Aiding Truman," *New York Times*, September 9, 1948.

25. Letter, Ashby Gaskins to Louis T. Wright, April 9, 1950, Roy Wilkins Papers, Box 34, LOC.

26. Janken, *White,* 341.

27. George Streator, "Negro Hints White May Resign," *New York Times,* July 17, 1949, NAACP Papers, Part 2, Box A610, LOC.

28. Letter, Roy Wilkins to Hubert Delaney, November 1, 1949; letter, Hubert Delaney to Roy Wilkins, November 9, 1949, both from Arthur Spingarn Papers, Reel 17, LOC. The NAACP's annual report for 1949 quotes two conflicting figures for 1948 membership. The introduction to the report stated that membership was almost half a million strong. However, later in the report, the figure of 383,000 is quoted. Delaney cites the greater figure in his November 9 letter to Wilkins.

29. Minutes of NAACP staff meeting, October 7, 1949, Roy Wilkins Papers, Box 21, LOC.

30. Report, Acting Secretary for the February 1950 meeting of the NAACP Board of Directors, Papers of the NAACP, Part 1, Reel 7, UCL.

31. Lindsay White to Louis Wright, February 7, 1950. Roy Wilkins Papers, Box 21, LOC; Roy Wilkins to Louis Wright, February 13, 1950, NAACP Papers, Part 2, Box A187, LOC.

32. Memorandum, Henry Lee Moon to Roy Wilkins, February 8, 1950, NAACP Papers, Part 2, Box A616, LOC. In the draft of the memorandum, Moon had written that he believed the prime objective of the statement should be to salvage the Association, indicating how serious he considered the situation to be. The sentence was later changed to "halt the Association's present loss of membership."

33. Minutes, Board of Directors meeting, February 14, 1950, Arthur Spingarn Papers, Reel 38, LOC.

34. Letter, Jane Bolin to Arthur Spingarn, March 9, 1950, Arthur Spingarn Papers, Box 20, Reel 17, LOC; Martha Biondi, *To Stand and Fight: The Struggle for Civil Rights in Postwar New York City* (Cambridge, MA: Harvard University Press, 2003), 167; Jacqueline A. McLeod, *Daughter of the Empire State: The Life of Judge Jane Bolin* (Champaign: University of Illinois Press, 2011), 100.

35. Resolutions adopted by the 41st Annual Convention of the NAACP, Boston, Mass., June 23, 1950, NAACP Papers, Part 2, Box K2, LOC.

36. Minutes of NAACP Board of Directors meeting, March 13, 1950, Papers of the NAACP, Part 17, Reel 24, UCL.

37. Letter, Roy Wilkins to William Walker, April 28, 1950, NAACP Papers, Part 2, Box A610, LOC; letter, Roy Wilkins to Walter White, April 28, 1950, Walter and Poppy Cannon White Papers, Box 8, Folder 25, Beinecke Rare Book and Manuscript Library, Yale University; James Hicks, "NAACP Crisis Set?" May 6, 1950, *The Afro-American,* NAACP Papers, Part 2, Box A610, LOC; editorial, "Civil War in the NAACP," *Pittsburgh Courier,* February 25, 1960, Arthur Spingarn Papers, Reel 58, LOC.

38. Roy Wilkins to Edward Dudley, April 29, 1950, Roy Wilkins Papers, Box 3, LOC.

39. Eleanor Roosevelt to Roy Wilkins, April 4, 1950, Roy Wilkins Papers, Box 30, LOC.

40. Roy Wilkins to Maceo Smith, May 2, 1950, NAACP Papers, Part 2, Box A616, LOC. See also Janken, *White,* 349–353, for White's perspective of the leadership battle.

41. "Report of Special Committee on Top Level Staff Organization," undated, NAACP Papers, Part 2, A610, LOC.

42. Janken, *White,* 353.

43. The NAACP's lobbying activities meant it could not apply for tax-exempt status and therefore any contributions would also not be tax exempt. To avoid this, the Legal Defense and Educational Fund was formed in March 1940 as a separate charitable organization to the NAACP for taxation purposes. The Inc. Fund would focus on legal issues while coordinating with the NAACP's program and sharing board members. Mark Tushnet, *Making Civil Rights Law: Thurgood Marshall and the Supreme Court, 1936–1961* (New York: Oxford University Press, 1994), 27. However, until the early 1960s, the activities of the LDF were intertwined with the NAACP, and for the purposes of clarity in this chapter, the two will be treated as one organization.

44. *Sweatt v. Painter,* 339 U.S. 629 (1950), *McLaurin v. Oklahoma State Regents,* 339 U.S. 637 (1950), *Henderson v. United States,* 339 U.S. 816 (1950); Jack Greenberg, *Race Relations and American Law* (New York: Columbia University Press, 1962), 121.

45. Mark Tushnet, *The NAACP's Legal Strategy against Segregated Education, 1925–1950* (Chapel Hill: University of North Carolina Press, 2005), 135. See also Michael J. Klarman, *From Jim Crow to Civil Rights: The Supreme Court and the Struggle for Racial Equality* (New York: Oxford University Press, 2004), and Richard Kluger, *Simple Justice: The History of* Brown v. Board of Education *and Black America's Struggle for Equality* (New York: Vintage Books, 1977). The importance of *Brown* to the civil rights movement has been debated many times since the ruling. Michael Klarman has been one of the most provocative proponents of the argument that *Brown* was not that important a step in dismantling segregation, and has argued that rather than hastening the end of segregation *Brown* was simply one of many factors that illustrated a shift in America's attitude to race that had been evolving for some time. Michael Klarman, "*Brown,* Radical Change, and the Civil Rights Movement," *Virginia Law Review* 80 (1994): 7–150; Michael J. Klarman, *From Jim Crow to Civil Rights: The Supreme Court and the Struggle for Racial Equality* (New York: Oxford University Press, 2004).

46. *Brown v. Board of Education of Topeka,* 349 U.S. 294, http://www.law.cornell.edu/supct/html/historics/USSC_CR_0349_0294_ZS.html.

47. Wilkins, Columbia oral history transcript, 106.

48. Brief History of the National Association for the Advancement of Colored People, 1909–1959, to be included in the Subcommittee Hearing minutes, NAACP Papers, Part 3, Box A73, LOC; memorandum, Gloster Current to branch and budget committees, October 8, 1954, NAACP, Part 3, Box A613, LOC.

49. Gilbert Jonas, *Freedom's Sword: The NAACP and the Struggle against Racism in America, 1909–1969* (New York: Routledge, 2005), 305.

50. Memorandum from Roy Wilkins to the NAACP board of directors, September 12, 1955, Roy Wilkins Papers, Box 29, LOC.

51. Juan Williams, *Thurgood Marshall: American Revolutionary* (New York: Times Books, 1998), 244–250.

52. Board of Directors meeting in Executive Session, April 11, 1955, NAACP Papers, Part 2, Box A611, LOC.

53. Press release, "Press Hails Choice of Wilkins as Wise, Logical, Appropriate," April 21, 1955, NAACP Papers, Part 2, Box A611, LOC.

54. Ibid.; "Roy Wilkins: New NAACP Chief a Quiet Fighter," *St. Petersburg Times*, May 29, 1955, NAACP Papers, Part 2, Box A611, LOC.

55. "NAACP's Top Man," *Ebony*, July 1955, NAACP Papers, Part 2, Box A611, LOC.

3. A Strategy for Freedom

1. "Roy Wilkins: New NAACP Chief a Quiet Fighter," *St. Petersburg Times*, May 29, 1955, NAACP Papers, Part 2, Box A611, LOC.

2. Letter, Roy Wilkins to Barbee William Durham, May 2, 1955, Roy Wilkins Papers, Box 3, General correspondence folder, 1955, LOC.

3. John Morsell, interview by John H. Britton, Director, Civil Rights Documentation Project, November 1, 1967, transcript, 4–5, Ralph J. Bunche Oral History Collection, Moorland-Spingarn Research Center, Howard University, Washington, DC (hereafter MSRC).

4. "Mississippi Terror," *The Crisis* 62, no. 10 (December 1955): 623–624.

5. Telegram, Roy Wilkins to branch leaders, February 23, 1956, NAACP Papers, Part 3, Box A175, LOC.

6. Letter, Roy Wilkins to Martin Luther King, March 8, 1956; letter, Roy Wilkins to Martin Luther King, April 12, 1956; both NAACP Papers, Part 3, Box A273, LOC.

7. Roy Wilkins with Tom Mathews, *Standing Fast: The Autobiography of Roy Wilkins* (Boston: Da Capo Press, 1994), 237–238; letter, Roy Wilkins to Alex Bradford, March 27, 1956, NAACP Papers, Part 3, Box A275, LOC.

8. Telegram, Roy Wilkins to Franklin Williams, March 8, 1956, NAACP Papers, Part 3, Box A273, LOC.

9. Lucy was eventually awarded a master's degree in elementary education

from the University of Alabama in 1992. See E. Culpepper Clark, *The Schoolhouse Door: Segregation's Last Stand at the University of Alabama* (Tuscaloosa: University of Alabama Press, 2007) for a detailed history of the battle to integrate the University of Alabama.

10. *Browder v. Gayle*, 142 F. Supp. 707 (1956).

11. Letter, James Peck to Roy Wilkins, January 26, 1958; letter, Roy Wilkins to James Peck, February 4, 1958; letter, Roy Wilkins to James Peck, December 16, 1957; all NAACP Papers, Part 3, Box A317, LOC; see also J. Mills Thornton, "Challenge and Response in the Montgomery Bus Boycott of 1955–1956," *Alabama Review* 33 (July 1980): 163–235.

12. Letter, Roy Wilkins to James Peck, February 4, 1958, NAACP Papers, Part 3, Box A317, LOC.

13. Ibid.

14. Mark Tushnet, *Making Civil Rights Law: Thurgood Marshall and the Supreme Court, 1936–1961* (New York: Oxford University Press, 1994), 305–306.

15. Address, Roy Wilkins to the NAACP annual convention, San Francisco, CA, July 1, 1956, Roy Wilkins Papers, Box 53, LOC.

16. Circular from Arnold Aronson, May 11, 1956, NAACP Papers, Box A205, LOC.

17. August Meier and John H. Bracey, "The NAACP as a Reform Movement, 1909–1965," *Journal of Southern History* 59 (February 1993): 22.

18. Kevin M. Schultz, "The FEPC and the Legacy of the Labor-Based Civil Rights Movement of the 1940s," *Labor History* 49, no. 1 (2008): 82.

19. Taylor Branch, *Parting the Waters: America in the King Years, 1954–1963* (New York: Touchstone Books, 1988), 839.

20. Members of the LCCR included the AFL, the CIO, the National Urban League, the National Women's Political Caucus, the American Jewish Congress, the Catholic Interracial Council, the Presbyterian Church, the Anti-Defamation League, and the National Council of Catholic Women.

21. Denton L. Watson, ed., *The Papers of Clarence Mitchell Jr.*, vol. 3, *NAACP Labor Secretary and Director of the NAACP Washington Bureau, 1946–1950* (Athens: Ohio University Press, 2010), xxxiii–xc.

22. Eisenhower's view of civil rights has recently been reassessed. The traditional view is that he was indifferent at best to the problems of African Americans, but this assertion has been challenged by David A. Nichols in *A Matter of Justice: Eisenhower and the Beginning of the Civil Rights Revolution* (New York: Simon & Schuster, 2007).

23. Keynote address by Roy Wilkins to National Delegate Assembly for Civil Rights, March 4, 1956, NAACP Papers, Part 21, Reel 12, LOC.

24. Wilkins with Mathews, *Standing Fast*, 241.

25. Pamphlet, NAACP fact sheet on Negro registration and voting (undated; circa 1960), NAACP Papers, Part 3, Box A246, LOC.

26. Letter, Roy Wilkins to E. Frederic Morrow, June 17, 1957, NAACP Papers, Part 3, Box A71, LOC.

27. Wilkins with Mathews, *Standing Fast,* 238.

28. "Uptown Lowdown with Jimmy Booker," *New York Amsterdam News,* May 12, 1956, NAACP Papers, Part 3, Box A317, LOC.

29. Roger Wilkins, interview by author, Washington, DC, August 16, 2006.

30. Wilkins with Mathews, *Standing Fast,* 219.

31. Adam Fairclough, *Race and Democracy: The Civil Rights Struggle in Louisiana, 1915–1971* (Athens: University of Georgia Press, 1995), 209.

32. Ibid.; Mark Tushnet, *Making Civil Rights Law,* 283; chronology of events leading to the trial of the State of Alabama's injunction against the NAACP in Montgomery County, Circuit Court, December 27, 1961, NAACP Papers, Part 3, Box A273, LOC.

33. Tushnet, *Making Civil Rights Law,* 285; Juan Williams, *Thurgood Marshall: American Revolutionary* (New York: Times Books, 1998), 259.

34. Letter, Roy Wilkins to John Boatwright, February 13, 1957, NAACP Papers, Part 3, Box A272, LOC.

35. For a more detailed examination of the NAACP's legal battles in Florida, see Steven F. Lawson, *Civil Rights Crossroads: Nation, Community, and the Black Freedom Struggle* (Lexington: University Press of Kentucky, 2005), 204–216.

36. Letter, Roy Wilkins to Daisy Bates, February 25, 1957, NAACP Papers, Part 3, Box A274, LOC.

37. Memorandum prepared by Theodore Leskes of the American Jewish Committee, May 7, 1957, NAACP Papers, Part 3, Box J4, LOC.

38. Memorandum from the desk of the Executive Secretary, March 1958, NAACP Papers, Part 3, Box A316, LOC.

39. Letter, Roy Wilkins to William Walker, April 15, 1958, NAACP Papers, Part 3, Box A238, LOC.

40. Report to the Annual Meeting (undated; circa January 1957), NAACP Papers, Part 3, Box J6, LOC.

41. Press release, "NAACP Set to Appeal Injunction in Texas," October 25, 1956; letter, Thurgood Marshall to A. Maceo Smith, September 19, 1956; both NAACP Papers, Part 3, Box A272, LOC; W. Marvin Dulaney, "Whatever Happened to the Civil Rights Movement in Dallas, Texas?" in John Dittmer, George C. Wright, W. Marvin Dulaney, and Kathleen Underwood, *Essays on the American Civil Rights Movement* (College Station: Texas A&M University Press, 1993), 76–78; Tushnet, *Making Civil Rights Law,* 272–273.

42. Tushnet, *Making Civil Rights Law,* 272–273; Walter F. Murphy, "The South Counterattacks: The Anti-NAACP Laws," *Western Political Quarterly* 12, no. 2 (June 1959): 377; memorandum, Robert Carter to Roy Wilkins, July 18, 1957, NAACP Papers, Part 3, Box A281, LOC.

43. *Sweatt v. Painter,* 339 U.S. 629 (1950); Tushnet, *Making Civil Rights Law,* 273.

44. Letter, Roy Wilkins to W. J. Durham, May 31, 1957, NAACP Papers, Part 3, Box A272, LOC.

45. Tushnet, *Making Civil Rights Law,* 273.

46. Jack Greenberg, *Crusaders in the Courts* (New York: Basic Books, 1994), 220.

47. Tushnet, *Making Civil Rights Law,* 310–311.

48. Minutes of the Executive Committee of the Board of Directors, Inc. Fund, April 4, 1956, NAACP Papers, Part 3, Box A237, LOC.

49. Wilkins with Mathews, *Standing Fast,* 260; Tushnet, *Making Civil Rights Law,* 310; Williams, *Thurgood Marshall,* 260–261.

50. Report on the NAACP Legal Program and the Relationship of the Inc. Fund to that Program, December 21, 1961, Arthur Spingarn Papers, Reel 47, LOC.

51. Nichols, *A Matter of Justice,* 143–144; statement, Roy Wilkins to Ted Poston of the New York Post, January 2, 1957, NAACP Papers, Part 3, Box A304, LOC. In the fall of 1956 an uprising had taken place in Hungary against the Soviet-backed government. The uprising was crushed by the Soviet military, which quickly imposed an even harsher regime.

52. Telegram, Roy Wilkins to Senator Herbert Lehman (D-NY), December 31, 1956, NAACP Papers, Box A205, LOC; Letter, Roy Wilkins to Senator George Allot (R-CO), December 18, 1956, NAACP Papers, Part 3, Box A66, LOC; Wilkins with Mathews, *Standing Fast,* 243.

53. Wilkins with Mathews, *Standing Fast,* 243.

54. Steven F. Lawson, *Black Ballots: Voting Rights in the South, 1944–1969* (Lanham, MD: Lexington Books, 1999), 167.

55. "NAACP Leader Warns Senators," *New York Times,* February 19, 1957; testimony, Roy Wilkins to the House Judiciary Committee, February 5, 1957, Roy Wilkins Papers, Box 54, LOC.

56. The first amendment authorized the Civil Rights Commission to investigate alleged violations of voting rights, and the second proposed that anyone charged with contempt of the act must be provided with legal representation if the accused could not afford one; Denton L. Watson, *The Lion in the Lobby: Clarence Mitchell Jr.'s Struggle for the Passage of Civil Rights Laws.* (New York: Morrow, 1990), 377.

57. Letter, Roy Wilkins to The Staff, July 17, 1957, Subject: Senate Action on the Civil Rights Bill, NAACP Papers, Part 21, Reel 8, LOC.

58. Address of Roy Wilkins to the 48th Annual NAACP Convention, Detroit, June 30, 1957, NAACP Papers, Part 3, Box A6, LOC.

59. Memorandum, "The New Civil Rights Act," draft, unsigned and undated, Roy Wilkins Papers, Box 21, LOC.

60. Wilkins with Mathews, *Standing Fast*, 243.

61. Ibid.

62. Memorandum, August 7, 1957, Arthur Spingarn Papers, Box 23, LOC. Johnson apparently shared this view. According to George Reedy, who was a member of the Senate leader's staff at the time, Johnson believed that passing any bill, however weak, raised the possibility of passing more far-reaching legislation at a later date. Letter, George Reedy to Michael Gillette, June 2, 1982, Oral history transcripts, Reedy XAC84–52, Lyndon B. Johnson Library, Austin, Texas (hereafter LBJL).

63. Suggested statement to President by Clarence Mitchell, June 19, 1958, NAACP Papers, Part 3, Box A72, LOC.

64. John A. Kirk, *Redefining the Color Line: Black Activism in Little Rock, Arkansas, 1940–1970* (Gainesville: University Press of Florida, 2005), 115. The Little Rock crisis is also discussed at length in Numan V. Bartley, *The Rise of Massive Resistance: Race and Politics during the 1950s* (Baton Rouge: Louisiana State University Press, 1997), 251–269, and Kenneth O'Reilly, "Racial Integration: The Battle General Eisenhower Chose Not to Fight," *Journal of Blacks in Higher Education* 18 (Winter 1997–1998): 110–119.

65. Williams, *Thurgood Marshall*, 267; Wilkins with Mathews, *Standing Fast*, 251.

66. Greenberg, *Crusaders in the Courts*, 241.

67. Memorandum for the files signed by Rocco C. Siciliano, June 24, 1958, Subject: Meeting of Negro Leaders with the President, June 23, 1958, LBJL.

68. Ibid.

69. Ibid. Siciliano's report differs in tone from Wilkins's recollection of the meeting, reproduced in his autobiography, in which he recounts a significantly more skeptical attitude and claims to have challenged the president's actions in Little Rock; Wilkins with Mathews, *Standing Fast*, 257.

70. Branch, *Parting the Waters*, 236.

71. The idea for the SCLC was discussed initially at a conference in Atlanta, Georgia, in January 1957. It took the name the Southern Christian Leadership Conference in August 1957 at the organization's first conference in Montgomery, Alabama. Adam Fairclough, *To Redeem the Soul of America: The Southern Christian Leadership Conference and Martin Luther King, Jr.* (Athens: University of Georgia Press, 2001), 32. See also Clayborne Carson, "Martin Luther King, Jr.: Charismatic Leadership in a Mass Struggle," *Journal of American History* 74 (September 1987): 448–454; and Adam Fairclough, "The Preachers and the People: The Origins and Early Years of the Southern Christian Leadership Conference, 1955–1959," *Journal of Southern History* 52 (August 1986): 403–440.

72. John Brooks, report, Southern Christian Leadership Conference Meeting, Clarksdale, Mississippi, June 1, 1958, NAACP Papers, Part 3, Box A211, LOC.

73. Letter, Medgar Evers to Roy Wilkins, March 11, 1957; letter, Roy Wilkins to Medgar Evers, April 2, 1957; both NAACP Papers, Part 3, Box A211, LOC. Pamphlet, "This Is SCLC," reprinted in August Meier, Elliott Rudwick, and Francis L. Broderick, eds., *Black Protest Thought in the Twentieth Century* (Indianapolis: Bobbs-Merrill, 1971), 303; Louis Lomax, *The Negro Revolt* (New York: Signet Books, 1963), 94–95. In response to King's request that a member of the NAACP's national staff join the national advisory committee of the SCLC, Reverend Edward Odom, the NAACP's church secretary, was selected by Wilkins to serve in that capacity. Letter, Roy Wilkins to Martin Luther King, January 20, 1958, NAACP Papers, Part 3, Box A211, LOC.

74. "NAACP Secretary Answers Chet Huntley," *The Crisis*, March 1959, 149–153.

75. George Lewis, "'A Gigantic Battle to Win Mens' Minds': The NAACP's Public Relations Department and Post-*Brown* Propaganda," in Kevern Verney and Lee Sartain, eds., *Long Is the Way and Hard: One Hundred Years of the NAACP* (Fayetteville: University of Arkansas Press, 2009), 30–31; Aniko Bodroghkozy, *Equal Time: Television and the Civil Rights Movement* (Champaign: University of Illinois Press, 2012), 71–74. See also Sasha Torres, *Black, White, and in Color: Television and Black Civil Rights* (Princeton: Princeton University Press, 2003).

76. Letter, Stanley Levison to Roy Wilkins, September 1958. See Adam Fairclough, *Martin Luther King, Jr.* (Athens: University of Georgia Press, 1995), 144.

77. Letter, James Peck to Roy Wilkins, January 26, 1958, NAACP Papers, Part 3, Box A317, LOC.

78. Letter, Roy Wilkins to James Peck, February 4, 1958, NAACP Papers, Part 3, Box A317, LOC.

79. Timothy B. Tyson, "Robert F. Williams, 'Black Power,' and the Roots of the African American Freedom Struggle," *Journal of American History* 85 (September 1998): 550; Timothy B. Tyson, *Radio Free Dixie: Robert F. Williams and the Roots of Black Power* (Chapel Hill: University of North Carolina Press, 1999), 81.

80. Letter, Harold Williams, Executive Secretary, Cleveland branch of the NAACP, to Gloster Current, February 12, 1960, NAACP Papers, Part 3, Box A334, LOC.

81. Pamphlet, "The Single Issue in the Robert Williams Case," July 1959, NAACP Papers, Part 3, Box I22, LOC; letter, Roy Wilkins to Bolza Baxter, May 21, 1959, NAACP Papers, Part 3, Box A334, LOC; "NAACP Leader Urges 'Violence,'" *New York Times*, May 7, 1959; letter, Roy Wilkins to Robert Williams, June 9, 1959, NAACP Papers, Part 3, Box A334, LOC.

82. Grif Stockley, *Daisy Bates: Civil Rights Crusader from Arkansas* (Jackson: University of Mississippi Press, 2005), 194–195; Lomax, *The Negro Revolt*, 113–114; Williams, *Thurgood Marshall*, 281–282; Wilkins with Mathews,

Standing Fast, 265; Tyson, "Robert F. Williams," 558–559; Draft Report of the NAACP Resolutions Committee (Internal Affairs) (undated), NAACP Papers, Part 3, Box A10, LOC; Resolution by the Committee of Branches, June 8, 1959, Arthur Spingarn Papers, Reel 23, LOC.

83. James L. Hicks, "Leadership," New York *Amsterdam News,* April 19, 1958; May 3, 1958; May 10, 1958; May 24, 1958; June 7, 1958; NAACP Papers, Part 3, Box A261, LOC.

84. Hicks, "Leadership," June 7, 1958.

85. Ibid.

86. Hicks, "Leadership," May 3, 1958.

87. Gretchen Cassel Eick, *Dissent in Wichita: The Civil Rights Movement in the Midwest, 1954–1972* (Urbana: University of Illinois Press, 2001), 5.

88. Ibid., 9; Aldon Morris, "Black Southern Student Sit-in Movement: An Analysis of Internal Organization," *American Sociological Review* 46 (December 1981): 750; memorandum, Herbert Wright to Roy Wilkins and Gloster Current, March 30, 1959, NAACP Papers, Part 3, Box A290, LOC.

4. Politics and Protest

1. William H. Chafe, *Civilities and Civil Rights: Greensboro, North Carolina and the Black Struggle for Equality* (New York: Oxford University Press, 1980), 82–101; August Meier and Elliott Rudwick, *CORE: A Study in the Civil Rights Movement, 1942–1968* (Urbana: University of Illinois Press, 1975), 101; Aldon Morris, "Black Southern Student Sit-in Movement: An Analysis of Internal Organization," *American Sociological Review* 46 (December 1981): 756; Manning Marable, *Race, Reform, and Rebellion: The Second Reconstruction in Black America, 1945–1990* (Jackson: University of Mississippi Press, 1991), 61–65.

2. Meier and Rudwick, *CORE,* 102. The sit-in protests are examined in detail in Chafe, *Civilities and Civil Rights.*

3. Memorandum, Roy Wilkins to Branches and Youth Councils in the South, February 19, 1960, NAACP Papers, Part 3, Box A289, LOC.

4. Memorandum, Roy Wilkins to Youth Chapters and College Chapters in the North, February 19, 1960, NAACP Papers, Part 3, Box A289, LOC.

5. Claude Sitbon, "Negro Sitdowns Stir Fear of Wider Unrest in South," *New York Times,* February 15, 1960; memo from Roy Wilkins to Gloster Current and Herbert Wright, February 15, 1960, NAACP Papers, Part 3, Box A310, LOC.

6. Memorandum, John Morsell to Executive Staff, February 29, 1960, NAACP Papers, Part 3, Box A310, LOC.

7. Memorandum, Robert Carter to John Morsell, March 17, 1960; memorandum, Mildred Bond to John Morsell, March 21, 1960; both NAACP Papers, Part 3, Box A310, LOC.

8. Memorandum, Calvin Banks to John Morsell, March 21, 1960; memorandum, Herbert Hill to John Morsell, March 21, 1960; both NAACP Papers, Part 3, Box A310, LOC.

9. Memorandum, Gloster Current to Roy Wilkins and John Morsell, March 22, 1960, NAACP Papers, Part 3, Box A310, LOC.

10. Memorandum, Roy Wilkins to Robert Carter, Gloster Current, James Farmer, Herbert Hill, Henry Lee Moon, and John Morsell, March 16, 1960, NAACP Papers, Part 3, Box A289, LOC; memorandum, Roy Wilkins to All Officers of NAACP State Conferences, Branches, Youth Councils, and College Chapters, March 16, 1960, NAACP Papers, Part 3, Box I22, LOC.

11. Memorandum, Gloster Current to Roy Wilkins, October 6, 1960, NAACP Papers, Part 3, Box A290, LOC.

12. Ibid.

13. Clayborne Carson, *In Struggle: SNCC and the Black Awakening of the 1960s* (Cambridge, MA: Harvard University Press, 1995), 23. Lawson quote from August Meier, Elliott Rudwick, and Francis L. Broderick, eds., *Black Protest Thought in the Twentieth Century*, 2nd ed. (Indianapolis: Bobbs Merrill, 1971), 314; Claude Sitton, "Negro Criticizes NAACP Tactics," *New York Times*, April 17, 1960; memorandum, Roy Wilkins to Gloster Current, James Farmer, Herbert Hill, Henry Lee Moon, John Morsell, and Herbert Wright, April 18, 1960, NAACP Papers, Part 3, Box A211, LOC.

14. According to a memorandum to Roy Wilkins from John Brooks, Lawson was alleged to have said in his speech that "the top leadership of the SCLC is not in harmony with the NAACP," although that does not appear to be the case according to a transcript of the speech reprinted in Meier, Rudwick, and Broderick, *Black Protest Thought*, 308–315; memorandum, John Brooks to Roy Wilkins, April 20, 1960, NAACP Papers, Part 3, Box A211, LOC.

15. Memorandum, John M. Brooks to Roy Wilkins, April 20, 1960; letter, James Lawson to Roy Wilkins, May 9, 1960; letter, Roy Wilkins to James Lawson, May 13, 1960; letter, Roy Wilkins to Dr. Benjamin Mays, May 19, 1960; all NAACP Papers, Part 3, Box A211, LOC. David Garrow, *Bearing the Cross: Martin Luther King, Jr., and the Southern Christian Leadership Conference* (New York: Quill, 1986), 134.

16. Garrow, *Bearing the Cross*, 134.

17. Letter, Roy Wilkins to Dr. Benjamin Mays, May 19, 1960, NAACP Papers, Part 3, A211, LOC.

18. Memorandum, Henry Lee Moon to Roy Wilkins, April 18, 1960; memorandum, Gloster Current to Roy Wilkins, April 18, 1960; both NAACP Papers, Part 3, Box A211, LOC. Memorandum, Herbert Wright to Roy Wilkins, March 3, 1960, Papers of the NAACP, Supplement to Part 17, Reel 10, Microfilm, UCL.

19. Louis E. Lomax, "The Negro Revolt against 'The Negro Leaders,'" *Harper's*, June 1960, 42–43.

20. Ibid., 48.

21. NAACP Annual Report, 1960, NAACP Papers, Part 3, Box 114, LOC; Stephen G. N. Tuck, *Beyond Atlanta: The Struggle for Racial Equality in Georgia, 1940–1980* (Athens: University of Georgia Press, 2001), 134; flyers, "Don't Buy Anything for Easter" and "A Message for Freedom-Loving Americans," NAACP Papers, Part 3, Box A227, LOC.

22. Adam Fairclough, *Race and Democracy: The Civil Rights Struggle in Louisiana, 1915–1971* (Athens: University of Georgia Press, 1995), 283.

23. Memorandum, Roy Wilkins to NAACP branch offices, April 1960, Papers of the NAACP, Part 21, Reel 22, Microfilm, UCL.

24. Ibid.

25. Minutes, NAACP staff conference, July 18–19, 1961, NAACP Papers, Part 3, Box A310, LOC.

26. Farnsworth Fowle, "NAACP Warns Two Conventions," *New York Times,* June 27, 1960.

27. NAACP Factsheet on Negro Registration and Voting (undated), Presidential Campaign of 1960, NAACP Papers, Part 3, Box A246, LOC.

28. Congressional Civil Rights Record of Presidential Candidates, June 10, 1960, produced by the Washington Bureau of the NAACP, NAACP Papers, Part 3, Box A7, LOC.

29. Letter, Roy Wilkins to Senator Kennedy, May 29, 1958, NAACP Papers, Part 3, A174, LOC; Nick Bryant, *The Bystander: John F. Kennedy and the Struggle for Black Equality* (New York: Basic Books, 2006), 88–89.

30. Bryant, *The Bystander,* 90.

31. Farnsworth Fowle, "Wilkins Praises Nixon on Rights," *New York Times,* June 21, 1960.

32. Bryant, *The Bystander,* 92.

33. Farnsworth Fowle, "NAACP Praises Nixon, Others," *New York Times,* June 21, 1960.

34. "Johnson 'Doer' Wilkins Agrees," *New Orleans Times Picayune,* July 19, 1960; Clayton Knowles, "Wilkins Defends Plank on Rights," *New York Times,* July 18, 1960.

35. NAACP Papers, Part 9, Box 118, LOC.

36. Memorandum, Arnold Aronson, Secretary of the LCCR, to Cooperating Organizations, August 5, 1960, NAACP Papers, Part 3, Box A246, LOC.

37. Press Release, "Roy Wilkins, the Civil Rights Planks Compared," July 28, 1960, NAACP Papers, Part 3, Box A31, LOC.

38. Bryant, *The Bystander,* 144–145; Democratic Party Platform of 1960, The American Presidency Project, http://www.presidency.ucsb.edu/ws/index.php?pid=29602; William M. Blair, "Strongest Plank on Rights Voted over Threat of Fight," *New York Times,* July 12, 1960.

39. Statement of Roy Wilkins before the Platform Committee of the Demo-

cratic National Convention, Los Angeles, California, July 7, 1960, NAACP Papers, Part 3, Box A246, LOC.

40. Text of Republican Planks on Civil Rights, Defense and Education and Conclusion to the Platform, American Presidency Project, http://www.presidency.ucsb.edu/ws/index.php?pid=25839; William M. Blair, "Firm Rights Plank Offered by Nixon," *New York Times,* July 22, 1960.

41. Letter, Roy Wilkins to A. C. Tompkins, August 18, 1960, NAACP Papers, Part 3, Box A246, LOC.

42. Letter, Roy Wilkins to Carter Wesley, September 8, 1960, NAACP Papers, Part 3, Box A246, LOC.

43. Jack Bass, *Unlikely Heroes: A Vivid Account of the Implementation of the Brown Decision in the South by Southern Federal Judges Committed to the Rule of Law* (Tuscaloosa: University of Alabama Press, 1990), 116; Harris Wofford, *Of Kennedys and Kings* (Pittsburgh: University of Pittsburgh Press, 1992), 111–118; Bryant, *The Bystander,* 185; Garrow, *Bearing the Cross,* 147; Adam Fairclough, *To Redeem the Soul of America: The Southern Christian Leadership Conference and Martin Luther King, Jr.* (Athens: University of Georgia Press, 2001), 75; address, Roy Wilkins to Newark, NJ, NAACP branch, November 2, 1960, NAACP Papers, Part 3, Box A304, LOC; Roy Wilkins with Tom Mathews, *Standing Fast: The Autobiography of Roy Wilkins* (New York: Da Capo Press, 1994), 279; Anthony Lewis, *Portrait of a Decade: The Second American Revolution* (New York: Random House, 1964), 115–116; Clifford Kuhn, "'There's a Footnote to History!' Memory and the History of Martin Luther King's October 1960 Arrest and Its Aftermath," *Journal of American History* 84 (September 1997): 590.

44. Annual Report, NAACP Annual Report for 1960, NAACP Papers, Part 3, Box I14, LOC.

45. Speech, Roy Wilkins to South Carolina State Conference of NAACP branches, November 20, 1960, NAACP Papers, Part 3, Box A304, LOC; Doug McAdam, *Political Process and the Development of Black Insurgency, 1930–1970* (Chicago: University of Chicago Press, 1982), 158; Bryant, *The Bystander,* 187; Annual Report, NAACP Annual Report for 1960, NAACP Papers, Part 3, Box I14, LOC.

46. Roy Wilkins, interview with Berl Bernhard, August 13, 1964, transcript, p. 5, John F. Kennedy Library, Boston, MA (hereafter JFKL); Wilkins with Mathews, *Standing Fast,* 280; Bryant, *The Bystander,* 206; Mark Stern, *Calculating Visions: Kennedy, Johnson, and Civil Rights* (New Brunswick: Rutgers University Press, 1992), 42.

47. Letter, Roy Wilkins to Theodore Sorensen, February 7, 1961, NAACP Papers, Part 3, Box A175, LOC.

48. "President's View on Rights Scored," *New York Times,* May 11, 1961; May 12, 1961.

49. Speech by Roy Wilkins to the Community Brotherhood Dinner of the

Stamford Interfaith Council, February 8, 1961, NAACP Papers, Part 3, Box A304, LOC.

50. Bryant, *The Bystander*, 206–207.

51. Letter, Roy Wilkins to Harris Wofford, April 5, 1961, JFKL, http://www.jfklibrary.org/Asset-Viewer/RbvfZID58EujvNxPmXnBPQ.aspx#.

52. Ibid.

53. Speech by Roy Wilkins to the Community Brotherhood Dinner of the Stamford Interfaith Council, February 8, 1961, NAACP Papers, Part 3, Box A304, LOC.

54. Ibid.

55. Memorandum, Harris Wofford to Kenneth O'Donnell, October 4, 1961; memorandum, Louis Martin to O'Donnell, June 20, 1961; memorandum, Harris Wofford to Kenneth O'Donnell, July 11, 1961; all in Civil Rights during the Kennedy Administration, 1961–1963, Part 1, Reel 1, RSC.

56. Meier and Rudwick, *CORE*, 135. See also Raymond Arsenault, *Freedom Riders: 1961 and the Struggle for Racial Justice* (New York: Oxford University Press, 2006); and Derek Charles Catsam, *Freedom's Main Line: The Journey of Reconciliation and the Freedom Rides* (Lexington: University Press of Kentucky, 2009).

57. Arsenault, *Freedom Riders*, 109.

58. Transcript, telephone conversation between Rev. P. B. Walker and Gloster Current, April 18, 1961, NAACP Papers, Part 3, Box A199, LOC.

59. Letter, Medgar Evers to Gordon Carey, May 4, 1961, NAACP Papers, Part 3, Box A136, LOC; Arsenault, *Freedom Riders*, 334–335.

60. Howell Raines, *My Soul Is Rested: The Story of the Civil Rights Movement in the Deep South* (New York: Penguin, 1983), 116; Arsenault, *Freedom Riders*, 153–154.

61. Remarks, June 7, 1961, NAACP Papers, LOC; memorandum to branches, youth councils, college chapters, and state conferences, May 25, 1961; and AP wire story clarifying the position of the NAACP regarding the Freedom Rides, June 14, 1961; both NAACP Papers, Part 3, Box A136, LOC.

62. Wilkins with Mathews, *Standing Fast*, 283.

63. James Farmer, *Lay Bare the Heart: An Autobiography of the Civil Rights Movement* (Fort Worth: Texas Christian University Press, 1985), 12–14; letter, James Farmer to Roy Wilkins, June 12, 1961, NAACP Papers, Part 3, Box A199, LOC.

64. Memorandum, Roy Wilkins to Presidents and Advisers of NAACP College Chapters, May 26, 1961, NAACP Papers, Part 3, Box A136, LOC.

65. Memorandum, Herbert Wright to Roy Wilkins and Gloster Current, June 2, 1961; "Freedom Riders Find Charleston, SC a Contrast to Jackson, Miss.," unattributed newspaper article, June 16, 1961; both NAACP Papers, Part 3, Box A136, LOC.

66. Remarks, Roy Wilkins at a mass meeting of the Jackson, Mississippi, branch of the NAACP, June 7, 1961; Associated Press newswire report, Freedom Riders, Jackson, Mississippi, June 8, 1960; "Jackson Arrests 9 'Freedom Riders,'" *New York Daily Mirror,* June 8, 1961; all NAACP Papers, Part 3, Box A136, LOC.

67. Newswire report, Clarification of the NAACP's position on the Freedom Rides, June 15, 1960, NAACP Papers, Part 3, Box A136, LOC; William O. Walker, "CORE, A New Dimension," *Pittsburgh Courier,* June 17, 1961; "Going to Jail Is Only Half the Battle," *Cleveland Call and Post,* June 17, 1961; both NAACP Papers, Part 3, Box A199, LOC.

68. Mary L. Dudziak, *Cold War Civil Rights: Race and the Image of American Democracy* (Princeton: Princeton University Press, 2000), 159–162; Bryant, *The Bystander,* 265–266; Nicholas Katzenbach, *Some of It Was Fun: Working with RFK and LBJ* (New York: W. W. Norton, 2008), 44–48.

69. Letter, Roy Wilkins to Theodore Sorensen, February 7, 1961, NAACP Papers, Part 3, Box A175, LOC.

70. Bryant, *The Bystander,* 265–266; Katzenbach, *Some of It Was Fun,* 44–48; Richard Reeves, *President Kennedy: Profile of Power* (New York: Simon & Schuster, 1993), 132–133; Meier and Rudwick, *CORE,* 139–140; Arsenault, *Freedom Riders,* 221–223.

71. Wilkins, interview with Bernhard, JFKL, 10.

72. Walker, *Pittsburgh Courier,* June 17, 1961; "Going to Jail Is Only Half the Battle," *Cleveland Call and Post,* June 17, 1961, NAACP Papers, Part 3, Box A199, LOC; Farmer, *Lay Bare the Heart,* 207–208; Meier and Rudwick, *CORE,* 144.

73. Memorandum, Gloster Current to Roy Wilkins, May 16, 1960, NAACP Papers, Part 3, Box A289, LOC.

74. "Confused Crusade," *Time,* January 12, 1962.

75. Letter, Helen Phelps to Gloster Current, October 4, 1961, NAACP Papers, Part 3, Box A199, LOC.

76. Letter, Lillian Tonnaire-Taylor, Chief of Bureau for Lynx, to Roy Wilkins, January 22, 1962, NAACP Papers, Part 3, Box A314, LOC. Lynx was a French photographic and news agency.

77. Stern, *Calculating Visions,* 63, 66; Manfred Berg, *The Ticket to Freedom: The NAACP and the Struggle for Black Political Integration* (Gainesville: University of Florida Press, 2005), 181. Berg and Stern cite slightly different figures for the total budget. Stern cites a total figure of $885,000, while Berg claims that the VEP disbursed $870,000 between April 1961 and November 1964.

78. The five organizations were the NAACP, SNCC, SCLC, CORE, and the Urban League.

79. Memorandum, The Structure and Activities of NAACP in Voter Registration, unattributed and undated, but the memorandum formed part of the

NAACP's submission to the Taconic Foundation for a request for funding, so it is likely to have been composed during the latter half of 1961. NAACP Papers, Part 3, Box A271, LOC.

80. Letter, John Brooks to Roy Wilkins, February 27, 1961, NAACP Papers, Part 3, Box A266, LOC.

81. Memorandum, John Morsell to Roy Wilkins, September 27, 1961, NAACP Papers, Part 3, Box A271, LOC.

82. Berg, *Ticket to Freedom,* 181.

83. Memorandum from Henry Lee Moon to Roy Wilkins, August 28, 1961; letter from Roy Wilkins to Stephen Currier, August 31, 1961; letter from Stephen Currier to Roy Wilkins, September 8, 1961; all from NAACP Papers, Part 3, Box A271, LOC.

84. Letter, Roy Wilkins to Leslie Dunbar, October 17, 1961, NAACP Papers, Part 3, Box A271, LOC.

85. Ibid.

86. James Forman, *The Making of Black Revolutionaries* (Seattle: University of Washington Press, 1997), 266.

87. NAACP Annual Report 1962, NAACP Papers, Part 3, Box I14, LOC.

88. Memorandum, John Morsell to Presidents of Branches, State Conferences, and Youth Councils, October 19, 1962, NAACP Papers, Part 3, Box A271, LOC.

89. Transcript, Summary of telephone conversation with Vernon Jordan and Gloster Current, December 14, 1961, NAACP Papers, Part 3, Box A277, LOC; Garrow, *Bearing the Cross,* 178; Fairclough, *To Redeem the Soul,* 87; Taylor Branch, *Parting the Waters: America in the King Years, 1954–1963* (New York: Touchstone Books, 1988), 526. For more on the Albany Movement see Fairclough, *To Redeem the Soul,* 85–109; Carson, *In Struggle,* 56–65; Tuck, *Beyond Atlanta,* 147–153; Garrow, *Bearing the Cross,* 173–230; and Branch, *Parting the Waters,* 524–561.

90. Summary of telephone conversation between Vernon Jordan and Gloster Current, December 14, 1961; summary of telephone conversations between Vernon Jordan, Ruby Hurley, and Gloster Current, December 18, 1961; both NAACP Papers, LOC.

91. Aldon Morris, *The Origins of the Civil Rights Movement: Black Communities Organizing for Change* (New York: Free Press, 1984), 250.

92. Report on the NAACP Legal Program and the Relationship of the Inc. Fund to that Program, December 21, 1961, Arthur Spingarn Papers, Reel 47, LOC; Greenberg, *Crusaders in the Courts,* 292; "Along the NAACP Battlefront," *The Crisis,* February 1962, 111.

93. Memorandum, Roy Wilkins to Presidents of Branches, State Conferences, and Youth Groups, November 28, 1962, NAACP Papers, Part 3, Box I13, LOC.

94. Letter, Ralph Stuart Smith, Press Attaché, US Embassy, Paris, to Roy

Wilkins, October 11, 1962; letter, Ralph A. Dungan, Special Assistant to the President, to Roy Wilkins, November 8, 1962; both NAACP Papers, Part 3, Box A313, LOC.

95. Constance Baker Motley, *Equal Justice under Law* (New York: Farrar Strauss and Giroux, 1998), 178. See also Charles W. Eagles, *The Price of Defiance: James Meredith and the Integration of Ole Miss* (Chapel Hill: University of North Carolina Press, 2009), and William Doyle, *An American Insurrection: James Meredith and the Battle of Oxford, Mississippi, 1962* (New York: Anchor, 2003) for a detailed examination of Meredith's attempt to enter "Ole Miss."

96. Bryant, *The Bystander,* 351; Reeves, *Profile of Power,* 364.

97. Letter, Roy Wilkins to Lionel Rogosin, undated, NAACP Papers, Part 3, Box A228, LOC.

98. John Dittmer, *Local People: The Struggle for Civil Rights in Mississippi* (Urbana: University of Illinois Press, 1995), 138–142; Bryant, *The Bystander,* 331–356; Jack Greenberg, *Crusaders in the Courts* (New York: Basic Books, 1994), 318–332.

99. Bryant, *The Bystander,* 359; Reeves, *Profile of Power,* 431–432.

100. Press release, "JFK Message 'Admirable' but Not Enough," February 28, 1963, NAACP Papers, Part 3, A175, LOC.

101. Memorandum, Calvin Banks to Roy Wilkins, June 28, 1961, NAACP Papers, Part 3, Box A251, LOC.

102. Garrow, *Bearing the Cross,* 228; Fairclough, *To Redeem the Soul,* 126.

103. The causes and political effects of the Birmingham campaign are examined in detail in Fairclough, *To Redeem the Soul,* 111–139; Garrow, *Bearing the Cross,* 231–263; Stern, *Calculating Visions,* 81–85; Bryant, *The Bystander,* 381–395; Reeves, *Profile of Power,* 482–506; and Branch, *Parting the Water,* 671–802.

104. Garrow, *Bearing the Cross,* 228; Fairclough, *To Redeem the Soul,* 126; Sasha Torres, *Black, White, and in Color: Television and Black Civil Rights* (Princeton: Princeton University Press, 2003), 28–29.

105. Bryant, *The Bystander,* 392–393; Stern, *Calculating Visions,* 80; Fairclough, *To Redeem The Soul,* 135–139.

106. Roy Wilkins, interview with Robert Wright, April 29, 1970, New York City, Ralph J. Bunche Collection, MSRC, 49.

107. Dittmer, *Local People,* 160; memorandum, Gloster Current to Ruby Hurley, Clarence Laws, L. C. Bates, Medgar Evers, Vernon Jordan, Willie B. Ludden, Charles McLean, I. DeQuincey Newman, Robert Saunders, U. Simpson Tate, May 13, 1963, NAACP Papers, Part 3, Box A236, LOC.

108. Memorandum, Current to Hurley et al., May 13, 1963, NAACP Papers, Part 3, Box A236, LOC.

109. Dittmer, *Local People,* 162–163.

110. Telegram, Roy Wilkins to all Branch Presidents, May 28, 1963, Roy Wilkins Papers, Box 27, LOC.

111. Taylor Branch, *Pillar of Fire: America in the King Years, 1963–1965* (New York: Simon & Schuster, 1998), 101.

112. Ibid.

113. "Roy Wilkins Is Arrested at Jackson," *New York Times,* June 2, 1963; letter, Dr. L. H. Holman to Roy Wilkins, June 3, 1963; letter, Percy Sutton to Roy Wilkins, June 3, 1963; both NAACP Papers, Part 3, Box A231, LOC. Zoe A. Colley, *Ain't Scared of Your Jail: Arrest, Imprisonment, and the Civil Rights Movement* (Gainesville: University of Florida Press, 2012), 78.

114. Dittmer, *Local People,* 164.

115. Ibid., 165.

116. Radio and Television Report to the American People on Civil Rights, President John F. Kennedy, The White House, June 11, 1963, JFKL, http://civilrights.jfklibrary.org/Media-Assets/address-to-the-American-People.aspx#A-Moral-Issue--The-Presidents-Promise.

117. Telegram, Roy Wilkins to President Kennedy, June 12, 1963, NAACP Papers, Part 3, Box A174, LOC.

118. Wilkins with Mathews, *Standing Fast,* 290. Michael Vinson Williams's *Medgar Evers: Mississippi Martyr* (Fayetteville: University of Arkansas Press, 2011) is a long overdue biography of this courageous and dedicated civil rights activist.

119. Dittmer, *Local People,* 165.

120. Branch, *Parting the Waters,* 829; Garrow, *Bearing the Cross,* 269.

121. Roger Wilkins, *A Man's Life: An Autobiography* (Woodbridge, CT: Ox Bow Press, 1991), 122; Branch, *Parting the Waters,* 831. Evers's murder is examined in detail in Adam Nossiter, *Of Long Memory: Mississippi and the Murder of Medgar Evers* (Reading, MA: Addison Wesley, 1995).

122. "Clash Erupts after Funeral of Negro Leader in Jackson," *Hartford Courant,* June 16, 1963; "Life and Death in Jackson," *Time* magazine, June 21, 1963.

123. "NAACP Leader Assails Other Civil Rights Groups," *New York Times,* June 17, 1963; Foster Hailey, "Four Direct Action Groups Seek Funds and Support for their Cause," *New York Times,* June 23, 1963; Anita Ehrman, "Wilkins Hits Rival Negro Rights Units," *Washington Post,* June 17, 1963; "Wilkins Brings Negro Split Out in the Open," *Long Island Press,* June 17, 1963.

124. Ehrman, *Washington Post,* June 17, 1963.

125. Telegram, James Stamps to Roy Wilkins, June 19, 1963; letter, Roy Wilkins to James Stamps, June 26, 1963; both NAACP Papers, Part 3, Box A294, LOC.

126. Letter, Wilkins to Stamps, June 26, 1963.

127. Interview, Roy Wilkins speaking with Robert Penn Warren, New York City, April 7, 1964, Tape 3, http://whospeaks.library.vanderbilt.edu/interview/roy-wilkins.

128. Roy Wilkins, "NAACP Backs Civil Rights Bill but Holds It Is Not Strong Enough," part of a symposium written by prominent black leaders and published during August and September 1963 by the *St. Louis Post Dispatch,* reprint, NAACP Papers, Part 3, Box I17, LOC; press release, "Wilkins Sees JFK's Proposals as Not Meeting Today's Needs," June 22, 1963, NAACP Papers, Part 3, Box A175, LOC.

129. Press release, "Wilkins Sees JFK's Proposals as Not Meeting Today's Needs."

130. Memorandum, From the LCCR to participating organizations (undated but presumably late July 1963), NAACP Papers, Part 3, Box A206, LOC.

131. Pamphlet, "Humiliation Stalks Them," Reprint of Roy Wilkins testimony in support of the public accommodations section of the proposed civil rights bill being considered by the Senate Commerce Committee, August 1963, NAACP Papers, Part 3, Box A233, LOC.

132. Ibid.

133. Ibid.

134. Ibid.; Denton L. Watson, *The Lion in the Lobby: Clarence Mitchell Jr.'s Struggle for the Passage of Civil Rights Laws* (New York: Morrow, 1990), 564–565.

135. Mary McGrory, "Wilkins States the Case," July 23, 1963, *New York Post,* LCCR Papers, Part 1, Box I42, LOC.

136. Ibid.

137. "Wilkins Cautions on Mass Protests," *New York Times,* June 21, 1963.

138. Berg, *Ticket to Freedom,* 205.

139. John Lewis with Michael D'Orso, *Walking with the Wind: A Memoir of the Movement* (New York: Harcourt Brace, 1998), 208.

140. Ibid.; Branch, *Parting the Waters,* 847.

141. Lewis with D'Orso, *Walking with the Wind,* 208.

142. Statement (undated but following the July 2, 1963, meeting, and unsigned), Bayard Rustin Papers, Box 31, LOC.

143. Draft statement, "The heads of the six active civil rights organizations calling for discipline in connection with the Washington March of August 28, 1963," Bayard Rustin Papers, Box 31, LOC.

144. Christopher Robert Reed, *The Chicago NAACP and the Rise of Professional Leadership, 1910–1966* (Bloomington: Indiana University Press, 1997), 198.

145. Wallace Terry, "Mayor and Cleric Jeered at Chicago Rights Rally," *Washington Post,* July 5, 1963.

146. Ibid., 198; Branch, *Parting the Waters,* 848.

147. Margaret McElheny, "NAACP Opens Sessions; More Mass Protests Seen," *Washington Post,* July 2, 1963.

148. Extract from NAACP Annual Report, 1963, NAACP Papers, Part 3, Box I14, LOC.

149. Memorandum, Father Brown to Gloster Current, December 20, 1963,

NAACP Papers, Part 3, Box C24, LOC. See also David R. Colbourn and Jane L. Landers, *The African American Heritage of Florida* (Gainesville: University Press of Florida, 1995).

150. Remarks, Roy Wilkins at the March on Washington, August 28, 1963, NAACP Papers, Part 3, Box A227, LOC.

151. Memorandum, John Morsell to NAACP staff members, August 21, 1963, NAACP Papers, Part 3, Box A227, LOC.

152. Bryant, *The Bystander*, 436; Stern, *Calculating Visions*, 105.

153. Stern, *Calculating Visions*, 105; Reeves, *Profile in Power*, 585.

154. Watson, *Lion in the Lobby*, 571–574; Bryant, *The Bystander*, 448–449; Stern, *Calculating Visions*, 108–109; Reeves, *Profile in Power*, 628–629.

155. Watson, *Lion in the Lobby*, 573.

156. Telegram, Roy Wilkins to Members of Congress, October 29, 1963, NAACP Papers, Part 3, Box A72, LOC.

157. Reeves, *Profile in Power*, 629–630.

158. Bryant, *The Bystander*, 449; Watson, *Lion in the Lobby*, 578.

159. Transcript, Roy Wilkins remarks to the Forum of the Temple Emmanuel Brotherhood, Worcester, MA, October 21, 1963, Roy Wilkins Papers, Box 56, LOC; memorandum, Arnold Aronson to Cooperating Organizations, November 18, 1963, NAACP Papers, Part 3, Box A206, LOC.

160. Wilkins with Mathews, *Standing Fast*, 294; "An Appreciation of Kennedy: Dr. King and Wilkins on Rights," *New York Herald Tribune*, Saturday, November 24, 1963, NAACP Papers, Part 3, Box I16, LOC.

5. All the Way with LBJ

1. "An Appreciation of Kennedy: Dr King and Wilkins on Rights," *New York Herald Tribune*, November 24, 1963, NAACP Papers, Part 3, Box I16, LOC.

2. Mark Stern, *Calculating Visions: Kennedy, Johnson, and Civil Rights* (New Brunswick: Rutgers University Press, 1992), 160; Robert Dallek, *Flawed Giant: Lyndon Johnson and His Times, 1961–1973* (New York: Oxford University Press, 1998), 112.

3. Transcript, President Johnson's Address to Joint Session of Congress, November 27, 1963, LBJL, http://www.lbjlib.utexas.edu/johnson/archives.hom/speeches.hom/631127.asp.

4. Both the comment and the press statement were reprinted in the Secretary's report to the Board of Directors, December 9, 1963, NAACP Papers, Part 3, Box A40, LOC.

5. Layhmond Robinson, "Negroes Praise Johnson Speech," *New York Times*, November 28, 1963.

6. Recording of telephone conversation between Lee White and Lyndon Johnson, December 12, 1963, Tape no. K6312.18, Recordings and Transcripts of Conversations and Meetings, LBJL.

7. Recording of telephone conversation between Lyndon B. Johnson and Lee White, December 26, 1963, 9.47 p.m., Citation no. 63121827, LBJL; Dallek, *Flawed Giant*, 112.

8. Nick Bryant, *The Bystander: John F. Kennedy and the Struggle for Black Equality* (New York: Basic Books, 2006), 459.

9. Robert Caro, *The Years of Lyndon Johnson: The Passage of Power* (New York: Knopf, 2012), 488.

10. Roy Wilkins with Tom Mathews, *Standing Fast: The Autobiography of Roy Wilkins* (Boston: Da Capo Press, 1994), 296; Caro, *Passage of Power*, 489.

11. Dallek, *Flawed Giant*, 113.

12. Steven F. Lawson, "Mixing Moderation with Militancy," in *The Johnson Years*, vol. 3, *LBJ at Home and Abroad*, ed. Robert Divine (Lawrence: University Press of Kansas, 1994), 84.

13. Ibid., 84–85; transcript, Harry McPherson Oral History Interview 5 by T. H. Baker, April 4, 1969, Internet Copy, LBJL, http://www.lbjlibrary.net/assets/documents/archives/oral_histories/mcpherson/mcpher05.pdf.

14. Caro, *Passage of Power*, 496.

15. Memorandum, Lawrence O'Brien to Lyndon Johnson, November 29, 1963, White House Central File, named file, Roy Wilkins, LBJL; Caro, *Passage of Power*, 496.

16. Transcript, Roy Wilkins Oral History Interview 1, April 1, 1969, by Thomas H. Baker, p. 7, LBJL.

17. Stern also cites his segregationist rhetoric during his 1948 senatorial campaign in Stern, *Calculating Visions*, 115.

18. Letter from Lyndon Johnson to Hurschel Mericle, Chairman of the Beaumont Taxpayers for Segregation and Clean Government, March 29, 1957; letter from Lyndon Johnson to Mrs. Wayne Pigg, February 22, 1957, Legislative files, 1957–58, Box 289, LBJL. Both the letters and Johnson's replies are representative of many similar exchanges from this period in the Johnson archives.

19. Dallek, *Flawed Giant*, 26.

20. Between November 1963 and March 1964, Johnson met or spoke with Martin Luther King twice, Whitney Young four times, and James Farmer three times. Schedule of meetings between President Johnson and civil rights leaders, 1963–1968, Legislative Background, voting rights act of 1965, Box 1, LBJL.

21. Recording of telephone conversation between Lyndon B. Johnson and Roy Wilkins, January 6, 1964, 5.12 p.m., Citation no. 1200, Recordings and Transcripts of Conversations and Meetings, LBJL.

22. Anthony Lewis, "Civil Rights Issue: Administration Will Be Judged to Large Degree by the Fate of This Bill," *New York Times*, December 8, 1963.

23. Recording of telephone conversation between Lyndon B. Johnson and Roy Wilkins, January 6, 1964, 5.12 p.m.

24. Dirksen was minority leader of the Senate and as such was of great strategic importance in ensuring the passage of the legislation.

25. Memorandum, Arnold Aronson to Cooperating Organizations, November 18, 1963, NAACP Papers, Part 3, Box A206, LOC.

26. Layhmond Robinson, "NAACP to Ask Voters to Purge Civil Rights Foes," *New York Times*, December 2, 1963.

27. Memorandum, Arnold Aronson to Cooperating Organizations, February 11, 1964, NAACP Papers, Part 3, Box A206, LOC; Denton L. Watson, *The Lion in the Lobby: Clarence Mitchell Jr.'s Struggle for the Passage of Civil Rights Laws* (New York: Morrow, 1990), 593. See also Joseph Rauh, "The Role of the Leadership Conference on Civil Rights in the Civil Rights Struggle of 1963–1964," in *The Civil Rights Act of 1964: The Passage of the Law That Ended Racial Segregation*, ed. Robert D. Loevy (Albany: State University of New York Press, 1997), 49–75.

28. Memorandum, February 11, 1964, NAACP Papers, Part 3, Box A206, LOC.

29. Ibid.; memorandum, Roy Wilkins to NAACP Branch Presidents, March 24, 1964, NAACP Papers, Part 3, Box A72, LOC.

30. Report of the Executive Secretary for the month of April 1964, May 11, 1964, NAACP Papers, Part 3, Box A40, LOC; Monthly Report of the Washington Bureau, May 8, 1964; Arthur Spingarn Papers, Reel 47, LOC.

31. Report of the Executive Secretary for May 1964 (undated, but after the June 19 vote), NAACP Papers, Part 3, Box A40, LOC.

32. Memorandum, Arnold Aronson to Cooperating Organizations, June 10, 1964, LCCR Papers, I37, LOC.

33. Recording of telephone conversation between Lyndon B. Johnson and Roy Wilkins, July 2, 1964, 12:05 p.m., Citation no. 4120, Recordings and Transcripts of Conversations and Meetings, LBJL.

34. Watson, *Lion in the Lobby*, 620; Wilkins with Mathews, *Standing Fast*, 302.

35. Annual Report of Roy Wilkins, January 4, 1965, NAACP Papers, Box 3, AI14, LOC; Wilkins with Mathews, *Standing Fast*, 302.

36. Letter, Clarence Mitchell to Roy Wilkins, December 22, 1964, Roy Wilkins Papers, Box 7, LOC.

37. "Two Kinds of Leadership," *Augusta Herald*, June 23, 1964.

38. M. S. Handler, "NAACP Keeps Moderate View," *New York Times*, June 24, 1964.

39. Memorandum, Roy Wilkins to Alfred Baker Lewis, February 19, 1965, NAACP Papers, Part 3, Box A33, LOC.

40. Jack M. Bloom, *Class, Race, and the Civil Rights Movement* (Bloomington: University of Indiana Press, 1987), 199.

41. Report, Executive Secretary's report to the NAACP Board of Directors, July and August 1964, NAACP Papers, Part 3, Box A32, LOC.

42. Roy Wilkins, "What Now? One Negro Leader's Answer," *New York Times*, August 16, 1964.

43. Letter, Perry Weiss to Roy Wilkins, August 16, 1964; Roy Wilkins to Perry Weiss, August 20, 1964; both NAACP Papers, Part 3, Box A40, LOC.

44. Letter, Roy Wilkins to Senator Barry Goldwater, May 13, 1964, NAACP Papers, Part 3, Box A40, LOC.

45. M. S. Handler, "NAACP Opposes Goldwater's Bid," *New York Times,* June 28, 1964; Roy Wilkins, *Saturday Review,* September 28, 1964.

46. M. S. Handler, "Wilkins Assails Goldwater," *New York Times,* July 4, 1964.

47. John Lewis, with Michael D'Orso, *Walking with the Wind: A Memoir of the Movement* (New York: Harcourt Brace & Co., 1998), 284; Stern, *Calculating Visions,* 192–193; telegram, Roy Wilkins to Martin Luther King, James Farmer, Whitney Young, A. Philip Randolph, and John Lewis, July 22, 1964, cited in Report of the Executive Secretary to Board of Directors for July and August 1964, NAACP Papers, Part 3, Box A40, LOC.

48. Recording of telephone conversation between Lyndon B. Johnson and Roy Wilkins, July 28, 1964, 11.00 a.m., Citation no. 4361, Recordings and Transcripts of Conversations and Meetings, LBJL.

49. Ibid.; Bruce Miroff, "Presidential Leverage over Social Movements: The Johnson White House and Civil Rights," *Journal of Politics* 43 (February 1981): 12–13.

50. Margery McEllheny, "NAACP Open Sessions," *Washington Post,* July 2, 1963.

51. David Garrow, *Bearing the Cross: Martin Luther King, Jr., and the Southern Christian Leadership Conference* (New York: Quill, 1986), 343; Taylor Branch, *Parting the Waters: America in the King Years, 1954–1963* (New York: Touchstone Books, 1988), 424; August Meier and Elliott Rudwick, *CORE: A Study in the Civil Rights Movement, 1942–1968* (Urbana: University of Illinois Press, 1975), 324; Adam Fairclough, *To Redeem the Soul of America: The Southern Christian Leadership Conference and Martin Luther King, Jr.* (Athens: University of Georgia Press, 2001), 200; Stern, *Calculating Visions,* 197; Lewis with D'Orso, *Walking with the Wind,* 284.

52. Report, Minutes of the Board of Directors' meeting, September 14, 1964, Roy Wilkins Papers, Box 16, LOC; Meier and Rudwick, *CORE,* 324; Garrow, *Bearing the Cross,* 324; Lewis, *Walking with the Wind,* 284.

53. Transcript, James Farmer Oral History Interview II, April 1, 1969, by Thomas H. Baker, Internet Copy, LBJL, http://www.lbjlibrary.net/assets/documents/archives/oral_histories/farmer/farmer2.pdf.

54. Text of Statements by Negro Leaders, *New York Times,* July 30, 1964; also reprinted in the Report of the Executive Secretary for July and August 1964, NAACP Papers, Part 3, Box A32, LOC.

55. Ibid.

56. "Key Negro Groups Call on Members to Curb Protests," July 30, 1964,

New York Times; text of Statements by Negro Leaders, *New York Times*, July 30, 1964.

57. R. W. Apple, "Negro Leaders Split Over Call to Curtail Drive," *New York Times*, July 31, 1964; Garrow, *Bearing the Cross*, 343; Branch, *Parting the Waters*, 424; Meier and Rudwick, *CORE*, 324; Fairclough, *To Redeem the Soul*, 200; Stern, *Calculating Visions*, 197; Lewis, *Walking with the Wind*, 284.

58. Clayborne Carson, *In Struggle: SNCC and the Black Awakening of the 1960s* (Cambridge, MA: Harvard University Press, 1995), 112–114.

59. Report, Special Mississippi Investigation Committee of the NAACP, July 23, 1964, NAACP Papers, Part 3, Box A200, LOC.

60. John Dittmer, *Local People: The Struggle for Civil Rights in Mississippi* (Urbana: University of Illinois Press, 1995), 118–119. Although the NAACP was heavily involved in the formation of COFO (Medgar Evers was one of the founders and Aaron Henry, the Association's state president in Mississippi, was COFO's president), by 1964 SNCC was the primary driver of its activities.

61. Memorandum, Laplois Ashford to Roy Wilkins, May 25, 1964; letter, Aaron Henry to Gloster Current, May 30, 1964; memorandum, Gloster Current to Roy Wilkins, John Morsell, and Clarence Mitchell, July 22, 1964; all NAACP Papers, Part 3, Box A212, LOC.

62. Memorandum, Gloster Current to Roy Wilkins, April 9, 1964, NAACP Papers, Part 3, Box A212, LOC. The field secretary Current refers to is Charles Evers, Medgar Evers's brother, who assumed the role on his brother's death with little support from the national office.

63. Herbert Hill, transcript of interview by Simon Hall, May 16, 2000. Thanks to Simon Hall for the use of this transcript.

64. James Booker, "Move to Drop Wilkins?" *Amsterdam News*, January 18, 1964; "The Revolt against Roy Wilkins," *New York Courier*, January 28, 1964, NAACP Papers, Part 3, Box A317, LOC; letter, J. M. Tinsley, member of the National Board of the NAACP, to Roy Wilkins (undated but presumably January 1964), Roy Wilkins Papers, Box 7, LOC.

65. Letter, Roy Wilkins to Executive staff, January 27, 1964, NAACP Papers, Part 3, Box A311, LOC.

66. "The Revolt against Roy Wilkins," *New York Courier*, January 28, 1964, Part 3, Box A317, LOC.

67. Fred Powledge, "Who Leads the Negro?" *New York Times*, January 13, 1964.

68. More on the New York school boycott can be found in Clarence Taylor and Milton A. Galamison, *Knocking at Our Own Door: Milton A. Galamison and the Struggle to Integrate New York City Schools* (Lanham, MD: Lexington Books, 2000).

69. "Who Leads the Negro?" *New York Times*, January 13, 1964; Fred Powledge, "New Rights Leaders," *New York Times*, February 6, 1964.

70. "The Revolt against Roy Wilkins," *New York Courier,* January 28, 1964.

71. Fred Powledge, "NAACP Rebels Seek Board Posts," *New York Times,* December 8, 1964; Fred Powledge, "Militants Press for NAACP Role," *New York Times,* October 5, 1964.

72. M. S. Handler, "NAACP to Help Implement Laws," *New York Times,* July 4, 1965. The decline in membership was also cause for concern. After rising to over 534,500 by the end of 1963, it had fallen to just under 456,000 a year later.

73. Report, Conclusions of the Management Survey Commissioned by the NAACP and Completed by Lennon/Rose, August 1964, NAACP Papers, Part 3, Box A316, LOC; Minutes, Board of Directors meeting, April 13, 1964, Roy Wilkins Papers, Box 16, LOC.

74. Letter to Bishop Spottswood from Roy Wilkins, December 31, 1963, Roy Wilkins Papers, Box 29, LOC.

75. Notes, Interview between Althea Simmons and Sam Rose, December 18–19, 1963, Roy Wilkins Papers, Box 29, LOC.

76. Judge Nathaniel Jones, interview by the author, December 15, 2007.

77. Notes, interview between Althea Simmons and Sam Rose, December 18–19, 1963.

78. Ibid.

79. Organizational chart, Organization and Conference Manual, West Coast Region, May 1953, Arthur Spingarn Papers, Reel 35, LOC.

80. Conclusions of the management survey commissioned by the NAACP and completed by Lennon/Rose, August 1964, NAACP Papers, Part 3, Box A316, LOC.

81. Report, Results of management survey completed by Lennon/Rose, March 20, 1964, Roy Wilkins Papers, Box 29, LOC. Another recommendation made by the consultants was to computerize the national office. This was done, at some expense, but was a notorious failure. Interview with John Morsell conducted by John H. Britton, director, Civil Rights Documentation Project, November 1, 1967, MSRC, 29.

82. Memorandum to underwrite core program budget of NAACP Special Contribution Fund (undated but circa 1970), Roy Wilkins Papers, Box 31, LOC.

83. Annual Report, 1964, NAACP Papers, Part 3, Box I14, LOC.

84. Memorandum, Gloster Current to Roy Wilkins, April 9, 1964, NAACP Papers, Part 3, Box A30, LOC.

85. Press Release, "Reorganization Program Adopted by NAACP Board," September 15, 1964, NAACP Papers, Part 3, Box A316, LOC.

86. Recording of telephone conversation between Roy Wilkins and President Johnson, August 15, 1964, Citation no. 4940, LBJL.

87. Fairclough, *Better Day Coming,* 287. John Dittmer devotes a chapter to the challenge of the MFDP in Atlantic City in detail in *Local People,* 272–302.

88. Fairclough, *Better Day Coming*, 288.

89. Lewis with D'Orso, *Walking with the Wind*, 291.

90. Chana Kai Lee, *For Freedom's Sake: The Life of Fannie Lou Hamer* (Urbana: University of Illinois Press, 2000), 100; Kay Mills and Marian Wright Edelman, *This Little Light of Mine: The Life of Fannie Lou Hamer* (Lexington: University Press of Kentucky, 1994), 128. James Forman tells a similar, albeit less abrasive, story in his biography, *The Making of Black Revolutionaries* (Seattle: University of Washington Press, 1997), 388.

91. Johnson won by a 486–52 margin in the Electoral College, and his share of the popular vote was the largest vote by the greatest margin and percentage won by a US president up to that point. Dallek, *Flawed Giant*, 183–184.

92. Manfred Berg, *The Ticket to Freedom: The NAACP and the Struggle for Black Political Integration* (Gainesville: University of Florida Press, 2005), 213. The *New York Times* cited a similar statistic in a preliminary survey conducted by the newspaper: M. S. Handler, "Negroes a Major Factor in Johnson Victory," *New York Times*, November 5, 1964.

93. Department of Public Relations departmental reports, Executive Secretary Report, November 24, 1964, NAACP Papers, Part 3, Box A32, LOC.

94. Memorandum, Gloster Current to Roy Wilkins, June 23, 1965, NAACP Papers, Part 3, Box A307, LOC.

95. Tanner's remarks are cited in a memorandum from Roy Wilkins to the Executive Committee of the Board of Directors, February 8, 1965, Roy Wilkins Papers, Box 16, LOC.

96. Memorandum, Roy Wilkins to Alfred Baker Lewis, February 19, 1965, NAACP Papers, Part 3, Box A33, LOC.

97. "Vote of Confidence for Roy Wilkins; Nomination of Gov. Coleman Blasted," *Kansas City Call*, July 9, 1965, NAACP Papers, Part 3, Box I16, LOC; "NAACP Chief Denies Cabinet Post 'Deal,'" *Washington Post*, July 4, 1965.

98. Wilkins's denial is reprinted in a memorandum from Roy Wilkins to national board members, vice presidents, state conference presidents, branch and youth unit presidents, November 27, 1964, Roy Wilkins Papers, Box 16, LOC.

99. Recording of telephone conversation between Lyndon B. Johnson and Roy Wilkins, November 12, 1964, 11.10 a.m., Citation no. 6348, Recordings and Transcripts of Conversations and Meetings, LBJL.

100. Simeon Booker, "The Great Society," *Ebony*, August 1965.

101. Wilkins with Mathews, *Standing Fast*, 306. Johnson's biographer, Robert Dallek, supports Wilkins's assertion that Johnson was hesitant to introduce voting rights legislation in early 1965: *Flawed Giant*, 212.

102. James C. Harvey, *Black Civil Rights during the Johnson Administration* (Jackson: University and College Press of Mississippi, 1973), 29.

103. Fairclough, *Better Day Coming*, 290–291; David Garrow, *Protest at Selma: Martin Luther King, Jr., and the Voting Rights Act of 1965* (New Haven: Yale

University Press, 1973), 74–77; Garrow, *Bearing the Cross*, 398–399; Fairclough, *To Redeem the Soul*, 225–251; Taylor Branch, *At Canaan's Edge: America in the King Years, 1965–1968* (New York: Simon & Schuster, 2006), 140–161.

104. Garrow, *Protest at Selma*, 75.

105. Wilkins with Mathews, *Standing Fast*, 306.

106. Lyndon B. Johnson, Address to Congress: The American Promise, March 15, 1965, LBJL, http://www.lbjlib.utexas.edu/johnson/archives.hom/speeches.hom/650315.asp.

107. Ibid.; Dallek, *Flawed Giant*, 218–219.

108. Lyndon B. Johnson, Address to Congress, March 15, 1965, LBJL; "Rights Aides Hail Johnson Address," *New York Times*, March 16, 1965; telegram from Roy Wilkins to President Johnson, March 16, 1965, White House Central Files, named files, Roy Wilkins, LBJL; Wilkins with Mathews, *Standing Fast*, 307.

109. "Protests Spread over the Nation," *New York Times*, March 15, 1965; Farnsworth Fowle, "NAACP Urges Troops in Selma," *New York Times*, March 9, 1965.

110. "Violence in Selma Is Denounced by Political Leaders and Clergy," *New York Times*, March 10, 1965; Nicholas Katzenbach quoted in Howell Raines, *My Soul Is Rested: The Story of the Civil Rights Movement in the Deep South* (New York: Penguin, 1983), 337.

111. Report, Executive Director's report to the Board of Directors, March 1965, NAACP Papers, Part 3, Box A33, LOC.

112. Press Release, "March to Montgomery Hailed by Wilkins," April 3, 1964, NAACP Papers, Part 3, Box A272, LOC.

113. Wilkins with Mathews, *Standing Fast*, 309; Dallek, *Flawed Giant*, 211–221.

114. Katzenbach quoted in Raines, *My Soul Is Rested*, 337.

115. Berg, *Ticket to Freedom*, 215; Watson, *Lion in the Lobby*, 656–658. In June 2013, the Supreme Court struck down Section 4 of the Voting Rights Act, which established a formula to identify those states that must obtain federal approval before making changes to their electoral process. Although the Court declined to rule on Section 5, its ruling in *Shelby County v. Holder* effectively nullifies the core provisions of the act.

116. Richard L. Lyons, "Katzenbach Mutes Clamor for More Vote Bill Strength," *Washington Post*, March 25, 1965.

117. Ibid.; Berg, *Ticket to Freedom*, 216.

118. Berg, *Ticket to Freedom*, 216–217.

119. Letter from Lee White to Roy Wilkins, May 12, 1965, Legislative background to Voting Rights Act, Box 1, LBJL. See Gary May, *Bending toward Justice: The Voting Rights Act and the Transformation of American Democracy* (New York: Basic Books, 2013) for the most recent examination of the passage of the Voting Rights Act.

120. Harvey, *Black Civil Rights,* 34.

121. Memorandum, Arnold Aronson to Cooperating Organizations, August 2, 1965, LCCR Papers, Box 137, LOC. See also memorandum, Arnold Aronson to Cooperating Organizations, April 29, 1965; memorandum, Arnold Aronson to Cooperating Organizations, July 1, 1965; memorandum, Arnold Aronson to Cooperating Organizations, July 12, 1965; all LCCR Papers, Box 137, LOC.

122. C Vann Woodward, "After Watts—Where Is the Negro Revolution Headed?" *New York Times,* August 29, 1965.

123. Harvey, *Black Civil Rights,* 33.

124. Letter, Lee White to Roy Wilkins, May 25, 1965, White House Central Files, named files, Roy Wilkins, LBJL.

125. "Negro Registration in the South Has Increased Dramatically," *New York Times,* May 15, 1966; Fairclough, *Better Day Coming,* 324; Neil R. McMillen, "Black Enfranchisement in Mississippi: Federal Enforcement and Black Protest in the 1960s," *Journal of Southern History* 43, no. 3 (August 1977): 369; Robert Cook, *Sweet Land of Liberty: The African-American Struggle for Civil Rights in the Twentieth Century* (Harlow, Essex: Longman, 1998), 177; Berg, *Ticket to Freedom,* 185; Stephen G. N. Tuck, *Beyond Atlanta: The Struggle for Racial Equality in Georgia, 1940–1980* (Athens: University of Georgia Press, 2001), 214–215; Steven F. Lawson, *Running for Freedom: Civil Rights and Black Politics in America since 1941,* 3rd ed. (New York: Wiley-Blackwell, 2008), 118, 124. John Dittmer tells a less successful story of Mississippi in the months immediately following the passage of the Voting Rights Act, where the Johnson administration was reluctant to send in federal registrars: *Local People,* 390–391.

126. Memorandum, C. D. DeLoach to Mr. Mohr, November 27, 1964, Roy Wilkins Papers, Box 24, LOC.

127. David Garrow, *The FBI and Martin Luther King* (New York: W. W. Norton, 1981), 128, 271n41; Kenneth O'Reilly, *Racial Matters: The FBI's Secret File on Black America, 1960–1972* (New York: Free Press, 1989), 106–107.

128. Steven F. Lawson, *Civil Rights Crossroads: Nation, Community, and the Black Freedom Struggle* (Lexington: University Press of Kentucky, 2005), 89.

129. Handwritten notes for speeches at Amerika Haus, Berlin, April 30, 1965, and Chatham House, May 3, 1965, London, Roy Wilkins Papers, Box 57, LOC.

130. Letter, Elizabeth Brinton to Roy Wilkins, July 28, 1965, Roy Wilkins Papers, Box 23, LOC.

131. Summary of German Press Clippings, Roy Wilkins Papers, Box 23, LOC.

132. Wilkins with Mathews, *Standing Fast,* 311; David C. Carter, *The Music Has Gone Out of the Movement: Civil Rights and the Johnson Administration, 1965–1968* (Chapel Hill: University of North Carolina Press, 2009), 18.

133. President Lyndon B. Johnson's Commencement Address at Howard University: "To Fulfill These Rights," June 4, 1965, http://www.lbjlib.utexas.edu/johnson/archives.hom/speeches.hom/650604.asp.

134. Ibid.

135. Transcript, Keynote address by Roy Wilkins to the 56th annual convention of the NAACP, Denver, CO, June 28, 1965, NAACP Papers, Part 3, Box A20, LOC.

136. Lewis M. Simons, "'Poverty War Mere Illusion,' High NAACP Aide Charges," *Washington Post,* June 30, 1965.

137. Ibid.

138. Unemployment figures cited by the *New York Times* showed that in 1962 the nonwhite unemployment rate was 124 percent higher than that for whites, up from 64 percent in 1947. M. S. Handler, "Greater Poverty for the Negro Feared at NAACP Parley," *New York Times,* June 29, 1965.

139. US Department of Labor, *The Negro Family: The Case for National Action* (Washington, DC, 1965). The *ANNALS of the American Academy of Political and Social Science* dedicated an entire issue to a critical assessment of the report in January 2009, "The Moynihan Report Revisited: Lessons and Reflections after Four Decades" (vol. 621, no. 1).

140. James T. Patterson, *Freedom Is Not Enough: The Moynihan Report and America's Struggle over Black Family Life from LBJ to Obama* (New York: Basic Books, 2010), 71–73.

141. Daniel Patrick Moynihan, "The President and The Negro: The Moment Lost," *Commentary* (February 1967): 38. Wilkins's letter to Moynihan is quoted in Patterson, *Freedom Is Not Enough,* 82.

142. Moynihan, "The President and the Negro," 32.

143. Wilkins with Mathews, *Standing Fast,* 313.

144. Robert Weisbrot, *Freedom Bound: A History of America's Civil Rights Movement* (New York: Plume, 1991), 155.

145. Thomas F. Pettigrew, "Complexity and Change in American Racial Patterns: A Social Psychological View," *Daedalus* 94, no. 4 (Fall 1965): 981 (issue entitled "The Negro American").

146. Ibid., 982. Similar points were made by Weisbrot, *Freedom Bound,* 155; and Woodward, "After Watts," *New York Times,* August 29, 1965.

147. Nancy MacLean, *Freedom Is Not Enough: The Opening of the American Workplace* (Cambridge, MA: Harvard University Press, 2008), 107–109.

148. Fairclough, *Better Day Coming,* 296; Cook, *Sweet Land of Liberty,* 178; Bayard Rustin, "The Watts 'Manifesto' and the McCone Report," *Commentary,* March 1966, 29; Dallek, *Flawed Giant,* 223. Estimates of the cost of property damage in the riots vary widely, from $35 million to $200 million.

149. Executive Director's report, March 1966, NAACP Papers, Part 4, Box A10, LOC.

150. Moynihan, "The President and the Negro," 38.

151. "Inquiry on Causes Urged by Wilkins," *New York Times,* August 16, 1965. Whitney Young and Martin Luther King, however, urged using force to quash the riots.

152. Wilkins with Mathews, *Standing Fast,* 313; Roy Wilkins, "Fate of Race Relations in Hands of Both Races," *Los Angeles Times,* August 23, 1965.

153. Wilkins with Mathews, *Standing Fast,* 314.

6. A Crisis of Victory

1. Press release, "Wilkins Nears 10 Years as NAACP Top Executive," March 26, 1965, NAACP Papers, Part 3, Box A318, LOC. By 1965, membership had fallen to 440,538 from a peak of 534,710 in 1963.

2. Transcript, Remarks of Roy Wilkins at the Annual Meeting of the NAACP, New York City, January 3, 1966, NAACP Papers, Part 4, Box A15, LOC.

3. Gilbert Jonas, who was in charge of fund-raising for the SCF, devotes a chapter to the Special Contribution Fund in his book *Freedom's Sword: The NAACP and the Struggle against Racism in America, 1909–1969* (New York: Routledge, 2005), 357–388; "NAACP Annual Meeting," *The Crisis,* January–February 1967, 12.

4. Report, Ongoing and Prospective Programs of the NAACP for 1965 that Can Be Underwritten by Tax Exempt Contributions through the NAACP Special Contribution Fund, NAACP Papers, Part 3, Box A234, LOC; Remarks, Roy Wilkins, January 3, 1966, NAACP Papers.

5. Memo to Foundations to Underwrite Core Program Budget of NAACP Special Contribution Fund, undated, Roy Wilkins Papers, Box 31, LOC.

6. Recording of telephone conversation between Lyndon B. Johnson and Roy Wilkins, October 30, 1965, 4.03 p.m., Citation 9049, Recordings and Transcripts of Conversations and Meetings, LBJL.

7. Statement by Flint branch, April 10, 1965; telegram, John Morsell to President of NAACP branch, Flint, MI, April 14, 1965; both NAACP Papers, Part 3, Box A328, LOC. Letter, Edwin Peets, President of the NAACP Greenwich Village–Chelsea branch to President Johnson, August 5, 1965, NAACP, Box 18, White House Central Files, LBJL.

8. Berg, "Guns, Butter and Civil Rights," in David K. Adams and Cornelis A. Van Minnen, eds., *Aspects of War in American History* (Keele, Staffordshire: Keele University Press, 1997), 215; Simon Hall, *Peace and Freedom: The Civil Rights Movement and Antiwar Movements in the 1960s* (Philadelphia: University of Pennsylvania Press, 2005), 94–95.

9. Memorandum, Bill Moyers to Lyndon Johnson, August 30, 1965, White House Central Files, Roy Wilkins, LBJL.

10. Draft memorandum, Roy Wilkins to Branch, State Conference, Youth Council and College Chapter Presidents (undated but approximately July 29, 1965), NAACP Papers, Part 3, Box A328, LOC.

11. Letter, Roy Wilkins to Henry S. Smith, January 25, 1966, NAACP Papers, Part 4, Box A88, LOC.

12. Hall, *Peace and Freedom*, 87; Nancy J. Weiss, *Whitney M. Young, Jr. and the Struggle for Civil Rights* (Princeton: Princeton University Press, 1989), 158.

13. Manfred Berg, *The Ticket to Freedom: The NAACP and the Struggle for Black Political Integration* (Gainesville: University of Florida Press, 2005), 226.

14. Clayborne Carson, *In Struggle: SNCC and the Black Awakening of the 1960s* (Cambridge, MA: Harvard University Press, 1995), 188.

15. Roy Wilkins, "SNCC Does Not Speak for Whole Movement," January 15–16, 1966, White House Central Files, HU2 1/20/66–5/31/67, LBJL.

16. Robert Dallek, *Flawed Giant: Lyndon Johnson and His Times, 1961–1973* (New York: Oxford University Press, 1998), 290–291.

17. Ibid., 290.

18. Daniel Patrick Moynihan, "The President and The Negro: The Moment Lost," *Commentary*, February 1967, 32.

19. August Meier and John H. Bracey, "The NAACP as a Reform Movement, 1909–1965," *Journal of Southern History* 59 (February 1993): 29.

20. Hill's contribution to black labor rights has yet to be examined in depth. For an overview of his work, see Nancy MacLean, "Achieving the Promise of the Civil Rights Act: Herbert Hill and the NAACP's Fight for Jobs and Justice," *Labor: Studies in Working-Class History of the Americas* 3, no. 2 (2006): 13–19.

21. Dallek, *Flawed Giant*, 224–225; Lyndon B. Johnson, Commencement Address at Howard University, "To Fulfill These Rights," June 4, 1965, LBJL, http://www.lbjlib.utexas.edu/johnson/archives.hom/speeches.hom/650604. asp; Kevin L. Yuill, "The 1966 White House Conference on Civil Rights," *Historical Journal* 41 (March 1998): 276.

22. Yuill, "The 1966 White House Conference on Civil Rights," 259.

23. Carson, *In Struggle*, 203.

24. John Dittmer, *Local People: The Struggle for Civil Rights in Mississippi* (Urbana: University of Illinois Press, 1995), 389.

25. Details of the strategy meeting held in Memphis are examined from the perspective of each of the participants in their respective biographies and autobiographies: Stokely Carmichael with Ekwueme Michael Thelwell, *Ready for Revolution: The Life and Struggles of Stokely Carmichael (Kwame Ture)* (New York: Scribner, 2003), 491–500; Roy Wilkins with Tom Mathews, *Standing Fast: The Autobiography of Roy Wilkins* (New York: Da Capo Press, 1994), 315–316; David Garrow, *Bearing the Cross: Martin Luther King, Jr., and the Southern Christian Leadership Conference* (New York: Quill, 1986), 476–478; Weiss, *Whitney M. Young*, 111; Adam Fairclough, *To Redeem the Soul of America: The Southern Christian Leadership Conference and Martin Luther King, Jr.* (Athens: University of Georgia Press, 2001), 309–312.

26. Lance Hill, *The Deacons for Defense: Armed Resistance and the Civil Rights Movement* (Chapel Hill: University of North Carolina Press, 2004) remains the definitive account of the organization.

27. Carmichael with Thelwell, *Ready for Revolution,* 499–500.

28. Carmichael's actions are reported in several histories, including Carson, *In Struggle,* 207; Fairclough, *To Redeem the Soul,* 314; and Garrow, *Bearing the Cross,* 476–477.

29. Manifesto of the Meredith-Mississippi March, June 8, 1966, transmitted by telephone to NAACP headquarters, NAACP Papers, Part 4, Box A56, LOC.

30. Draft statement, Roy Wilkins, June 8, 1966 (unsent), NAACP Papers; Part 4, Box A81. Press release, "NAACP Supports Objectives of James Meredith's March," June 11, 1966, NAACP Papers, Part 4, Box A56, LOC.

31. Memorandum, Roy Wilkins to NAACP branch officers on Meredith March, Memphis to Jackson, June 10, 1966, NAACP Papers, Part 4, Box A56, LOC.

32. Roy Wilkins, "'New Militants' Have Altered Meredith's Idea," *Los Angeles Times,* June 20, 1966.

33. "Mississippi March Results: The Balance Is Favorable," *Los Angeles Times,* July 4, 1966.

34. Memorandum, Roy Wilkins to Delegates to the 57th Annual NAACP Convention, July 5, 1966, NAACP Papers, Part 4, Box A81, LOC; M. S. Handler, "Wilkins Assails CORE and SNCC, Hints Full Break," *New York Times,* July 8, 1966.

35. Berg, *Ticket to Freedom,* 229; Garrow, *Bearing the Cross,* 481.

36. Speech, Roy Wilkins to the 57th NAACP Annual Convention, Los Angeles, July 5, 1966, NAACP Papers, Part 4, Box A3, LOC.

37. Ibid.

38. Ibid.

39. Cited in William Brink and Louis Harris, *Black and White: A Study of U.S. Racial Attitudes Today* (New York: Simon & Schuster, [1967]), 120.

40. Wilkins with Mathews, *Standing Fast,* 322.

41. James Meredith, "Big Changes Are Coming," *Saturday Evening Post,* August 14, 1966, NAACP Papers, Part 4, Box A56, LOC.

42. Ibid.

43. Letter, Roy Wilkins to the Editor, *Saturday Evening Post,* August 11, 1966, NAACP Papers, Part 4, Box A56, LOC.

44. Memorandum, Willard Wirtz, Secretary of Labor, to unnamed recipients, August 8, 1967, White House Central Files, HU2/ST, LBJL. King was cited by 178 respondents, Carmichael by 52, and A. Philip Randolph by 24.

45. Draft memorandum, Roy Wilkins to Branches (undated but approximately June 15, 1966), NAACP Papers, Part 4, Box A61, LOC.

46. Wilkins with Mathews, *Standing Fast,* 323.

47. Roy Wilkins, "What Will the Nation Do?" *Los Angeles Times,* March 13, 1967.

48. Letter, Jack Tanner to Roy Wilkins, May 23, 1966; letter, Roy Wilkins to Jack Tanner, May 25, 1966; letter, Stephen Spottswood to Jack Tanner, June 16, 1966; all NAACP Papers, Part 4, Box A13, LOC.

49. Nicholas von Hoffman, "NAACP Keeps Unity but Finds It Difficult," *Washington Post,* July 9, 1966; "Use Black Power, Says NAACP Head," *Yakima Herald,* July 13, 1966, NAACP Papers, Part 4, Box A13, LOC.

50. Transcript, Statements made by Roy Wilkins on *Meet the Press,* August 21, 1966, NAACP Papers, Part 4, Box A83, LOC.

51. Memorandum, Harry McPherson to Lyndon Baines Johnson, September 12, 1966, Civil Rights during the Johnson Administration, Reel 11, RSC.

52. Memorandum, Nicholas Katzenbach to Harry McPherson, September 17, 1966, Civil Rights during the Johnson Administration, Reel 11, RSC.

53. Emmanuel Perlmutter, "16 Negroes Seized: Plot to Kill Wilkins and Young Charged," *New York Times,* June 22, 1967.

54. Note, Roy Wilkins to Minnie Wilkins, November 10, 1966, Roy Wilkins Papers, Box 76, LOC.

55. Speech, Dr. Martin Luther King Jr. to a meeting of Clergy and Laity Concerned about Vietnam at Riverside Church, New York City, April 4, 1967, The Martin Luther King Jr. Research and Education Institute, http://mlk-kpp01 .stanford.edu/kingweb/publications/speeches/Beyond_Vietnam.pdf.

56. Ibid. SNCC had issued a similarly militant rebuke of America's policy in Vietnam in January 1966, which Wilkins refuted with strong language in his weekly column, arguing that, while he disagreed with the principles of SNCC's condemnation of the war, the document was the result of "the snail's pace of racial justice in the United States." Roy Wilkins, January 15–16, 1966, White House Central Files, HU2 1/20/66–5/31/67, LBJL.

57. Roy Wilkins, "King Spoke for Self, Not for Civil Rights Movement," *Los Angeles Times,* April 17, 1967.

58. Harris poll, May 22, 1967, referenced in a memorandum from Fred Panzer to President Johnson, May 20, 1967, White House Central Files, HU2 1/20/66–5/31/67, Box 4, LBJL.

59. Berg, "Guns, Butter and Civil Rights," 213–238.

60. James E. Westheider, *Fighting on Two Fronts: African Americans and the Vietnam War* (New York: New York University Press, 1999), 24.

61. Spencer C. Tucker, *The Encyclopedia of the Vietnam War: A Political, Social, and Military History* (Oxford: Oxford University Press, 2000), 9; Westheider, *Fighting on Two Fronts,* 24. Blacks accounted for around 13 percent of the total population of the United States at this time.

62. Memorandum, Gloster Current to Roy Wilkins, April 16, 1967, NAACP Papers, Part 4, Box 89, LOC.

7. The Survivor

1. Roy Wilkins with Tom Mathews, *Standing Fast: The Autobiography of Roy Wilkins* (Boston: Da Capo Press, 1994), 326.

2. "Summary of Report by National Advisory Commission on Civil Disorders," *New York Times,* March 1, 1968.

3. Judge Nathaniel Jones, interview by author, December 15, 2007.

4. Memorandum, Harry McPherson to Joseph Califano, March 1, 1968, Box 39, FG632, LBJL.

5. "Summary of Report by National Advisory Commission on Civil Disorders," *New York Times,* March 1, 1968.

6. John Herbers, "Panel on Civil Disorders Calls for Drastic Action to Avoid Two-Society Nation," *New York Times,* March 1, 1968; memorandum, Joe Califano to Lyndon Baines Johnson, February 28, 1968, White House Central Files, Ex FG690, LBJL; US Riot Commission, *Report of the National Advisory Commission on Civil Disorders* (New York: The New York Times Co., 1968).

7. Sidney E. Zion, "Rights Leaders Support Criticism of Whites," *New York Times,* March 2, 1968; telegram, Martin Luther King to Roy Wilkins, March 4, 1968, NAACP Papers, Part 4, Box A237, LOC.

8. Robert Dallek, *Flawed Giant: Lyndon Johnson and His Times, 1961–1973* (New York: Oxford University Press, 1998), 516.

9. Memorandum, Joseph Califano to President Johnson, February 28, 1968, White House Central Files, Ex FG690; memorandum, Harry McPherson to Joe Califano, March 1, 1968, FG632, Box 39, LBJL.

10. Memorandum, Joseph Califano to President Johnson, March 2, 1968, White House Central Files, Ex FG690, LBJL.

11. "President Condemns Violence, Says US Is Shocked, Saddened," *Los Angeles Times,* April 5, 1968.

12. Clayborne Carson, *In Struggle: SNCC and the Black Awakening of the 1960s* (Cambridge, MA: Harvard University Press, 1995), 288.

13. "N.Y. Reaction to Slaying," *Christian Science Monitor,* April 6, 1968; "The Martyrdom of Martin Luther King, Jr.," *The Crisis,* April 1968, 115.

14. Report on the Special Planning Conference, February 23 and 24, 1968, Wilkins Papers, Box 17, LOC.

15. Dallek, *Flawed Giant,* 534.

16. August Meier and Elliott Rudwick, *CORE: A Study in the Civil Rights Movement, 1942–1968* (Urbana: University of Illinois Press, 1975), 428–429.

17. Summary of 1968 NAACP Convention Security Measures, submitted by Clarence Mitchell, July 26, 1968, NAACP Papers, Part 5, Box A7, LOC; Thomas A. Johnson, "NAACP Youths Quit Convention," *New York Times,* June 29, 1968.

18. August Meier and Elliott Rudwick, *Along the Color Line: Explorations in the Black Experience* (Urbana: University of Illinois Press, 1976), 256.

19. "Second Walkout by Young Turks Leaves NAACP Session in Chaos," *Washington Post,* June 30, 1968.

20. Meier and Rudwick, *Along the Color Line,* 257; "Ghetto Housing Program Announced," *The Crisis,* August–September 1968, 252–253.

21. Gilbert Jonas, *Freedom's Sword: The NAACP and the Struggle against Racism in America, 1909–1969* (New York: Routledge, 2005), 324.

22. Meier and Rudwick, *Along the Color Line*, 257.

23. Wilkins with Mathews, *Standing Fast*, 300; Earl Caldwell, "Wilkins, in Talk to CORE, Seeks to Close Negro Rift," *New York Times*, July 6, 1968; Jean M. White, "Wilkins Opposes Black Separatism," *Washington Post*, July 6, 1968, NAACP Papers, Part 4, Box A45, LOC.

24. Wilkins with Mathews, *Standing Fast*, 329.

25. Ibid., 330.

26. Lewis M. Steel, "Nine Men in Black Who Think White," *New York Times*, October 13, 1968.

27. Press Release, October 14, 1969, Roy Wilkins Papers, Box 31, LOC. Memorandum, Roy Wilkins to National Board Members, Presidents of State Conferences, Branches, Youth Councils and College Chapters, and Field Staff, October 24, 1968; letter, Robert Carter to Roy Wilkins, October 28, 1968; letter, Roy Wilkins to Robert Carter, October 29, 1968; memorandum, Roy Wilkins to Board of Directors, October 31, 1968; letter, Roy Wilkins to Eugene Reed, November 6, 1968; "The Substantive Issue in the Steel Case" (unattributed), December 6, 1968; all NAACP Papers, Part 4, Box A11, LOC. Letter, Robert Carter to Roy Wilkins, Oct. 28, 1968, Roy Wilkins Papers, Box 31, LOC. Judge Nathaniel Jones, interview by author, December 15, 2007. Wilkins with Mathews, *Standing Fast*, 331–332.

28. Statement of the staff attorneys of the General Counsel's office of the NAACP (undated; Wilkins gives the date as October 28, 1968); memorandum, Roy Wilkins to Members of the National Board of Directors, October 31, 1968, Roy Wilkins Papers, Box 31, LOC.

29. Robert L. Carter, *A Matter of Law: A Memoir of Struggle in the Cause of Equal Rights* (New York: New Press, 2005), 201.

30. Wilkins with Mathews, *Standing Fast*, 332.

31. Ibid., 333.

32. Jack Nelson and Ray Rogers, "Wilkins Blasts School Desegregation Decision," *Los Angeles Times*, July 4, 1969.

33. *Green v. County School Board of New Kent County*, 391 U.S. 430 (1968).

34. *Alexander v. Holmes County Board of Education*, 396 U.S. 1218 (1969); *The Crisis*, November 1969, 361.

35. James T. Patterson, *Brown v. Board of Education: A Civil Rights Milestone and Its Troubled Legacy* (Oxford: Oxford University Press, 2001), 155.

36. *Swann v. Charlotte-Mecklenburg Board of Education*, 402 U.S. 1 (1971).

37. Stephen G. N. Tuck, *Beyond Atlanta: The Struggle for Racial Equality in Georgia, 1940–1980* (Athens: University of Georgia Press, 2001), 212–213; Raymond Wolters, *Race and Education, 1954–2007* (Columbia: University of Missouri Press, 2009), 128. The first Atlanta Compromise refers to a speech given

by Booker T. Washington in 1895 in which he argued that blacks should pursue vocational skills rather than political power and "social equality," but that whites should bear responsibility for just treatment of black Americans.

38. "Voluntary Segregation—A Disaster," March 29, 1969, reprinted in Roy Wilkins, *Talking It Over* (1982; reprint, Norwalk, CT: M&B Publishing, 1994), 66–67.

39. Handwritten draft of telegram and press release issued of telegram exchange between Roy Wilkins and Bobby Seale, July 1, 1969; telegram, David Hilliard, chief of staff of the Black Panther Party, to Roy Wilkins, August 31, 1969; telegram, Roy Wilkins to David Hilliard, Black Panther Party HQ, September 4, 1969; telegram, Roy Innis to Roy Wilkins, December 6, 1969; letter, John Morsell to Gannel Taylor, January 20, 1970; all NAACP Papers, Part 6, Box A35, LOC.

40. Roy Wilkins and Ramsey Clark (Chairmen), *Search and Destroy: A Report by the Commission of Inquiry into the Black Panthers and the Police* (New York: Metropolitan Applied Research Center, 1973), 248–249; Matthew Fleischer, "Policing Revolution," *Los Angeles Times* magazine, April 2011. See Jakobi Williams, *From the Bullet to the Ballot: The Illinois Chapter of the Black Panther Party and Racial Coalition Politics in Chicago* (Chapel Hill: University of North Carolina Press, 2013) for more on the history of the Black Panther Party in Illinois and the events that led up to the deaths of Fred Hampton and Mark Clark.

41. "The Police vs. the Black Panthers," *The Crisis,* January 1970.

42. Memorandum, Roy Wilkins to adult branch officers, youth unit officers and state conference presidents, November 7, 1969, NAACP Papers, Part 4, Box A83, LOC; "NAACP Annual Meeting: January 11, 1971," *The Crisis,* March 1971, 61.

43. Jonas, *Freedom's Sword*, 326.

44. Vernon Jarrett, "Wilkins Brought Vision, Reality to Human Rights," *Evening Independent,* September 15, 1981; Orde Coombs, "The Long Good-Bye of Roy Wilkins," *New York* magazine, June 27, 1977, 95–97; Celeste Durant, "Roy Wilkins: Pushed off the Mountaintop," *Los Angeles Times,* August 24, 1977.

45. Statement, Roy Wilkins to the NAACP Board of Directors, July 1, 1976, Roy Wilkins Papers, Box 76, LOC.

46. Speech, Roy Wilkins to the 67th Annual Convention, July 1, 1976, Memphis, Tennessee, Roy Wilkins Papers, Box 76, LOC.

47. Walter Morrison, "Wilkins Dispute Threatens Image of NAACP," *Pittsburgh Press,* July 17, 1976.

48. Jonas, *Freedom's Sword*, 321.

49. Judge Nathaniel Jones, interview by author, December 15, 2007.

50. Report to the national board of directors of the NAACP of the Search and Screening Committee for a New Executive Director, November 6, 1976, Roy Wilkins Papers, Box 17, LOC.

51. "Wilkins Retires after 22 Years as NAACP Head," *Washington Post,* June 27, 1977.

52. Simeon Booker, "Roy Wilkins Showered with Affection as He Leaves Top NAACP Post," *Jet,* July 14, 1977.

53. Paul Delaney, "Tribute to Wilkins Unites Feuding NAACP Parley," *New York Times,* June 30, 1977.

54. Coombs, "The Long Good-Bye of Roy Wilkins," 95–97.

55. Celeste Durant, "Roy Wilkins: Pushed off the Mountaintop," *Los Angeles Times,* August 24, 1977.

56. Roy Wilkins, "Ghettoes Screaming for Help," *The Afro-American,* May 31, 1980.

57. David Garrow, "FBI Political Harassment and FBI Historiography: Analyzing Informants and Measuring Effects," *Public Historian* 10, no. 4 (Autumn 1988): 5–18; George Lardner, "Wilkins Denied Any Link to FBI Plot to Discredit Dr. King," *Washington Post,* May 31, 1978.

Conclusion

1. Warren Brown, "NAACP's Roy Wilkins Dies," *Washington Post,* September 9, 1981.

2. August Meier and John H. Bracey, "The NAACP as a Reform Movement, 1909–1965," *Journal of Southern History* 59 (February 1993): 22.

Bibliography

Archival Collections

Library of Congress, Washington, DC
NAACP Papers
Papers of the Leadership Conference on Civil Rights
Joseph L. Rauh Papers
Bayard Rustin Papers
Arthur Spingarn Papers
Roy Wilkins Papers

Lyndon B. Johnson Library, Austin, Texas
White House Central Files
Commission on Civil Rights (Box 375)
Civil Rights (Box 4, 7, 20, 22, 23, 24, 33, 56, 652)
Equality of the Races (Box 2–57)
Named files
Martin Luther King Jr.
NAACP
Roy Wilkins
Confidential File (Box 39)
Legislative File (Boxes 1–2, 289–291)
Administrative Histories
Department of Justice, Civil Rights Division (Parts 9–10)
Office Files of the White House Aides
Bellinger, Cecil
Califano, Joseph A.
Cater, Douglass
Gaither, James
McPherson, Harry C.
Panzer, Frederick
Reedy, George E.
White, Lee C.
Oral Histories
Califano, Joseph A.

Clark, Ramsey
Evers, Charles
Farmer, James
Katzenbach, Nicholas
Marshall, Burke
McPherson, Harry
Mitchell, Clarence
Rauh, Joseph L., Jr.
Valenti, Jack
Wilkins, Roy
Young, Whitney, M., Jr.

Note: The Johnson Library has also made available a substantial number of recordings of telephone conversations made by President Johnson. The recordings
are available online at http://www.lbjlib.utexas.edu/johnson/archives.hom/
Dictabelt.hom/content.asp. A selection of oral history transcripts is also available online via the Johnson Library: http://www.lbjlib.utexas.edu/johnson/
archives.hom/biopage.asp#anchor27458

**Beinecke Rare Book and Manuscript Library, Yale University, New
Haven, Connecticut**

Walter and Poppy Cannon White Papers (Box 8, 12)
James Weldon Johnson Papers (Box 24, 25)

**Moorland-Spingarn Research Center, Howard University, Washing-
ton, DC**

Ralph J. Bunche Oral History Collection
Carter, Robert
Current, Gloster
Farmer, James
Kennedy, Judge Joseph J.
King, Celes
Mitchell, Clarence
Morsell, John
Spingarn, Arthur
Wilkins, Roy
Williams, Robert F.

Roosevelt Study Center, Middelburg, The Netherlands

The Roosevelt Study Center is a research center devoted to modern American
history. It houses a large collection of microfiche copies of presidential archives as
well as the archives of some organizations involved in the civil rights movement.
Records of the Southern Christian Leadership Conference

Papers of the Student Nonviolent Coordinating Committee (SNCC)
Papers of W. E. B. Du Bois
Civil Rights during the Kennedy Administration, 1961–1963, Part 1
Civil Rights during the Kennedy Administration, 1961–1963, Part 2
President John F. Kennedy's Office Files
Note: These files incorporate the working files of President Kennedy. The parts reviewed for this work were:
> Special Correspondence, Speech, Legislative and Press Conference Files
> Staff Memoranda
> Departments and Agencies File
> Subjects File

Oral Histories

Farmer, James
Marshall, Burke
Marshall, Thurgood
Mitchell, Clarence
Wilkins, Roy

Daily diary of President Johnson, 1963–1969

Civil Rights during the Johnson Administration, 1963–1969

Federal Bureau of Investigation

Roy Wilkins: http://vault.fbi.gov/Roy Wilkins

University of Cambridge Library, Cambridge, UK

Papers of the NAACP, Parts 1–3

British Library, London

Tuskegee Institute News Clippings File
Note: The British Library holds a set of microfilm of press clippings collected by the Tuskegee Institute Department of Records and Research in Tuskegee, Alabama. The clippings cover the years 1899 to 1966 and were compiled from more than 300 American and international newspapers. The collection focuses primarily on African American issues.

Interviews by Author

Jack Greenberg, New York City, September 2007.
Nathaniel Jones, New York City, December 2007.
Roger Wilkins, Washington, DC, August 2006.

Books and Articles

Adams, David K., and Cornelis A. Van Minnen, eds. *Aspects of War in American History.* Keele, Staffordshire: Keele University Press, 1997.

Adelman, Lynn. "A Study of James Weldon Johnson." *Journal of Negro History* 52 (April 1967): 128–145.

Alinksy, Saul A. *Rules for Radicals: A Pragmatic Primer for Realistic Radicals.* 1971. Reprint, New York: Vintage Books, 1989.

Ames, Jessie Daniel. "Editorial Treatment of Lynchings." *Public Opinion Quarterly* 2 (January 1938): 77–84.

Anderson, Carol. *Eyes Off the Prize: The United Nations and the African American Struggle for Human Rights, 1944–1955.* Cambridge: Cambridge University Press, 2003.

Anderson, Jervis. *Bayard Rustin: The Trouble I've Seen.* Berkeley: University of California Press, 1998.

Anderson, Karen Tucker Anderson. "Last Hired, First Fired: Black Woman Workers during World War II." *Journal of American History* 69 (June 1982): 82–97.

Arsenault, Raymond. *Freedom Riders: 1961 and the Struggle for Racial Justice.* New York: Oxford University Press, 2006.

Autrey, Dorothy. "'Can These Bones Live?': The National Association for the Advancement of Colored People in Alabama, 1918–1930." *Journal of Negro History* 82 (Winter 1997): 1–12.

Banks, Waldo R. "Changing Attitudes towards the Negro in the United States: The Primary Causes." *Journal of Negro Education* 30 (Spring 1961): 87–93.

Barksdale, Marcellus. "Civil Rights Organization and the Indigenous Movement in Chapel Hill, NC, 1960–1965." *Phylon* 47 (1st Quarter 1986): 29–42.

Barnett, Claude A. "The Role of the Press, Radio and Motion Picture and Negro Morale." *Journal of Negro Education* 12 (Summer 1943): 474–489.

Bartley, Numan V. *The Rise of Massive Resistance: Race and Politics during the 1950s.* Baton Rouge: Louisiana State University Press, 1997.

Bass, Jack. *Unlikely Heroes: A Vivid Account of the Implementation of the Brown Decision in the South by Southern Federal Judges Committed to the Rule of Law.* Tuscaloosa: University of Alabama Press, 1990.

Bass, Jack, and Walter de Vries. *The Transformation of Southern Politics: Social Change and Political Consequence since 1945.* Athens: University of Georgia Press, 1995.

Bates, Beth Tompkins. *The Making of Black Detroit in the Age of Henry Ford.* Chapel Hill: University of North Carolina Press, 2012.

———. "A New Crowd Challenges the Agenda of the Old Guard in the NAACP, 1933–1941." *American Historical Review* 102 (April 1997): 340–377.

Beck, E. M., and Stewart Tolnay. "The Killing Fields of the Deep South: The

Market for Cotton and the Lynching of Blacks, 1882–1930."*American Sociological Review* 55 (August 1990): 526–539.

———. "Racial Violence and Black Migration in the American South, 1910 to 1930." *American Sociological Review* 57 (February 1992): 103–116.

Beck, Kent M. "What Was Liberalism in the 1950s?" *Political Science Quarterly* 102 (Summer 1987): 233–258.

Bell, W. Y., Jr. "The Negro Warrior's Home Front." *Phylon* 5 (3rd Quarter 1944): 271–278.

Berg, Manfred. "Black Civil Rights and Liberal Anticommunism: The NAACP in the Early Cold War." *Journal of American History* 94 (June 2007): 75–96.

———. *The Ticket to Freedom: The NAACP and the Struggle for Black Political Integration.* Gainesville: University of Florida Press, 2005.

Biles, Roger. "The Urban South in the Great Depression." *Journal of Southern History* 56 (February 1990): 71–100.

Biondi, Martha. *The Black Revolution on Campus.* Berkeley: University of California Press, 2012.

———. *To Stand and Fight: The Struggle for Civil Rights in Postwar New York City.* Cambridge, MA: Harvard University Press, 2003.

Blassinghame, John W. *The Slave Community: Plantation Life in the Antebellum South.* New York: Oxford University Press, 1979.

Blaustein, Albert P., and Robert L. Zagrando, eds. *Civil Rights and the American Negro.* New York: Washington Square Press, 1968.

Bloom, Jack M. *Class, Race, and the Civil Rights Movement.* Bloomington: University of Indiana Press, 1987.

Bodroghkozy, Aniko. *Equal Time: Television and the Civil Rights Movement.* Champaign: University of Illinois Press, 2012.

Bonjean, Charles M. "Community Leadership: A Case Study and Conceptual Refinement." *American Journal of Sociology* 68 (May 1963): 672–681.

Borstelmann, Thomas. *The Cold War and the Color Line: American Race Relations in the Global Arena.* Cambridge, MA: Harvard University Press, 2001.

Boulware, Marcus H. *The Oratory of Negro Leaders, 1900–1968.* Westport, CT: Negro Universities Press, 1969.

Branch, Taylor. *At Canaan's Edge: America in the King Years, 1965–1968.* New York: Simon & Schuster, 2006.

———. *Parting the Waters: America in the King Years, 1954–1963.* New York: Touchstone Books, 1988.

———. *Pillar of Fire: America in the King Years, 1963–1965.* New York: Simon & Schuster, 1998.

Branson, Herman. "The Training of Negroes for War Industries in World War II." *Journal of Negro Education* 12 (Summer 1943): 376–385.

Braungart, Margaret M., and Richard G. Braungart. "The Effects of the 1960s

Political Generation on Former Left- and Right-Wing Youth Activist Leaders." *Social Problems* 38 (August 1991): 297–315.

Brink, William, and Louis Harris. *Black and White: A Study of U.S. Racial Attitudes Today.* New York: Simon & Schuster [1967].

Brown-Nagin, Tomiko. *Courage to Dissent: Atlanta and the Long History of the Civil Rights Movement.* Oxford: Oxford University Press, 2011.

Bryant, Nick. *The Bystander: John F. Kennedy and the Struggle for Black Equality.* New York: Basic Books, 2006.

Bunche, Ralph J. "A Critical Analysis of the Tactics and Programs of Minority Groups." *Journal of Negro Education* 4 (July 1935): 308–320.

———. "A Critique of the New Deal Social Planning as It Affects Negroes." *Journal of Negro Education* 5 (January 1936): 59–65.

———. "The Programs of Organizations Devoted to the Improvement of the Status of the American Negro." *Journal of Negro Education* 8 (July 1939): 539–550.

Burk, Robert F. *The Eisenhower Administration and Black Civil Rights.* Knoxville: University of Tennessee Press, 1984.

Button, James W. *Blacks and Social Change: Impact of the Civil Rights Movement in Southern Communities.* Princeton: Princeton University Press, 1989.

Bynum, Thomas. *NAACP Youth and the Fight for Black Freedom, 1936–1965.* Knoxville: University of Tennessee Press, 2013.

Caplan, Marvin. *Farther Along: A Civil Rights Memoir.* Baton Rouge: Louisiana State University Press, 1999.

Carmichael, Stokely, and Charles V. Hamilton. *Black Power: The Politics of Liberation in America.* 1967. Rev. ed., Harmondsworth: Pelican Books, 1969.

Carmichael, Stokely, with Ekwueme Michael Thelwell. *Ready for Revolution: The Life and Struggles of Stokely Carmichael (Kwame Ture).* New York: Scribner, 2003.

Caro, Robert. *The Years of Lyndon Johnson: Master of the Senate.* New York: Vintage, 2002.

———. *The Years of Lyndon Johnson: Means of Ascent.* New York: Vintage, 1991.

———. *The Years of Lyndon Johnson: The Passage of Power.* New York: Knopf, 2012.

———. *The Years of Lyndon Johnson: The Path to Power.* New York: Vintage, 1990.

Carson, Clayborne. *In Struggle: SNCC and the Black Awakening of the 1960s.* Cambridge, MA: Harvard University Press, 1995.

———. "Martin Luther King, Jr.: Charismatic Leadership in a Mass Struggle." *Journal of American History* 74 (September 1987): 448–454.

———. "Two Cheers for *Brown v. Board of Education.*" *Journal of American History* 91 (June 2004): 26–31.

Carter, Dan. *Scottsboro: A Tragedy of the American South.* Baton Rouge: Louisiana State University Press, 1995.

Carter, David C. *The Music Has Gone Out of the Movement: Civil Rights and the Johnson Administration, 1965–1968*. Chapel Hill: University of North Carolina Press, 2009.

Carter, Robert L. *A Matter of Law: A Memoir of Struggle in the Cause of Equal Rights*. New York: New Press, 2005.

Cash, W. J. *The Mind of the South*. 1941. Rev. ed., New York: Vintage Books, 1991.

Catsam, Derek Charles. *Freedom's Main Line: The Journey to Reconciliation and the Freedom Rides*. Lexington: University Press of Kentucky, 2009.

Cell, John W. *The Highest Stage of White Supremacy: The Origins of Segregation in South Africa and the American South*. Cambridge: University of Cambridge Press, 1982.

Chafe, William H. *Civilities and Civil Rights: Greensboro, North Carolina and the Black Struggle for Equality*. New York: Oxford University Press, 1980.

Chafe, William H., Raymond Gavins, and Robert Korstad, eds. *Remembering Jim Crow: African Americans Tell about Life in the Segregated South*. New York: New Press, 2001.

Chappell, David L. *A Stone of Hope: Prophetic Religion and the Death of Jim Crow*. Chapel Hill: University of North Carolina Press, 2004.

Charles, Cleophus. "Roy Wilkins, the NAACP, and the Early Struggle for Civil Rights: Towards the Biography of a Man and a Movement in Microcosm, 1901–1939." PhD diss., Cornell University, 1981.

Clark, E. Culpepper. *The Schoolhouse Door: Segregation's Last Stand at the University of Alabama*. Tuscaloosa: University of Alabama Press, 2007.

Clark, Kenneth B. "Morale of the Negro on the Home Front: World Wars I and II." *Journal of Negro Education* 12 (Summer 1943): 417–428.

Clement, Rufus E. "The Strange Career of Jim Crow (Review)." *Journal of Southern History* 21 (November 1955): 557–559.

Cobb, Charles E., Jr. "From Stokely Carmichael to Kwame Ture." *Callaloo* 34, no. 1 (Winter 2011): 89–97.

Cohen, Robert, and David J. Snyder, eds. *Rebellion in Black and White: Southern Student Activism in the 1960s*. Baltimore: John Hopkins University Press, 2013.

Cohodas, Nadine. *The Band Played Dixie: Race and the Liberal Conscience at Ole Miss*. New York: Free Press, 1997.

Colaiaco, James A. "Martin Luther King Jr. and the Paradox of Nonviolent Direct Action." *Phylon* 47 (1st Quarter 1986): 16–28.

Colbourn, David R., and Jane L. Landers. *The African American Heritage of Florida*. Gainesville: University Press of Florida, 1995.

Colley. Zoe A. *Ain't Scared of Your Jail: Arrest, Imprisonment, and the Civil Rights Movement*. Gainesville: University of Florida Press, 2012.

Cone, James H. *Martin and Malcolm and America: A Dream or a Nightmare*. Maryknoll, NY: Orbis Books, 1992.

Contee, Clarence G. "Du Bois, the NAACP, and the Pan-African Congress of 1919." *Journal of Negro History* 57 (January 1972): 13–28.

Conyers, James L., ed. *Charles H. Houston: An Interdisciplinary Study of Civil Rights Leadership.* Lanham, MD: Lexington Books, 2012.

Cook, Mercer. "Race Relations as Seen by Recent French Visitors." *Phylon* 15 (2nd Quarter 1954): 121–138.

Cook, Robert. *Sweet Land of Liberty: The African-American Struggle for Civil Rights in the Twentieth Century.* Harlow, Essex: Longman, 1998.

Cosgrove, Stuart. "The Zoot-Suit and Style Warfare." *History Workshop Journal* 18 (Autumn 1984): 77–91.

Cox, Oliver C. "The Program of Negro Civil Rights Organization." *Journal of Negro Education* 20 (Summer 1951): 354–366.

Crespino, Joseph. *In Search of Another Country: Mississippi and the Conservative Counterrevolution.* Princeton: Princeton University Press, 2007.

Dailey, Jane, Glenda Elizabeth Gilmore, and Bryant Simon, eds. *Jumpin' Jim Crow: Southern Politics from Civil War to Civil Rights.* Princeton: Princeton University Press, 2000.

Dalfiume, Richard M. "The 'Forgotten Years' of the Negro Revolution." *Journal of American History* 55 (June 1968): 90–106.

———. "Military Segregation and the 1940 Presidential Election." *Phylon* 30 (1st Quarter 1969): 42–55.

Dallek, Robert. *Flawed Giant: Lyndon Johnson and His Times, 1961–1973.* New York: Oxford University Press, 1998.

Daniel, Pete. "Going among Strangers: Southern Reactions to World War II." *Journal of American History* 77 (December 1990): 886–911.

———. *Lost Revolutions: The South in the 1950s.* Chapel Hill: University of North Carolina Press, 2000.

Davis, John A., and Cornelius L. Golightly. "Negro Employment in the Federal Government." *Phylon* 6 (October 1945): 337–346.

D'Emilio, John. *Lost Prophet: The Life and Times of Bayard Rustin.* Chicago: University of Chicago Press, 2004.

Dittmer, John. *Local People: The Struggle for Civil Rights in Mississippi.* Urbana: University of Illinois Press, 1995.

Dittmer, John, George C. Wright, W. Marvin Dulaney, and Kathleen Underwood. *Essays on the American Civil Rights Movement.* College Station: Texas A&M University Press, 1993.

Divine, Robert A., ed. *The Johnson Years,* vol. 2: *Vietnam, the Environment, and Science.* Lawrence: University Press of Kansas, 1987.

———, ed. *The Johnson Years,* vol. 3: *LBJ At Home and Abroad.* Lawrence: University Press of Kansas, 1994.

Dollard, John. *Caste and Class in a Southern Town.* 3rd ed. Garden City, NY: Doubleday, 1949.

Doyle, William. *An American Insurrection: James Meredith and the Battle of Oxford, Mississippi, 1962.* New York: Anchor, 2003.

Drake, St. Clair. "The International Implications of Race and Race Relations." *Journal of Negro Education* 20 (Summer 1951): 261–278.

Dray, Philip. *At the Hands of Persons Unknown: The Lynching of Black America.* New York: Modern Library Paperbacks, 2002.

Drimmer, Melvin. "Roy Wilkins and the American Dream: A Review Essay." *Phylon* 45 (2nd Quarter 1984): 160–163.

Du Bois, W. E. B. *Darkwater: Voices from within the Veil.* 1920. Reprint, Mineola, NY: Dover Thrift Editions, 1999.

———. "Does the Negro Need Separate Schools?" *Journal of Negro Education* 4 (July 1935): 328–335.

———. *The Souls of Black Folk.* 1903. Reprint, New York: Bantam, 1989.

Dudziak, Mary L. "Birmingham, Addis Ababa, and the Image of America: Managing the Impact of Foreign Affairs on Civil Rights in the Kennedy Administration." Paper presented at colloquium "Directions in Postwar American History." Princeton University, 1998.

———. *"Brown* as a Cold War Case." *Journal of American History* 91 (June 2004): 32–42.

———. *Cold War Civil Rights: Race and the Image of American Democracy.* Princeton: Princeton University Press, 2000.

———. "Desegregation as a Cold War Imperative." *Stanford Law Review* 41 (November 1988): 61–120.

———. "Exporting American Dreams: Thurgood Marshall and the Constitution of Kenya." Working Paper No. 3-001. Princeton University, Program in Law and Public Affairs. Available from http://ssrn.com/abstract_id=380260.

———. "The March on Washington, at Home and Abroad." Olin Working Paper No. 99-2. USC Law School Working Paper Series. Available from http://papers.ssrn.com/paper.taf?abstract=895313.

Eagles, Charles W., ed. *The Civil Rights Movement in America.* Jackson: University Press of Mississippi, 1986.

———. *The Price of Defiance: James Meredith and the Integration of Ole Miss.* Chapel Hill: University of North Carolina Press, 2009.

Egerton, John. *Speak Now against the Day.* Chapel Hill: University of North Carolina Press, 1994.

Eick, Gretchen Cassel. *Dissent in Wichita: The Civil Rights Movement in the Midwest, 1954–1972.* Urbana: University of Illinois Press, 2001.

Elliott, Aprele. "Ella Baker: Free Agent in the Civil Rights Movement." *Journal of Black Studies* 26 (May 1996): 593–603.

Ellis, Mark. "'Closing Ranks' and 'Seeking Honors': W. E. B. Du Bois in World War I." *Journal of American History* 79 (June 1992): 96–124.

Emmons, Caroline. "'Somebody Has Got to Do That Work': Harry T. Moore and the Struggle for African-American Voting Rights in Florida." *Journal of Negro History* 82 (Spring 1997): 232–242.

Epstein, Lee, and C. K. Rowland. "Debunking the Myth of Interest Group Invincibility in the Courts." *American Political Science Review* 85 (March 1991): 205–217.

Eschen, Penny von. *Race against Empire*. Ithaca: Cornell University Press, 2001.

Evers-Williams, Myrlie, and Manning Marable, eds. *The Autobiography of Medgar Evers*. New York: Basic Civitas Books, 2006.

Fairclough, Adam. *Better Day Coming: Blacks and Equality, 1890–2000*. London: Penguin Books, 2001.

———. *A Class of Their Own: Black Teachers in the Segregated South*. Cambridge, MA: The Belknap Press of Harvard University Press, 2007.

———. "The Costs of *Brown*: Black Teachers and Social Integration." *Journal of American History* 91 (June 2004): 43–55.

———. *Martin Luther King, Jr.* Athens: University of Georgia Press, 1995.

———. "Martin Luther King, Jr. and the Quest for Nonviolent Social Change." *Phylon* 47 (1st Quarter 1986): 1–15.

———. "Martin Luther King, Jr. and the War in Vietnam." *Phylon* 45 (1st Quarter 1984): 19–39.

———. "The Preachers and the People: The Origins and Early Years of the Southern Christian Leadership Conference, 1955–1959." *Journal of Southern History* 52 (August 1986): 403–440.

———. *Race and Democracy: The Civil Rights Struggle in Louisiana, 1915–1971*. Athens: University of Georgia Press, 1995.

———. *To Redeem the Soul of America: The Southern Christian Leadership Conference and Martin Luther King, Jr.* Athens: University of Georgia Press, 2001.

Farmer, James. *Lay Bare the Heart: An Autobiography of the Civil Rights Movement*. Fort Worth: Texas Christian University Press, 1985.

Feldman, Glenn, ed. *Before* Brown: *Civil Rights and the White Backlash in the Modern South*. Tuscaloosa: University of Alabama Press, 2004.

Fernandez, Roberto M. "Structural Bases of Leadership in Intraorganizational Networks." *Social Psychological Quarterly* 54 (March 1991): 36–53.

Finkle, Lee. "The Conservative Aims of Militant Rhetoric: Black Protest during World War II." *Journal of American History* 60 (December 1973): 692–713.

———. *Forum for Protest: The Black Press during World War II*. Cranbury, NJ: Fairleigh Dickinson University Press, 1975.

Fischer, Roger A. "Racial Segregation in Ante Bellum New Orleans." *American Historical Review* 74 (February 1969): 926–937.

Fleming, Harold C. "The Federal Executive and Civil Rights, 1961–1965." *Daedalus* 94 (Fall 1965): 921–948.

Folmsbee, Stanley J. "The Origin of the First 'Jim Crow' Law." *Journal of Southern History* 15 (May 1949): 235–247.

Foreman, Clark. "The Decade of Hope." *Phylon* 12 (2nd Quarter 1951): 137–150.

Forman, James. *The Making of Black Revolutionaries.* Seattle: University of Washington Press, 1997.

Franklin, John Hope, and Isidore Starr, eds. *The Negro in Twentieth-Century America: A Reader on the Struggle for Civil Rights.* New York: Vintage Books, 1967.

Frazier, E. Franklin. *Black Bourgeoisie.* 1957. Reprint, New York: Free Press Paperbacks, 1990.

———. "The Status of the Negro in the American Social Order." *Journal of Negro Education* 4 (July 1935): 293–307.

Friedman, Tami J. "Exploiting the North-South Differential: Corporate Power, Southern Politics, and the Decline of Organized Labor after World War II." *Journal of American History* 95 (September 2008): 323–348.

Gaines, Kevin. "Rethinking Race and Class in African-American Struggles for Equality, 1885–1941." *American Historical Review* 102 (April 1997): 378–387.

———. *Uplifting the Race: Black Leadership, Politics, and Culture in the Twentieth Century.* Chapel Hill: University of North Carolina Press, 1996.

———. "Whose Integration Was It? An Introduction." *Journal of American History* 91 (June 2004): 19–25.

Garfinkel, Herbert. *When Negroes March.* New York: Atheneum, 1969.

Garrow, David. *Bearing the Cross: Martin Luther King, Jr., and the Southern Christian Leadership Conference.* New York: Quill, 1986.

———. *The FBI and Martin Luther King.* New York: W. W. Norton, 1981.

———. "FBI Political Harassment and FBI Historiography: Analyzing Informants and Measuring Effects." *Public Historian* 10, no. 4 (Autumn 1988): 5–18.

———. *Protest at Selma: Martin Luther King, Jr., and the Voting Rights Act of 1965.* New Haven: Yale University Press, 1973.

Gellman, Erik S. *Death Blow to Jim Crow: The National Negro Congress and the Rise of Militant Civil Rights.* Chapel Hill: University of North Carolina Press, 2012.

Gentile, Thomas. *March on Washington: August 28, 1963.* Washington, DC: New Day Publications, 1983.

Gilmore, Glenda Elizabeth. *Defying Dixie: The Radical Roots of Civil Rights, 1919–1950.* New York: W. W. Norton, 2008.

Gitlin, Todd. *The Whole World Is Watching: Mass Media in the Making and Unmaking of the New Left.* Berkeley: University of California Press, 1980.

Glazer, Nathan, and Daniel P. Moynihan. *Beyond the Melting Pot.* 2nd ed. Cambridge: MIT Press, 1991.

Goluboff, Risa L. *The Lost Promise of Civil Rights.* Cambridge, MA: Harvard University Press, 2007.

Goodman, James. *Stories of Scottsboro*. New York: Vintage, 1994.

Graham, Hugh Davies. *The Civil Rights Era: Origins and Development of National Policy*. Oxford: Oxford University Press, 1990.

Graves, John William. "Jim Crow in Arkansas: A Reconsideration of Urban Race Relations in the Post-Reconstruction South." *Journal of Southern History* 55 (August 1989): 421–448.

Greenberg, Jack. *Crusaders in the Courts*. New York: Basic Books, 1994.

———. *Race Relations and American Law*. New York: Columbia University Press, 1962.

Hahn, Steven. *A Nation under Our Feet: Black Political Struggles in the Rural South from Slavery to the Great Migration*. Cambridge, MA: The Belknap Press of Harvard University Press, 2003.

Halberstam, David. *The Children*. New York: Fawcett Books, 1999.

———. *The Fifties*. New York: Ballantine Books, 1994.

Hale, Grace Elizabeth. *Making Whiteness: The Culture of Segregation in the South, 1890–1940*. New York: Vintage Books, 1999.

Hall, Jacquelyn Dowd. "The Long Civil Rights Movement and the Political Uses of the Past." *Journal of American History* 91 (March 2005): 1233–1263.

Hall, Simon. "The NAACP, Black Power, and the African American Freedom Struggle, 1966–1969." *The Historian* 69 (Spring 2007): 49–82.

———. *Peace and Freedom: The Civil Rights Movement and Antiwar Movements in the 1960s*. Philadelphia: University of Pennsylvania Press, 2005.

———. "The Response of the Moderate Wing of the Civil Rights Movement to the War in Vietnam." *Historical Journal* 46 (September 2003): 669–701.

Hamilton, Dona Cooper, and Charles V. Hamilton. "The Dual Agenda of African American Organizations since the New Deal: Social Welfare Policies and Civil Rights." *Political Science Quarterly* 107 (Autumn 1992): 435–452.

Hampton, Henry, and Steve Fayer. *Voices of Freedom: An Oral History of the Civil Rights Movement from the 1950s through the 1980s*. London: Vintage Books, 1990.

Harris, J. William. "Etiquette, Lynching, and Racial Boundaries in Southern History: A Mississippi Example." *American Historical Review* 100 (April 1995): 387–410.

Harvey, James C. *Black Civil Rights during the Johnson Administration*. Jackson: University and College Press of Mississippi, 1973.

Hill, Lance. *The Deacons for Defense: Armed Resistance and the Civil Rights Movement*. Chapel Hill: University of North Carolina Press, 2004.

Hine, Darlene Clark. "Black Professionals and Race Consciousness: Origins of the Civil Rights Movement, 1890–1950." *Journal of American History* 89 (March 2003): 1279–1294.

———. *Black Victory: The Rise and Fall of the White Primary in Texas*. Columbia: University of Missouri Press, 2003.

Hixson, William B., Jr. "Moorfield Story and the Struggle for Equality." *Journal of American History* 55 (December 1968): 533–554.

Holmquist, June D. *They Chose Minnesota: A Survey of the State's Ethnic Groups.* St. Paul: Minnesota Historical Society Press, 2003.

Houston, Charles H. "Future Policies and Practices Which Should Govern the Relationship of the Federal Government to Negro Separate Schools." *Journal of Negro Education* 7 (July 1938): 460–462.

Howard, John R. *The Shifting Wind: The Supreme Court and Civil Rights from Reconstruction to Brown.* Albany: State University of New York Press, 1999.

Hudson-Weems, Clenora. "Resurrecting Emmett Till: The Catalyst of the Modern Civil Rights Movement." *Journal of Black Studies* 29 (November 1998): 179–188.

Hughes, Langston. *Fight for Freedom: The Story of the NAACP.* New York: Berkley Publishing, 1962.

Janken, Kenneth Robert. *White: The Biography of Walter White, Mr. NAACP.* New York: New Press, 2003.

Jenkins, J. Craig, and Craig M. Eckert. "Channeling Black Insurgency: Elite Patronage and Professional Social Movement Organizations in the Development of the Black Movement." *American Sociological Review* 51 (December 1986): 812–829.

Johnson, Guy B. "Negro Racial Movements and Leadership in the United States." *American Journal of Sociology* 43 (July 1937): 57–71.

Johnson, James Weldon. *The Autobiography of an Ex-Colored Man.* 1912. Reprint, Mineola, NY: Dover Publications, 1995.

Jonas, Gilbert. *Freedom's Sword: The NAACP and the Struggle against Racism in America, 1909–1969.* New York: Routledge, 2005.

Jordan, William. "'The Damnable Dilemma': African-American Accommodation and Protest during World War I." *Journal of American History* 81 (March 1995): 1562–1583.

Joseph, Peniel E., ed. *The Black Power Movement: Rethinking the Civil Rights–Black Power Era.* New York: Routledge, 2006.

———. "The Black Power Movement: A State of the Field." *Journal of American History* 96 (December 2009): 751–776.

Katzenbach, Nicholas de B. *Some of It Was Fun: Working with RFK and LBJ.* New York: W. W. Norton, 2008.

Kelley, Robin D. G. "We Are Not What We Seem: Rethinking Black Working-Class Opposition in the Jim Crow South." *Journal of American History* 1 (June 1993): 75–112.

Kellogg, Charles Flint. *NAACP: A History of the National Association for the Advancement of Colored People.* Vol. 1. Baltimore: John Hopkins University Press, 1967.

Killian, Lewis M. "Organization, Rationality, and Spontaneity in the Civil Rights Movement." *American Sociological Review* 49 (December 1984): 770–783.

King, Richard H. *Civil Rights and the Idea of Freedom.* Athens: University of Georgia Press, 1996.

Kirby, John B. "Ralph J. Bunche and Black Radical Thought in the 1930s." *Phylon* 35 (2nd Quarter 1974): 129–141.

Kirk, John A. *Redefining the Color Line: Black Activism in Little Rock, Arkansas, 1940–1970.* Gainesville: University Press of Florida, 2005.

Klarman, Michael. "*Brown*, Racial Change, and the Civil Rights Movement." *Virginia Law Review* 80 (1994): 7–150.

———. "Brown v. Board of Education: Facts and Political Correctness." *Virginia Law Review* 80 (1994): 185–199.

———. *From Jim Crow to Civil Rights: The Supreme Court and the Struggle for Racial Equality.* New York: Oxford University Press, 2004.

———. "How *Brown* Changed Race Relations: The Backlash Thesis." *Journal of American History* 81 (June 1994): 81–118.

Kluger, Richard. *Simple Justice: The History of* Brown v. Board of Education *and Black America's Struggle for Equality.* New York: Vintage Books, 1977.

Korstad, Robert, and Nelson Lichtenstein. "Opportunities Found and Lost: Labor, Radicals, and the Early Civil Rights Movement." *Journal of American History* 75 (December 1988): 786–811.

Kotlowski, Dean J. *Nixon's Civil Rights: Politics, Principle, and Policy.* Cambridge, MA: Harvard University Press, 2001.

Kuhn, Clifford. "'There's a Footnote to History!' Memory and the History of Martin Luther King's October 1960 Arrest and Its Aftermath." *Journal of American History* 84 (September 1997): 583–595.

Landry, Bart, and Kris Marsh. "The Evolution of the New Black Middle Class." *Annual Review of Sociology* 37 (2011): 73–378, C1–C3, 379–394.

Lawson, Steven F. *Black Ballots: Voting Rights in the South, 1944–1969.* Lanham, MD: Lexington Books, 1999.

———. *Civil Rights Crossroads: Nation, Community, and the Black Freedom Struggle.* Lexington: University Press of Kentucky, 2005.

———. *Running for Freedom: Civil Rights and Black Politics in America since 1941.* 3rd ed. New York: Wiley-Blackwell, 2008.

Lee, Chana Kai. *For Freedom's Sake: The Life of Fannie Lou Hamer.* Urbana: University of Illinois Press, 2000.

Lemann, Nicholas. *The Promised Land: The Great Black Migration and How It Changed America.* London: Macmillian, 1995.

LeMelle, Tilden J. "Race, International Relations, US Foreign Policy, and the African Liberation Struggle." *Journal of Black Studies* 3 (September 1972): 95–109.

Lewis, Anthony. *Portrait of a Decade: The Second American Revolution.* New York: Random House, 1964.

Lewis, David Levering. *King: A Critical Biography.* Baltimore: Pelican Books, 1971.

———. *W. E. B. Du Bois: The Fight for Equality and the American Century, 1919–1963.* New York: Henry Holt, 2000.

———. *W. E. B. Du Bois, 1868–1919: Biography of a Race.* New York: Henry Holt, 1993.

Lewis, George. *Massive Resistance: The White Response to the Civil Rights Movement.* London: Hodder Education Press, 2006.

Lewis, John, with Michael D'Orso. *Walking with the Wind: A Memoir of the Movement.* New York: Harcourt Brace, 1998.

Lewis, Roscoe E. "The Role of Pressure Groups in Maintaining Morale among Negroes." *Journal of Negro Education* 3 (Summer 1943): 464–473.

Litwack, Leon F. *Trouble in Mind: Black Southerners in the Age of Jim Crow.* New York: Vintage Books, 1999.

Loevy, Robert D., ed. *The Civil Rights Act of 1964: The Passage of the Law That Ended Racial Segregation.* Albany: State University of New York Press, 1997.

Lomax, Louis. *The Negro Revolt.* New York: Signet Books, 1963.

———. "The Negro Revolt against 'The Negro Leaders.'" *Harper's,* June 1960, 41–48.

Lott, Eric. "Double V, Double-Time: Bebop's Politics of Style." *Callaloo* 36 (Summer 1988): 597–605.

Lutz, Tom, and Susanna Ashton, eds. *These "Colored" United States: African American Essays from the 1920s.* New Brunswick: Rutgers University Press, 1996.

MacLean, Nancy. "Achieving the Promise of the Civil Rights Act: Herbert Hill and the NAACP's Fight for Jobs and Justice." *Labor: Studies in Working-Class History of the Americas* 3, no. 2 (2006): 13–19.

———. *Freedom Is Not Enough: The Opening of the American Workplace.* Cambridge, MA: Harvard University Press, 2008.

Marable, Manning. *Malcolm X: A Life of Reinvention.* New York: Viking, 2011.

———. *Race, Reform, and Rebellion: The Second Reconstruction in Black America, 1945–1990.* Jackson: University of Mississippi Press, 1991.

Marger, Martin N. "Social Movements Organizations and Response to Environmental Change: The NAACP, 1960–1973." *Social Problems* 32 (October 1984): 16–30.

Marsh, Charles. *God's Long Summer: Stories of Faith and Civil Rights.* Princeton: Princeton University Press, 1997.

Marshall, Ray. "The Negro and Organized Labor." *Journal of Negro Education* 32 (Autumn 1963): 375–389.

Martin, Charles H. "Communists and Blacks: The ILD and the Angelo Herndon Case." *Journal of Negro History* 64 (Spring 1979): 131–141.

———. "The International Labor Defense and Black America." *Labor History* 26 (Spring 1985): 165–194.

Martinez, Elizabeth Sutherland, ed. *Letters from Mississippi: Personal Reports from Civil Rights Volunteers of the 1964 Freedom Summer.* Brookline, MA: Zephyr Press, 2002.

May, Gary. *Bending toward Justice: The Voting Rights Act and the Transformation of American Democracy.* New York: Basic Books, 2013.

McAdam, Doug. *Political Process and the Development of Black Insurgency, 1930–1970.* Chicago: University of Chicago Press, 1982.

McCullough, David. *Truman.* New York: Simon & Schuster, 1992.

McGuire, Danielle L. "'It Was Like All of Us Had Been Raped': Sexual Violence, Community Mobilization, and the African American Freedom Struggle." *Journal of American History* 91 (December 2004): 906–931.

McGuire, Philip. "Desegregation of the Armed Forces: Black Leadership, Protest, and World War II." *Journal of Negro History* 68 (Spring 1983): 147–158.

McLeod, Jacqueline A. *Daughter of the Empire State: The Life of Judge Jane Bolin.* Champaign: University of Illinois Press, 2011.

McMillen, Neil R. "Black Enfranchisement in Mississippi: Federal Enforcement and Black Protest in the 1960s." *Journal of Southern History* 43, no. 3 (August 1977): 351–372.

———, ed. *Remaking Dixie: The Impact of World War II on the American South.* Jackson: University Press of Mississippi, 1997.

McNeil, Genna Rae. *Groundwork: Charles Hamilton Houston and the Struggle for Civil Rights.* Philadelphia: University of Pennsylvania Press, 1983.

McWorter, Gerald A., and Robert L. Crain. "Subcommunity Gladatorial Competition: Civil Rights Leadership as a Competitive Process." *Social Forces* 46 (September 1967): 8–21.

Meier, August. "Negro Protest Movements and Organizations." *Journal of Negro Education* 32 (Autumn 1963): 437–450.

———. "The Revolution against the NAACP: A Critical Appraisal of Louis E. Lomax's *The Negro Revolt.*" *Journal of Negro Education* 32 (Spring 1963): 146–152.

Meier, August, and John H. Bracey. "The NAACP as a Reform Movement, 1909–1965." *Journal of Southern History* 59 (February 1993): 3–30.

Meier, August, and Elliott Rudwick. *Along the Color Line: Explorations in the Black Experience.* Urbana: University of Illinois Press, 1976.

———. "Attorneys Black and White: A Case Study of Race Relations within the NAACP." *Journal of American History* 62 (March 1976): 913–946.

———. "The Boycott Movement against Jim Crow Streetcars in the South, 1900–1906." *Journal of American History* 55 (March 1969): 756–775.

———. *CORE: A Study in the Civil Rights Movement, 1942–1968.* Urbana: University of Illinois Press, 1975.

———. "Early Boycotts of Segregated Schools: The Case of Springfield, Ohio, 1922–1923." *American Quarterly* 20 (Winter 1968): 744–758.

———. "The First Freedom Ride." *Phylon* 30, no. 3 (3rd Quarter, 1969): 213–222.

———. *From Plantation to Ghetto*. Rev. ed. New York: Hill and Wang, 1970.

Meier, August, Elliott Rudwick, and John H. Bracey, eds. *Conflict and Competition in the Recent Black Protest Movement*. Belmont, CA: Wadsworth, 1971.

Meier, August, Elliott Rudwick, and Francis L. Broderick, eds. *Black Protest Thought in the Twentieth Century*. 2nd ed. Indianapolis: Bobbs-Merrill, 1971.

Mershon, Sherie, and Steven Schlossman. *Foxholes and Color Lines: Desegregating the U.S. Armed Forces*. Baltimore: Johns Hopkins University Press, 1998.

Metcalf, George R. *Black Profiles*. New York: McGraw-Hill, 1971.

Miller, James, *Remembering Scottsboro: The Legacy of an Infamous Trial*. Princeton: Princeton University Press, 2009.

Miller, James A., Susan D. Pennybacker, and Eve Rosenhaft. "Mother Ada Wright and the International Campaign to Free the Scottsboro Boys, 1931–1934." *American Historical Review* 106 (April 2001): 387–430.

Miller, Loren. *The Petitioners: The Story of the Supreme Court of the United States and the Negro*. New York: Pantheon Books, 1966.

Mills, Kay, and Marian Wright Edelman. *This Little Light of Mine: The Life of Fannie Lou Hamer*. Lexington: University Press of Kentucky, 1994.

Mills, Nicolaus. *Like a Holy Crusade: Mississippi 1964—The Turning of the Civil Rights Movement in America*. Chicago: Elephant Paperbacks, 1993.

Minchin, Timothy J. "Making Best Use of the New Laws: The NAACP and the Fight for Civil Rights in the South, 1965–1975." *Journal of Southern History* 74 (August 2008): 669–702.

Minkoff, Debra C. "Interorganizational Influences on the Founding of African-American Organizations, 1955–1985." *Sociological Review* 10 (March 1995): 51–79.

Miroff, Bruce. "Presidential Leverage over Social Movements: The Johnson White House and Civil Rights." *Journal of Politics* 43 (February 1981): 2–23.

Modell, John, Marc Goulden, and Sigurdur Magnusson. "World War II in the Lives of Black Americans: Some Findings and Interpretation." *Journal of American History* 76 (December 1989): 838–848.

Morris, Aldon. "Black Southern Student Sit-in Movement: An Analysis of Internal Organization." *American Sociological Review* 46 (December 1981): 744–767.

———. *The Origins of the Civil Rights Movement: Black Communities Organizing for Change*. New York: Free Press, 1984.

———. "Reflections on Social Movement Theory: Criticisms and Proposals." *Contemporary Sociology* 29 (May 2000): 445–454.

———. "A Retrospective on the Civil Rights Movement: Political and Intellectual Landmarks." *Annual Review of Sociology* 25 (1999): 517–539.

Morrison, Minion K. C. "Preconditions for Afro-American Leadership: Three Mississippi Towns." *Polity* 17 (Spring 1985): 504–529.

Motley, Constance Baker. *Equal Justice under Law*. New York: Farrar Strauss and Giroux, 1998.

Moynihan, Daniel Patrick. "The President and The Negro: The Moment Lost." *Commentary,* February 1967, 31–45.

Murphy, Walter F. "The South Counterattacks: The Anti-NAACP Laws." *Western Political Quarterly* 12, no. 2 (June 1959): 371–390.

Murray, Hugh T. "Changing America and the Changing Image of Scottsboro." *Phylon* 38 (1977): 82–92.

———. "The NAACP versus the Communist Party: The Scottsboro Rape Cases, 1931–1932." *Phylon* 28 (1967): 276–287.

Murray, Pauli. "The Historical Development of Race Laws in the United States." *Journal of Negro Education* 22 (Winter 1953): 4–15.

Myrdal, Gynnar. *An American Dilemma: The Negro Problem and American Democracy.* New York: Harper & Row, 1962.

Nabrit, James M., Jr. "Resort to the Courts as a Means of Eliminating 'Legalized' Segregation." *Journal of Negro Education* 20 (Summer 1951): 460–474.

Nelson, Bruce. "Organized Labor and the Struggle for Black Equality in Mobile during World War II." *Journal of American History* 80 (December 1993): 952–988.

Nelson, H. Viscount. "The Philadelphia NAACP: Race versus Class Consciousness during the Thirties." *Journal of Black Studies* 3 (1975): 255–276.

Nelson, Harold A. "Leadership and Change in an Evolutionary Movement: An Analysis of Change in the Leadership Structure of the Southern Civil Rights Movement." *Social Forces* 49 (March 1971): 353–371.

Neustadt, Richard E. *Presidential Power: The Politics of Leadership.* New York: Mentor Books, 1964.

Newby, I. A., ed. *The Development of Segregationist Thought.* Homewood, IL: Dorsey Press, 1968.

Nichols, David A. *A Matter of Justice: Eisenhower and the Beginning of the Civil Rights Revolution.* New York: Simon & Schuster, 2007.

Norrell, Robert J. "Caste in Steel: Jim Crow Careers in Birmingham, Alabama." *Journal of American History* 73 (December 1986): 669–694.

———. *The House I Live In: Race in the American Century.* Oxford: Oxford University Press, 2005.

Nossiter, Adam. *Of Long Memory: Mississippi and the Murder of Medgar Evers.* Reading, MA: Addison Wesley, 1995.

Ogbar, Jeffrey O. G. *Black Power: Radical Politics and African American Identity.* Baltimore: Johns Hopkins University Press, 2005.

———, ed. *Problems in American Civilization: The Civil Rights Movement.* Boston: Houghton Mifflin, 2002.

O'Reilly, Kenneth. "The FBI and the Politics of the Riots, 1964–1968." *Journal of American History* 75 (June 1988): 91–114.

———. "Racial Integration: The Battle General Eisenhower Chose Not to Fight." *Journal of Blacks in Higher Education* 18 (Winter 1997–1998): 110–119.

———. *Racial Matters: The FBI's Secret File on Black America, 1960–1972.* New York: Free Press, 1989.

Ovington, Mary White. *Black and White Sat Down Together: The Reminiscences of an NAACP Founder.* New York: Feminist Press, 1996.

———. "The National Association for the Advancement of Colored People." *Journal of Negro History* 9 (April 1924): 107–116.

Ownby, Ted, ed. *The Role of Ideas in the Civil Rights South.* Jackson: University Press of Mississippi, 2002.

Patterson, Haywood, and Earl Conrad. *Scottsboro Boy.* 1950. Rev. ed., New York: Bantam Books, 1962.

Patterson, James T. *Brown v. Board of Education: A Civil Rights Milestone and Its Troubled Legacy.* Oxford: Oxford University Press, 2001.

———. *The Eve of Destruction: How 1965 Transformed America.* New York: Basic Books, 2012.

———. *Freedom Is Not Enough: The Moynihan Report and America's Struggle over Black Family Life from LBJ to Obama.* New York: Basic Books, 2010.

Payne, Charles. *I've Got the Light of Freedom: The Organizing Tradition and the Mississippi Freedom Struggle.* Berkeley: University of California Press, 1995.

Perry, Bruce. *Malcolm: The Life of a Man Who Changed Black America.* New York: Station Hill. 1991.

Pettigrew, Thomas F. "Complexity and Change in American Racial Patterns: A Social Psychological View." Issue entitled "The Negro American." *Daedalus* 94, no. 4 (Fall 1965): 974–1008.

Pfeffer, Paula F. *A. Philip Randolph, Pioneer of the Civil Rights Movement.* Baton Rouge: Louisiana State University Press, 1990.

Pickens, William. *Bursting Bonds: The Autobiography of a "New Negro."* Bloomington: Indiana University Press, 1991.

Pitre, Merline, and Bruce A. Glasrud, eds. *Southern Black Women in the Modern Civil Rights Movement.* College Station: Texas A&M University Press, 2013.

Plummer, Brenda Gayle. *In Search of Power: African Americans in the Era of Decolonization, 1956–1974.* New York: Cambridge University Press, 2012.

———. *Rising Wind: Black Americans and U.S. Foreign Affairs, 1935–1960.* Chapel Hill: University of North Carolina Press, 1996.

———, ed. *Window on Freedom: Race, Civil Rights, and Foreign Affairs, 1945–1988.* Chapel Hill: University of North Carolina Press, 2003.

Popper, Micha. "The Development of Charismatic Leaders." *Political Psychology* 21 (December 2000): 729–744.

Prattis, P. L. "The Morale of the Negro in the Armed Services of the United States." *Journal of Negro Education* 12 (Summer 1943): 355–363.

———. "Race Relations and the Negro Press." *Phylon* 14 (4th Quarter 1953): 373–383.

Pryer, Margaret W., Austin W. Flint, and Bernard M. Bass. "Group Effectiveness and Consistency of Leadership." *Sociometry* 25 (December 1962): 391–397.

Rabinowitz, Howard N. "From Exclusion to Segregation: Southern Race Relations, 1865–1890." *Journal of American History* 63 (September 1976): 325–350.

———. "More than the Woodward Thesis: Assessing the Strange Career of Jim Crow." *Journal of American History* 75 (December 1988): 842–856.

———. *Race Relations in the Urban South, 1865–1890.* 1978. Reprint, Athens: University of Georgia Press, 1996.

Rable, George C. "The South and the Politics of Antilynching Legislation, 1920–1940." *Journal of Southern History* 51 (May 1985): 201–220.

Raines, Howell. *My Soul Is Rested: The Story of the Civil Rights Movement in the Deep South.* New York: Penguin, 1983.

Ransby, Barbara. *Ella Baker and the Black Freedom Movement: A Radical Democratic Vision.* Chapel Hill: University of North Carolina Press, 2003.

Ransom, Leon A. "Combating Discrimination in the Employment of Negroes in War Industries and Government Agencies." *Journal of Negro Education* 12 (Summer 1943): 405–416.

Record, Wilson. "American Racial Ideologies and Organizations in Transition." *Phylon* 26 (4th Quarter 1965): 315–329.

———. "Negro Intellectual Leadership in the National Association for the Advancement of Colored People, 1910–1940." *Phylon* 17 (4th Quarter 1956): 375–389.

———. *Race and Radicalism: The NAACP and the Communist Party in Conflict.* Ithaca, NY: Cornell University Press, 1964.

Reed, Christopher Robert. *The Chicago NAACP and the Rise of Professional Leadership, 1910–1966.* Bloomington: Indiana University Press, 1997.

Reed, Merl E. "FEPC and the Federal Agencies in the South." *Journal of Negro History* 65 (Winter 1980): 43–56.

———. *Seedtime for the Civil Rights Movement: The President's Committee on Fair Employment Practice, 1941–1946.* Baton Rouge: Louisiana State University Press, 1991.

Reeves, Richard. *President Kennedy: Profile of Power.* New York: Simon & Schuster, 1993.

Reid, Ira De A. "A Critical Summary: The Negro on the Home Front in World Wars I and II." *Journal of Negro Education* 3 (Summer 1943): 511–520.

Renshon, Stanley. "Personality and Family Dynamics in the Political Socialization Process." *American Journal of Political Science* 19 (February 1975): 63–80.

———. "Political Leadership as Social Capital: Governing in a Divided National Culture." *Political Psychology* 21 (March 2000): 199–226.

———. "A Preliminary Assessment of the Clinton Presidency: Character, Leadership, and Performance." *Political Psychology* 15 (June 1994): 375–394.

Rice, Roger, L. "Residential Segregation by Law, 1910–1917." *Journal of Southern History* 34 (May 1968): 179–199.

Roark, James L. "American Black Leaders: The Response to Colonialization and the Cold War, 1943–1953." *African Historical Studies* 4 (1971): 253–270.

Roberts, Gene, and Hank Klibanoff. *The Race Beat: The Press, The Civil Rights Struggle, and the Awakening of a Nation.* New York: Knopf, 2006.

Roberts, Thomas N. "The Negro in Government War Agencies." *Journal of Negro Education* 12 (Summer 1943): 367–375.

Robinson, Armistead L., and Patricia Sullivan, eds. *New Directions in Civil Rights Studies.* Charlottesville: University Press of Virginia, 1991.

Rollins, Judith. "Part of a Whole: The Interdependence of the Civil Rights Movement and Other Social Movements." *Phylon* 47 (1st Quarter 1986): 61–70.

Rosenberg, Jonathan, and Zachary Karabell. *Kennedy, Johnson, and the Quest for Justice: The Civil Rights Tapes.* New York: W. W. Norton, 2003.

Ross, B. Joyce. *J. E. Spingarn and the Rise of the NAACP.* New York: Atheneum, 1972.

Ross, Felecia G. Jones. "Mobilizing the Masses: The Cleveland Call and Post and the Scottsboro Incident." *Journal of Negro History* 84 (Winter 1999): 48–60.

Rudwick, Elliott M. "Du Bois' Last Year as *Crisis* Editor." *Journal of Negro Education* 27 (Autumn 1958): 526–533.

———. "The Niagara Movement." *Journal of Negro History* 42 (July 1957): 177–200.

Rustin, Bayard. "'Black Power' and Coalition Politics." *Commentary,* September 1966: 35–40.

———. "From Protest to Politics: The Future of the Civil Rights Movement." *Commentary,* February 1965, 25–31.

———. "The Watts 'Manifesto' and The McCone Report." *Commentary,* March 1966: 29–35.

Sartain, Lee. *Borders of Equality: The NAACP and the Baltimore Civil Rights Struggle, 1914–1970.* Jackson: University Press of Mississippi, 2013.

Schneider, Mark Robert. *We Return Fighting: The Civil Rights Movement in the Jazz Age.* Boston: Northeastern University Press, 2001.

Schnore, Leo F., and Philip C. Evenson. "Segregation in Southern Cities." *American Journal of Sociology* 72 (July 1966): 58–67.

Schultz, Kevin M. "The FEPC and the Legacy of the Labor-Based Civil Rights Movement of the 1940s." *Labor History* 49, no. 1 (2008): 71–92.

Sinsheimer, Joseph A. "The Freedom Vote of 1963: New Strategies of Racial Protest in Mississippi." *Journal of Southern History* 55 (May 1989): 217–244.

Sitkoff, Harvard. "Harry Truman and the Election of 1948: The Coming of Age of Civil Rights in American Politics." *Journal of Southern History* 37 (November 1971): 597–616.

———. *A New Deal for Blacks.* New York: Oxford University Press, 1978.

———. "Racial Militancy and Interracial Violence in the Second World War." *Journal of American History* 58 (December 1971): 661–681.

Smith, J. Clay, Jr. *Emancipation: The Making of the Black Lawyer, 1844–1944.* Philadelphia: University of Philadelphia Press, 1993.

Smith, John David, ed. *When Did Southern Segregation Begin?* Boston: Bedford/ St. Martin's, 2002.

Smith, Tom W. "The Polls: American Attitudes toward the Soviet Union and Communism." *Public Opinion Quarterly* 47 (Summer 1983): 277–292.

Sokol, Jason. *There Goes My Everything: White Southerners in the Age of Civil Rights, 1945–1975.* New York: Alfred A. Knopf, 2006.

Somers, Dale A. "Black and White in New Orleans: A Study in Urban Race Relations, 1865–1900." *Journal of Southern History* 40 (February 1974): 19–42.

Stein, Judith. *The World of Marcus Garvey: Race and Class in Modern Society.* Baton Rouge: Louisiana State University Press, 1986.

Steinberg, Blema S. "Indira Gandhi: The Relationship between Personality Profile and Leadership Style." *Political Psychology* 26 (October 2005): 755–789.

Stern, Mark. *Calculating Visions: Kennedy, Johnson, and Civil Rights.* New Brunswick: Rutgers University Press, 1992.

Sternsher, Bernard, ed. *The Negro in Depression and War.* Chicago: Quadrangle Books, 1969.

Stockley, Grif. *Daisy Bates: Civil Rights Crusader from Arkansas.* Jackson: University of Mississippi Press, 2005.

Stoper, Emily. "The Student Nonviolent Coordinating Committee: Rise and Fall of a Redemptive Organization." *Journal of Black Studies* 8 (September 1977): 13–34.

Stuart, Jack. "A Note on William English Walling and His 'Cousin,' W. E. B. Du Bois." *Journal of Negro History* 82 (Spring 1997): 270–274.

Sugrue, Thomas J. "Crabgrass-Roots Politics: Race, Rights, and the Reaction against Liberalism in the Urban North, 1940–1964." *Journal of American History* 82 (September 1995): 551–578.

———. *Sweet Land of Liberty: The Forgotten Struggle for Civil Rights in the North.* New York: Random House, 2008.

Sullivan, Patricia. *Lift Every Voice: The NAACP and the Making of the Civil Rights Movement.* New York: New Press, 2009.

Surace, Samuel J., and Melvin Seeman. "Some Correlates of Civil Rights Action." *Social Forces* 46 (December 1967): 197–207.

Taylor, Clarence, and Milton A. Galamison. *Knocking at Our Own Door: Milton A. Galamison and the Struggle to Integrate New York City Schools.* Lanham, MD: Lexington Books, 2000.

Thompson, Daniel C. "Civil Rights Leadership (An Opinion Study)." *Journal of Negro Education* 32 (Autumn 1963): 426–436.

Thornton, J. Mills. "Challenge and Response in the Montgomery Bus Boycott of 1955–1956." *Alabama Review* 33 (July 1980): 163–235.

———. *Dividing Lines: Municipal Politics and the Struggle for Civil Rights in Montgomery, Birmingham, and Selma*. Tuscaloosa: University of Alabama Press, 2002.

Torres, Sasha. *Black, White, and in Color: Television and Black Civil Rights*. Princeton: Princeton University Press, 2003.

Tuck, Stephen G. N. *Beyond Atlanta: The Struggle for Racial Equality in Georgia, 1940–1980*. Athens: University of Georgia Press, 2001.

Tucker, Spencer C. *The Encyclopedia of the Vietnam War: A Political, Social, and Military History*. Oxford: Oxford University Press, 2000.

Tushnet, Mark. *Making Civil Rights Law: Thurgood Marshall and the Supreme Court, 1936–1961*. New York: Oxford University Press, 1994.

———. *The NAACP's Legal Strategy against Segregated Education, 1925–1950*. Chapel Hill: University of North Carolina Press, 2005.

———. "The Politics of Equality in Constitutional Law: The Equal Protection Clause, Dr. Du Bois, and Charles Hamilton Houston." *Journal of American History* 74 (December 1987): 884–903.

Tyson, Timothy B. *Radio Free Dixie: Robert F. Williams and the Roots of Black Power*. Chapel Hill: University of North Carolina Press, 1999.

———. "Robert F. Williams, 'Black Power,' and the Roots of the African American Freedom Struggle." *Journal of American History* 85 (September 1998): 540–570.

Umoja, Akinyele O. "The Ballot and the Bullet; A Comparative Analysis of Armed Resistance in the Civil Rights Movement." *Journal of Black Studies* 29 (March 1999): 558–578.

US Department of Labor. *The Negro Family: The Case for National Action*. Washington, DC, 1965.

US Riot Commission. *Report of the National Advisory Commission on Civil Disorders*. New York: The New York Times Co., 1968.

Verney, Kevern, and Lee Sartain, eds. *Long Is the Way and Hard: One Hundred Years of the NAACP*. Fayetteville: University of Arkansas Press, 2009.

Vose, Clement. *Caucasians Only: The Supreme Court, the NAACP, and the Restrictive Covenant Cases*. Berkeley: University of California Press, 1959.

Waldrep, Christopher. "War of Words: The Controversy over the Definition of Lynching, 1899–1940." *Journal of Southern History* 66 (February 2000): 75–100.

Ward, Brian. *Radio and the Struggle for Civil Rights in the South*. Gainesville: University of Florida Press, 2004.

Ward, Brian, and Tony Badger, eds. *The Making of Martin Luther King and the Civil Rights Movement*. London: Macmillan Press, 1996.

Ware, Gilbert. "Lobbying as a Means of Protest: The NAACP as an Agent of Equality." *Journal of Negro Education* 33 (Spring 1964): 103–110.

———. "The NAACP–Inc. Fund Alliance: Its Strategy, Power, and Destruction." *Journal of Negro Education* 63 (Summer 1994): 323–335.

Warren, Robert Penn. *Segregation: The Inner Conflict in the South.* New York: Modern Library Paperbacks, 1956.

———. *Who Speaks for the Negro?* New York: Random House. 1965.

Washington, Booker T. *Up From Slavery.* 1901. Reprint, New York: Dover Publications, 1995.

Watson, Denton L. "Assessing the Role of the NAACP in the Civil Rights Movement." *The Historian* 55, no. 3 (Spring 1993): 453–468.

———. *The Lion in the Lobby: Clarence Mitchell Jr.'s Struggle for the Passage of Civil Rights Laws.* New York: Morrow, 1990.

———, ed. *The Papers of Clarence Mitchell Jr.* Vol. 3, *NAACP Labor Secretary and Director of the NAACP Washington Bureau, 1946–1950.* Athens: Ohio University Press, 2010.

———, ed. *The Papers of Clarence Mitchell Jr.* Vol. 4, *Director of the NAACP Washington Bureau, 1951–1954.* Athens: Ohio University Press, 2010.

Watters, Pat. *Down to Now: Reflections on the Southern Civil Rights Movement.* 1971. Rev. ed., Athens: University of Georgia Press, 1993.

Weaver, Robert C. "The Employment of the Negro in War Industries." *Journal of Negro Education* 12 (Summer 1943): 386–396.

———. "The NAACP Today." *Journal of Negro Education* 29 (Autumn 1960): 421–425.

Wedin, Carolyn. *Inheritors of the Spirit: Mary White Ovington and the Founding of the NAACP.* New York: John Wiley, 1998.

Weinberger, Stephen. "*The Birth of a Nation* and the Making of the NAACP." *Journal of American Studies* 45 (February 2011): 77–93.

Weisbrot, Robert. *Freedom Bound: A History of America's Civil Rights Movement.* New York: Plume, 1991.

Weiss, Nancy J. *Farewell to the Party of Lincoln: Black Politics in the Age of FDR.* Princeton: Princeton University Press, 1983.

———. *Whitney M. Young, Jr. and the Struggle for Civil Rights.* Princeton: Princeton University Press, 1989.

Westheider, James E. *Fighting on Two Fronts: African Americans and the Vietnam War.* New York: New York University Press, 1999.

White, Walter. *A Man Called White: The Autobiography of Walter White.* New York: Viking Press, 1948.

———. *Rope and Faggot: A Biography of Judge Lynch.* 1929. Reprint, Notre Dame, IN: University of Notre Dame Press, 2001.

Whitfield, Stephen J. *A Death in the Delta.* Baltimore: John Hopkins University Press, 1988.

Whyte, William H. *The Organization Man.* 1956. Reprint, London: Penguin Books, 1961.

Wildavsky, Aaron. "The Goldwater Phenomenon: Purists, Politicians, and the Two-Party System." *Review of Politics* 27 (July 1965): 386–413.

Wilkins, Roger. *A Man's Life: An Autobiography.* Woodbridge, CT: Ox Bow Press, 1991.

Wilkins, Roy. "Adult Education Program of the NAACP." *Journal of Negro Education* 14 (Summer 1945): 403–406.

———. "The Future of the Negro Voter in the United States." *Journal of Negro Education* 26 (Summer 1957): 424–431.

———. "Next Steps in Education for Racial Understanding." *Journal of Negro Education* 13 (Summer 1944): 432–440.

———. "The Role of the National Association for the Advancement of Colored People in the Desegregation Process." *Social Problems* 2 (April 1955): 201–204.

———. *Talking It Over.* 1982. Reprint, Norwalk, CT: M&B Publishing, 1994.

Wilkins, Roy, and Ramsey Clark. *Search and Destroy: A Report by the Commission of Inquiry into the Black Panthers and the Police.* New York: Metropolitan Applied Research Center, 1973.

Wilkins, Roy, with Tom Mathews. *Standing Fast: The Autobiography of Roy Wilkins.* Boston: Da Capo Press, 1994.

Williams, Jakobi. *From the Bullet to the Ballot: The Illinois Chapter of the Black Panther Party and Racial Coalition Politics in Chicago.* Chapel Hill: University of North Carolina Press, 2013.

Williams, Joel. *After Slavery: The Negro in South Carolina during Reconstruction, 1861–1877.* 1965. Rev. ed., New York: Norton Library, 1975.

———. *The Crucible of Race: Black-White Relations in the American South since Emancipation.* New York: Oxford University Press, 1984.

Williams, Juan. *Thurgood Marshall: American Revolutionary.* New York: Times Books, 1998.

Williams, Michael Vinson. *Medgar Evers: Mississippi Martyr.* Fayetteville: University of Arkansas Press, 2011.

Wilson, Sondra Kathryn, ed. *In Search of Democracy: The NAACP Writings of James Weldon Johnson, Walter White, and Roy Wilkins (1920–1977).* New York: Oxford University Press, 1999.

Wirmark, Bo. "Nonviolent Methods and the American Civil Rights Movement, 1955–1965." *Journal of Peace Research* 11 (1974): 115–132.

Wish, Harvey. "Negro Education and the Progressive Movement." *Journal of Negro History* 49 (July 1964): 184–200.

Wofford, Harris. *Of Kennedys and Kings.* Pittsburgh: University of Pittsburgh Press, 1992.

Wolters, Raymond. *Race and Education, 1954–2007.* Columbia: University of Missouri Press, 2009.

Woodward, C. Vann. *The Burden of Southern History.* 3rd ed. Baton Rouge: Louisiana State University Press, 1993.

———. "*Strange Career* Critics: Long May They Persevere." *Journal of American History* 75 (December 1988): 857–868.

———. *The Strange Career of Jim Crow*. 3rd rev. ed. Oxford: Oxford University Press, 1974.

Wynn, Neil A. *The African American Experience during World War II*. Lanham, MD: Rowman & Littlefield, 2010.

———. *The Afro American and the Second World War*. London: Paul Elek, 1976.

———. "The 'Good War': The Second World War and Postwar American Society." *Journal of Contemporary History* 31 (July 1996): 463–482.

———. "The Impact of the Second World War on the American Negro." *Journal of Contemporary History* 6 (1971): 42–53.

Yarbrough, Tinsley E. *A Passion for Justice: J. Waties Waring and Civil Rights*. New York: Oxford University Press, 1987.

Young, Andrew. *An Easy Burden: The Civil Rights Movement and the Transformation of America*. New York: Harper Collins, 1996.

Yuill, Kevin L. "The 1966 White House Conference on Civil Rights." *Historical Journal* 41 (March 1998): 259–282.

Zaleznik, Abraham. "Managers and Leaders: Are They Different?" *Harvard Business Review* (March–April 1992): 2–11. www.hbr.org. Reprint: R0401G.

Zangrando, Robert L. "The NAACP and the Federal Antilynching Bill, 1934–1940." *Journal of Negro History* 50 (April 1965): 106–117.

———. *The NAACP Crusade against Lynching, 1909–1950*. Philadelphia: Temple University Press, 1980.

Zinn, Howard. *SNCC: The New Abolitionists*. Westport, CT: Greenwood Press, 1965.

Index

Great Depression: impact on the
NAACP, 21–22; New Deal
programs and black Americans,
18–19
Great Society, 145–146
Greensboro (NC) sit-in protests,
81–82
*Green v. County School Board of New
Kent County,* 185

Hamer, Fannie Lou, 143–144
Hammond, John, 35, 45
Hampton, Fred, 187, 188
Harper's, 86
Harris, Abram, 21
Hastie, William, 48–49
Hayling, Robert, 117
Heineman, Ben, 164
Henderson v. United States, 49
Henry, Aaron, 96
Hickenlooper, Bourke, 130
Hicks, James, 79–80
Higginbotham, Leon, 127
Hill, Herbert, 83, 138, 155, 164
Holman, L. H., 110
Holmes, Hamilton, 95
Hooks, Benjamin, 192
Hoover, J. Edgar, 151–152
Houston, Charles, 18, 23–24, 49
Howard University: Johnson's
speech at, 153–154
Hunter, Charlayne, 95
Huntley, Chet, 76
Hurley, Ruby, 103

Inc. Fund (NAACP Legal Defense
and Educational Fund), 49, 67,
68, 104–105
institutional racism: effects of,
156–157

integration: black separatism and
challenges to goal of, 167, 169,
181, 186–187; of public schools
(*see* school integration); Wilkins's
views on, 2, 7, 169, 193–194,
197. *See also* desegregation
International Labor Defense (ILD),
16–17

Jackson (MS) movement, 108–110
Jackson, Jimmie Lee, 147
Jackson, Marvel, 10
Johns committee, 65–66
Johnson, James Weldon, 12
Johnson, Lyndon B.: 1957 Civil
Rights Act and, 70–71, 126;
1964 Democratic National
Convention and, 143; 1965
Voting Rights Act, 147–148;
1966 White House conference
on civil rights, 164–165;
administration's concerns over
rift in civil rights movement,
172–173; Kerner Commission
and, 177, 178–179; NAACP
dissatisfaction with
administration of, 154–155;
political alliance with Wilkins,
123–127, 145; role in 1964
Civil Rights Act, 123–125,
128–129, 131; speech at
Howard University, 153–154;
Wilkins on, 71, 89–90, 123,
124, 148
Joint Committee on National
Recovery (JCNR), 19
Jonas, Gilbert, 7
Jones, Madison, 30, 43–44
Jones, Nathaniel, 177, 184
Jones, Walter B., 65

White, Lindsay, 42, 45
White, Walter: background and
    leadership style, 12–13, 34, 35,
    36, 40–41; clashes with W. E. B.
    Du Bois, 13–14, 41; health
    problems and death of, 37, 51;
    marriage to Poppy Cannon,
    41–42; NAACP leadership
    crisis of 1949–1950 and, 42,
    47–49; Scottsboro case and,
    16–17; Wilkins and, 11, 28,
    35, 47
white racism, 8, 156–157, 178
Wichita (KS) sit-in protests, 80
Wilkins, Armeda, 5, 10
Wilkins, Asberry, 5
Wilkins, Earl, 5, 10, 26
Wilkins, Mayfield, 5–6
Wilkins, Roger, 26
Wilkins, Roy: 1960 presidential
    campaign and, 87–91;
    achievements and legacy of,
    197–200; alleged role in FBI
    investigations of King, 151–152,
    194–195; appointed executive
    secretary of NAACP, 52, 53;
    on armed self-defense, 77–78;
    on Black Power and separatism,
    167, 168–169, 182, 186–187;
    cancer diagnoses, 37, 189;
    civil rights philosophy and
    guiding convictions of, 169,
    193–194, 197–198; college
    years and early professional
    life, 7–11; criticism of, 77,
    79–80, 138–140, 144; defense
    of NAACP and criticism of
    other civil rights organizations,
    84–85, 100, 112–113, 167, 170;
    detached approach of, 2, 63;

on direct action and boycotts,
    3, 56–57, 58–59, 63, 77, 108,
    139; early involvement and
    first job with NAACP, 11–14;
    editorship of The Crisis, 19–21;
    on Eisenhower, 69, 73; events
    and controversy surrounding
    retirement of, 189–193; family
    history and early life of, 5–7;
    final illness and death of, 1,
    195; frugality of, 6–7, 199;
    international travels, 105–106,
    152–153, 189; involvement
    with Scottsboro case, 17; as
    leader of LCCR, 60, 198 (see
    also Leadership Conference on
    Civil Rights [LCCR]); NAACP
    leadership crisis of 1949–1950
    and, 42–49; on NAACP
    organizational problems, 29–30,
    33–35, 36–37; newspaper
    column of, 194; on Nixon, 91,
    185; "racial defense policy"
    of, 83; relations/comparisons
    with other civil rights leaders,
    63, 97, 151–152, 165–166,
    170–171, 197; relations with
    Lyndon Johnson (see Johnson,
    Lyndon B.); relations with John
    F. Kennedy (see Kennedy, John
    F.); role in Jackson movement,
    109–110; role in March on
    Washington, 115, 118–119; role
    in NAACP levee investigation,
    15–16; role in passage of 1957
    Civil Rights Act, 69–72; role
    in passage of 1964 Civil Rights
    Act, 113–115, 119–120, 127–
    132; role in Selma campaign,
    148–149; support for Moynihan

CIVIL RIGHTS AND THE STRUGGLE FOR BLACK EQUALITY
IN THE TWENTIETH CENTURY

SERIES EDITORS
Steven F. Lawson, Rutgers University
Cynthia Griggs Fleming, University of Tennessee

Freedom's Main Line: The Journey of Reconciliation and the Freedom Rides
Derek Charles Catsam

Subversive Southerner: Anne Braden and the Struggle for Racial Justice in the Cold War South
Catherine Fosl

Constructing Affirmative Action: The Struggle for Equal Employment Opportunity
David Hamilton Golland

Sidelined: How American Sports Challenged the Black Freedom Struggle
Simon Henderson

Becoming King: Martin Luther King Jr. and the Making of a National Leader
Troy Jackson

Civil Rights in the Gateway to the South: Louisville, Kentucky, 1945–1980
Tracy E. K'Meyer

In Peace and Freedom: My Journey in Selma
Bernard LaFayette Jr. and Kathryn Lee Johnson

Democracy Rising: South Carolina and the Fight for Black Equality since 1865
Peter F. Lau

Civil Rights Crossroads: Nation, Community, and the Black Freedom Struggle
Steven F. Lawson